Chinese Classical Gardens of Suzhou

China Architecture and Building Press
Liu Dun-zhen

Translator: Chen Lixian
English Text Editor: Joseph C. Wang

McGraw-Hill, Inc.
New York   San Francisco   Washington, D.C.   Auckland   Bogotá
Caracas   Lisbon   London   Madrid   Mexico City
Milan   Montreal   New Delhi   San Juan
Singapore   Sydney   Tokyo   Toronto

Library of Congress Catalog No. 92-41-042

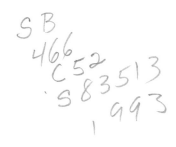

Previously published in Chinese by the China Architecture and Building Press.

1 2 3 4 5 6 7 8 9 0   HAL/HAL   9 8 7 6 5 4 3 2

ISBN   0-07-010876-5

The sponsoring editor for this book was Joel E. Stein, the editing supervisor was Caroline Levine, the designer was Susan Maksuta, and the production supervisor was Suzanne W. Babeuf. This book was set in Goudy by Six West Design. Photo and art layout: Nicholas A. Bernini.

Printed and bound by Arcata Graphics/Halliday.

Contents

PART 2   *Chinese Classical Gardens*

part One
Theory and Methods

I

Introduction

Classical gardens in China attained a high artistic level and possessed a unique architectural style; they occupied an important place in the development of garden building in the world. Not only did they have a great influence upon the art of gardening in other Asian countries like Japan, they also influenced the design of parks and gardens in Western Europe, especially in England, in the second half of the eighteenth century.

The classical gardens in Suzhou are representative specimens of privately owned gardens in southern China; and hence, the Suzhou gardens that are preserved today are priceless treasures of Chinese cultural heritage (Fig. I-1). A careful study of these historically valuable gardens and a summing up of their characteristic features would help to advance and develop the art of garden building, both in China and elsewhere.

Generally speaking, Chinese gardens of the past fall into two main types: On the one hand there are the imperial gardens and parks, and on the other the private residential gardens of high ranking officials, big landowners, and wealthy merchants. Most of the imperial gardens and parks are attached to summer or winter palaces, and usually are located in the suburbs. They are built on a grand scale, often taking up several hundred hectares of land, such as the ones at Yihe Yuan (The Summer Palace) of Beijing and Bishu Shanzhuang (The Imperial Summer Resort) in Chengde. Several imperial gardens that were built inside the capital, right next to the palaces or imperial residences, are also fairly large, such as the gardens at Sanhai (The Three Seas Park), Beihai (The North Sea Park), Zhonghai (The Central Sea), and Nanhai (The South Sea) of Beijing.

The layout of these imperial gardens and parks is based chiefly on the rearranging and reshaping of natural hills and lakes, and building pavilions, halls, and other structures around them; flowers and trees planted in their proper place enhanced the beautiful scenery. The buildings are generally large, multicolored, and have an abundance of meadows and groves and a great variety of flowers and plants around them.

Private gardens, on the other hand, usually are built within the city limits, right next to private residences. They generally are smaller, occupying an average of one tenth hectare of land, with the largest not exceeding a 6 or 7 hectares. These private gardens are laid out mainly in units of small areas where scenery can be observed from a short distance. Although differences in the political and economic status of the owners necessarily led to different characteristics in the different gardens, there were many similarities in the techniques employed for scenic effects.

In the conception and arrangement of scenery in garden planning, emphasis in most cases is placed on the imitation of nature. This design principle, which led to the tortuous, irregular, and free patterns of arrangement in buildings, hillocks, pools, and flowers and trees usually differs from the regulated geometrical patterns common in gardens of continental Europe. In both the imperial gardens and parks and the privately owned gardens, there are always a good number of architectural units built into compounds or closed courtyards. In both cases, the piling up of rocks into hillocks invariably adds to the variegated beauty of the garden scenery. Also, in these classical Chinese gardens there is the usual expression of the traditional architectural style and the cultivation of indigenous plants.

In Chinese history most gardens were constructed in national and provincial capitals where many aristocratic families, high ranking officials, big land owners, and wealthy merchants dwelt.[1] Also, these gardens were built near economically developed areas and important trade centers such as Wuxin in the Southern Song Dynasty (now Huzhou in Zhejiang Province), Suzhou in the Ming and Qing Dynasties, and Hangzhou in the middle of the Qing Dynasty. Good examples of this may be found in numerous private gardens in Suzhou.

According to historical records, gardens were first constructed in Suzhou and its environs in the Jin Dynasty when its capital was moved to South China.[2] Up until the Tang Dynasty, there were not many gardens in that part of the country. In the period of the Five Dynasties (907–960 A.D.), the whole district around Suzhou was little disturbed by war, and it became one of the most prosperous areas in China. When Qian Liu and his son made Hangzhou their capital and built the city walls and palaces there on a grand scale, Suzhou became their chief stronghold, and many aristocrats and high government officials constructed their gardens there. In A *Chronicle of Happy Gardens* written by Zhu Changwen of the Northern Song Dynasty, we are told:

> During the rule of the Qian family, Yuanliao, Prince of Guangling and a son of Qian Liu, lived in Suzhou. He liked to build gardens with tree groves. His followers tried to please him, and many of them constructed gardens with terraces and ponds. Quite a number of the remains of these gardens may still be found inside the city of Suzhou today.[3]

Sun Chengyou, a general of the Qian regime, also built many gardens and ponds there. Cangland Ting Garden (Surging-Wave-Pavilion Garden), the oldest, well-preserved garden in Suzhou, was built and rebuilt a number of times over several dynasties on the historical site of one of Sun Chengyou's gardens. In the last year of the Northern Song Dynasty, garden construction in Suzhou was already a common practice. Later, in the Southern Song dynasty, more gardens and private residences were built in Suzhou.

Not only were there many privately owned gardens within the city limits, but private residences with gardens were also built in rapid succession by aristocrats and landowners in areas of scenic beauty in suburban districts such as Shihu Shan (Stone-Lake Hill), Yaofeng Shan (Yao-Peak Hill), Tianchi Shan (Sky-Lake Hill), Dongtingdong Shan (East Dongting Hill), and Dongtingxi Shan (West Dongting Hill).[4] In the Ming and Qing Dynasties, when China's feudal society was on the wane, economically prosperous districts south of the Changjiang (Yangtse) River became concentrated regions of privately owned gardens.[5] Garden-building activities in Suzhou again reached a new height.

Finally, following the Taiping Uprising, a number of officials came to Suzhou one after another with their ill-gotten wealth, and they, too, built many private residences and gardens, which brought about another wave of garden construction in Suzhou.[6] Such was the social background for the building of numerous gardens in Suzhou in the last years of the Qing Dynasty.

The economy in the several large cities south of the Changjiang (Yangtse) River either depended chiefly on trade, or was dominated by the rise of handicraft arts. In some cases, these municipalities simply served as centers of consumption to provide luxuries for high officials and big landowners.

Just as there were different circumstances for the different cities, so the number and the size of the gardens and the state of their preservation in these cities also varied. Suzhou was an important city in southern China, which dated back to the Spring-Autumn period and to the Western Han and Eastern Han Dynasties. It was important not only for its high level of production in agriculture, but also for its silk goods and other handicraft arts. Though the city suffered several times from war damages throughout the centuries from the Tang Dynasty up to the Opium Wars, it recovered quickly each time and remained prosperous.

There was a higher level of culture in the city than in all other municipalities in the provinces of southeast China. During the Ming and the Qing Dynasties, numerous scholars of this district passed the state examinations and eventually obtained high government posts. They all amassed considerable wealth and returned home to Suzhou in their old age to buy land and estates and build private gardens and residences. Other high-ranking officials and big landowners, hearing of the beautiful scenery and comfortable living in and around Suzhou, also came to retire to this city and construct gardens there.

Of course, Suzhou was different in many ways from Luoyang in the Tang and the Northern Song Dynasties, Wuxing in the Southern Song Dynasty, and Nanjing in the Ming Dynasty, though all of these cities, like Suzhou, were centers of consumption for high officials and big landowners. As a result, over the course of time, many well-known gardens of the past were purchased by successive owners, but their original appearance was generally preserved; some were reconstructed or replenished with added splendor. In the areas south of the Changjiang (Yangtse) River in the Qing Dynasty, although Suzhou, Yanghou, and Hangzhou were the three cities equally renowned for their garden architecture, there were many more privately owned gardens in Suzhou than in the other two municipalities.

The chief tasks in the construction of gardens in China always have been piling up the hillocks or rockeries and diverting water to form the pools. Of the two, the former is comparatively easy, while the latter is more difficult. South of the Changjiang (Yangtse) River there are many lakes and ponds interwoven with rivers and brooks, so the conditions are especially favorable in this part of the country for constructing garden pools.

Rocks are essential for building hillocks or rockeries, and they are best if they are small and exquisite, odd shaped, and transparent. The Taihu rocks from the Dongtingxi Shan (The West Dongting Hill) near Suzhou are multicolored and full of cavities and creases; they have been well known throughout the country ever since the Tang Dynasty. Fine quality rocks can be gathered in Wajiabu in Huzhou, Bin Shan in Wuxing, Ma'an Shan in Kunshan, Huang Shan in Changzhou, Zhanggong Cave, Shanjuan Cave, and Jiangshan Cave in Yixing; those from Chuan Shan and Daxian Shan in Zhenjiang, Longtang in Jurong, and Qinglong Shan, in Nanjiang, and from the districts of Changshu and Hangzhou, are all easily available, though slightly inferior in quality.

Yellow rocks may be found in all the places mentioned above, but especially in Yaofeng Shan, Qionglong Shan, Shangfang Shan, Qizi Shan, and Lingyan Shan in Suzhou, and in Yang Shan in Xushuguan near Wuxi. There the rocks are hard, with veined surfaces, and white, yellow, red, and purple tints.

This easy availability of good rocks and water provides favorable conditions for the development of gardens in the south Jiangsu and north Zhejiang provinces.

Records and relics of gardens that were built before the Han Dynasty are sadly lacking, and a good deal of research is needed. However, beginning with the Western Han and Eastern Han Dynasties, records of gardens increased with time. For instance, Lin Wu or Xiao, king of the Liang Dynasty, as well as Yuan Guanghan, Liang Chi, and others were all known to have built gardens, dug pools, and piled hillocks that imitated nature. Liu Wu's Tu Yuan (Rabbit Garden) linked his palace with the adjacent temple, and it extended for tens of kilometers.

The buildings in Yuan Guanghan's garden extended in an almost continuous sequence. The garden was dotted with so many pavilions and long corridors that one could not go through the entire garden even in several hours' time. [7] This shows that in Chinese garden planning the design technique of linking up numerous buildings with pools and hillocks has had a tradition of more than two thousand years. But this was only one aspect of garden design in ancient China. There was yet another aspect.

In the years of Zhengshi, during the Wei Kingdom, in the era of the Three Kingdoms, many officials and literati used to indulge in metaphysics and cynicism, expressing their feelings amidst an environment of hills and rills, and considering hermetic seclusion the noblest way of life. Under the influence of Buddhism, this attitude toward gardening became even more common after the Western Jin and Eastern Jin Dynasties.

During the Northern and Southern Dynasties, more and more officials and literati engaged in the art of painting, and there was the birth of a school of "literati painters" midway in the Tang Dynasty. These painters considered themselves cultured and refined, and they designed and built gardens of their own in which they were able to express their poetic feelings and pictorial thoughts. Representative literati painters of the time included Song Zhiwen, Wang Wei, and Bai Juyi. In essence, the so-called "poetic feelings and pictorial thoughts" were no more than the sentiment expressed in the poems and paintings of literati painters who instilled these sentiments into their gardens in order to create artistic objects to their own liking. For instance, pools and hillocks in gardens symbolically implied that the proprietors dwelt among the hills and rested upon the rocks, or lived their lives in seclusion and away from human society; rocky peaks were used to symbolize famous peaks and sacred mountains and to suggest that the owners of the gardens were refined scholars and recluses; the pine, the bamboo, and the plum were meant to represent "the three friends in the winter season," aloof and proud; while the lotus was analogous to a "thoroughgoing gentleman" who "emerges from the mud and is yet unsoiled."

Such self-eulogy, with the above cited metaphorical significance assigned to various scenic items in the gardens, generally was displayed by inscribed titles, couplets, garden chronicles, and on paintings with verses inscribed. For example, the inscription of the title of Yuanxing Tang (Distant-fragrance Hall) in Zhouzheng Yuan (The Humble Administrator's Garden) was derived from the poetic phrase, "The more distant the fragrance is, the more delicate it is," which may be found in Ai lian Shuo (Essay on Fondness for the Lotus) by Zhou Dunyi of the Song Dynasty; the inscription of "With-Whom-to-Sit Lounge" on the Shanmian Ting (Fan-Shaped Pavilion) in Zhouzheng Yuan (The Humble

Administrator's Garden) was condensed from two lines of a verse by Su Shi, "With whom to sit, the bright moon and the soft wind and me."[8]

Chinese paintings of hills and and rivulets had one thing in common with classical Chinese gardens: their attempt to imitate nature. For this reason, more and more painters after the Southern Song Dynasty participated in planning and designing gardens. These activities had a profound effect on promoting the art of gardening in China in the past centuries. In fact, in the area south of the Changjiang (Yangtse) River, people such as Zhang Nanyuan, Zhou Bingzhong, and Ji Cheng of the Ming Dynasty, and Zhang Lian, Zhang Ran, Ye Tao, Ge Yuliang, of the Qing Dynasty, were all both good painters and renowned garden designers. Actually, it was through practice that they learned the technique of garden construction before they adopted garden planning as their profession and offered their services to influential clients. Ji Cheng, the most important of them, wrote a book entitled *Yuan Ye* (*Garden Building*), which in a sense represented the peak of achievement in the technique of garden building in the South near the end of the Ming Dynasty.

The artisans who built the gardens accumulated and handed down experience from the long years of practical work they devoted to improving their skill and fine technique in garden construction. According to historical records, the artisans of Luoyang in the Northern Song Dynasty had already adopted grafting as a method of introducing new varieties of flowers and trees.[9] There were also craftsmen known as "hill artisans" who specialized in the construction of rockeries during the Southern Song dynasty. [10]

The technical skill of the garden construction artisans south of the Changjiang (Yangtse) river in the Ming Dynasty was more advanced, as chronicled in *Records on Visits to the West Lake*, by Tian Rucheng of the Ming Dynasty. A certain artisan named Lu of Hangzhou "piled up heaps of peaks and hills crests, and broke up ravines, with such great skill and proficiency that he was called Lu the piler of hills." According to another record from a book titled *Chronicles of Social Customs of the Wu District* in the Ming Dynasty, there was an artisan in Suzhou who "knew the art of planting trees and piling hills" and was known as the "Garden Man."[11] Some of the gardens were even constructed by artisans who made direct copies of the scenic objects they observed in the hills.[12]

All these records give us a general picture of how the artisans were engaged in actual garden construction, from the Northern and Southern Song Dynasties down to the Ming Dynasty. In *Leisurely Sentiments Jotted Down*, written by Li Yu during the reign of Emperor Kangxi of the Qing Dynasty, the author wrote:

> There are a number of artists whose bosoms are full of hills and ravines and whose pen brushes are entwined with mists and clouds. If you ask them to paint rivers and inscribe hills, they can picture a thousand cliffs and ten thousand ravines in a jiffy, but if you ask them to pile up small pieces of rock in a private study, they can do nothing about it, and you seem to be asking a blind man to show you the way. Experts in piling up rockeries were never those who could write poetry or paint pictures; yet when one saw them casually lifting a rock and placing it upside down it instantly became grey and forceful as in calligraphy or tortuous and graceful as in a painting.[13]

This passage relates to the real conditions in those bygone days and tells us that those who had a real mastery of the technique of building parks were the artisans who spent their whole lives in constructing gardens, but whose names and deeds never appeared in historical records. The above records also remind us that the art of construction of China's classical gardens had a long history of distant origin and that the high degree of artistic excellence evolved only through many generations of artisans.

An actual investigation shows that except for Canglang Ting (The Surging-Wave-Pavilion Garden) and a few gardens attached to guild halls, ancestral halls, or Buddhist temples, most of the preserved classical gardens in Suzhou, are privately owned. Historical records tell us that Canglang Ting (The Surging-Wave-Pavilion Garden) dated back to the mid-Northern Song Dynasty; Shizilin (The Forest of the Lions Garden) was first built in the last years of the Yuan Dynasty; and Yi Pu (Art Orchard), Zhuozheng Yuan (The Humble Administrator's Garden), Wufeng Yuan (The Five-Peak Garden), Liu Yuan (The Lingering-Here Garden), Xi Yuan (West Garden), Fangcao Yuan (Fragrant-Grass Garden), and Qiayin Yuan (Harmony-Heritage Garden) were first constructed between the middle period and the last years of the Ming Dynasty. But the farther back a garden can be traced in history, the more numerous repairs and reconstructions it must have gone through, with the result that probably little is left today of its original appearance, which must have been changed beyond recognition.

The gardens other than those mentioned above were built during the Qing Dynasty, and most of them were first built or reconstructed after the reign of Emperor Tongzhi. By the end of the 1940s most of the classical gardens had been either partly demolished or completely destroyed. The reconstruction work started in 1953, after which the old gardens were reopened to the public one after the other.

Notes:

1. Many records are extant on the construction of gardens in Changan and Luoyang in the Han Dynasty, in Luoyang in the state of the Northern Wei of the Northern and Southern Dynasties, in Jiankang in the South Dynasties, in Changan and Luoyang in the Tang Dynasty, in Dongjing (East Capital) and Xijing (West Capital) in the Northern Song Dynasty, in Linan in the Southern Song Dynasty, in Nanjing (South Capital) and Beijing (North Capital) in the Ming Dynasty, and in Beijing in the Qing Dynasty.
2. A garden built by Gu Pijiang, as recorded in the "Biography of Wang Xianzhi" in *The History of Jin Dynasty* (Jin Shu).
3. See "Records of Construction Project," in vol. 119 of *Collections of Books Ancient and Modern*.
4. See vol. 39 of *Annals of Wu Country*, published in the Minguo period.
5. See a *Record of Visits to Several Gardens in Jinling*, by Wang Shizhen; also *Accounts of Gardens in Loudong*, and other annals of different localities.
6. Gu Wenbin, the builder of Yi Yuan (Happy Garden), Shen Bingcheng, the owner of Ou Yuan (Twin Garden), and Ren Daorong, who owned many residences and gardens, were all directly responsible for the massacres of revolutionaries during the peasants' risings in the Qing Dynasty.
7. See *Random Records of the Western Capital*, by Liu Xin of the Han Dynasty.
8. See "Rouged Lips," a poem by Su Shi, in *Complete Poems of the Song Dynasty*, p. 324.
9. See an entry on Renfeng Yuan Garden, owned by the Li family, in *Annals of Famous Gardens in Luoyang*, by Li Gefei of the Song Dynasty.
10. See "Miscellaneous Information in the Year Kui-Xin," by Zhou Mi of the Song dynasty, as recorded in *A Miscellany of Unofficial Records*, edited by Shuang Jun of the Ming Dynasty.

11. See "A Record of Suzhou Customs," by Huang Xingzeng, as collected in *A Hundred Mounds Mimicking the Hills*.
12. See an entry on "Yilao Garden" in vol. 39 of *Annals of Wu Country*, written in the Minguo period.
13. See entry on "Mountain Rocks," No. 5, in vol. 9 of *Leisurely Sentiments Jotted Down*.

II
Layout

The classical gardens in Suzhou functioned as an amalgam of living quarters for rest and observation and a locale for an assorted display of the arts. But in order to realize these combined functions within the limited area of a private garden, there was the urgent problem of housing a goodly number of buildings in a small space, and installing many attractive details such as artificial "hills and rills." This called for great skill in garden construction.

Chinese artisans of the past had accumulated much experience: On the one hand they had created the architectural styles befitting the requirements of garden construction and had blended into one entity the buildings, flowers and trees, and hills and rills, while on the other hand, they had put into practice the idea of "nature in miniature" for recreating natural scenery. Thus, in their garden planning they employed numerous devices such as contrast, foil effect, relative dimensions, sequence in depth, scenes in contraposition, and the "borrowing" of a distant scene, so that one can "see a broad expanse through a small object," "make a few items surpass many," and "take in a variety of views within a limited space." Due to historical limitations, however, the problem of overcrowded space and overconcentration of buildings and rockeries at times could not be satisfactorily resolved with the above-mentioned devices.

The specific plan for the layout of each garden in Suzhou varies according to its size, topography, and the scenic items involved. The gardens enclosed within the residences generally are placed either in front of or behind the main hall or study, and consist chiefly of halls in several courtyards adorned with pools and rockeries, flowers and trees, pavilions and corridors, to provide outdoor scenery (Figs. II-1 through II-9). Small-sized gardens that are detached from residences usually are the expansion and elaboration of residential-type gardens. They can also comprise a main-landscape area surrounded by a number of small courts, providing numerous scenic objects in a more complex pattern (Figs. II-10 through II-13). Chang Yuan (Carefree Garden) and Hu Yuan (Kettle Garden) are typical examples of such small-size gardens (See Chaps. XVIII and XIX). In the case of medium-sized and large gardens, there are many more scenic objects, and usually the gates open onto the streets, making these gardens entirely independent of the residences.[1] (See Chaps. VII, VIII, XI, XII, XIII, etc.). The common layout of these gardens is as follows: The main hall serving as the center of activities is placed opposite the rockeries, pools, flowers, and trees as scenic objects in contraposition, while between the hall area, the rockeries and the pool there are pavilions, water pavilions, two-story halls and two-story pavilions. The main hall is surrounded by courtyards and other smaller scenic areas, which are to be linked up with foot-path and winding corridors to form a complete whole that is liveable, observable, and enjoyable. The following discussions and analyses on design principles and devices are made from observations of existing and preserved gardens that serve as concrete examples for continued research studies.

Scenic Areas and Spaces

In the classical gardens of Suzhou in order to create a kaleidoscopic series of scenes within a restricted space, the garden space generally is divided into several scenic areas. In fairly large gardens generally there would be several separate areas, each having its own scenic theme and its peculiar characteristics. This is one of the basic devices for creating a rich variety of scenes as well as a feeling of extensive spaces. It was used in all the classical gardens in China—not alone in the gardens of Suzhou but also in the imperial gardens such as the Yuanmingyuan (Imperial Round and Bright Garden), Yihe Yuan (The Summer Palace) in Beijing, and Bishu Shanzhuang (The Imperial Summer Resort) in Chengde. However, in dividing scenic areas there should always be a clear distinction between the primary and the secondary ones, and there should be a fit proportion between tortuous areas and open spaces so that there is plenty of variety and contrast, rich in details but not fragmentary.

Since the pool and the rockery usually take up a lot of space, the space containing the main pool and the rockery generally is designated as the garden's main scenic area, and is surrounded by several secondary ones. The adoption of this device is obvious in practically all the preserved gardens in Suzhou. At the same time, just one scenic feature in the main scenic area should be emphasized; for instance, the hillock is given prominence in Huanxiu Shanzhuang (The Mountain Villa of Encircled Elegance), whereas the watery area is especially well arranged in Wangshi Yuan (The Retired Fisherman's Garden) and Zhouzheng Yuan (The Humble Administrator's Garden). In each case, one particular scenic object dominates, and there is something unique in the garden.

In fact, no matter whether a garden is large or small, once this effect is achieved, the whole place would leave a profound impression on the visitors even if there were design defects elsewhere. So, in the case of the rockery in Canglang Ting (Surging-Wave-Pavilion Garden), the dense bamboo grove and the thickly overgrown wooded region would give one a striking impression of the hilly scene (see Chap. X). But if the hillock were to appear dwarfish or the watery region to seem pent up, the whole garden would appear to hang loosely together and lack a focal point.

The rockery in Huanxiu Shanzhuang (The Mountain Villa of Encircled Elegance) is smaller than those in Yi Yuan (Happy Garden); yet it gives an impression of great vitality. Likewise, the watery area of Wangshi Yuan (The Retired Fisherman's Garden) may only be about half the size of that in Yi Yuan (Happy Garden), yet it appears rather broad and spacious (see Chaps. XI and XII). In both cases, it is not the actual height of the hillock or the width of the pool, but rather the device of highlighting a certain scenic theme that brings about the desirable effect of "seeing a broad expanse in a small object."

The emphasis on one scenic theme of course must be supported by a great variety of other scenes. In the classical gardens of Suzhou, the chief scenic theme in the central scenic area usually consists of a hillock and a pool, but generally there is a variety of scenic themes for the other smaller scenic areas: In one case the main feature would be flowers and trees, such as the peony, magnolia, laurel, maple, a bamboo grove, and so on; in another area the main theme would be the watery area (as for instance water courts, paved walks across the top of the pool, water pavilions and so forth); in a third case the theme would be a rocky peak (such as the scene at the Salute-to-the-Peak Hall, the Bowing-to-the-Stone Hall, or the Salute-to-the-Peak-and-Pointing-at-the-Cypress Hall, and so forth). In other areas there would be a mixed scenic theme of a rocky peak, flowers and trees, and a pool.

Nevertheless, in most gardens, a rocky peak is chosen as the chief scenic theme. This is because a rocky peak may assume a great variety of shapes, so that by virtue of its central positioning in a courtyard or in front of a building, its unique appearance can easily create a favorable impression. That is why for many centuries after the Northern and Southern Dynasties quite a number of officials and landowners were engaged in an indefatigable search for odd-shaped rocks.[2] Only toward the end of the Qing Dynasty, when big, uncleft rocky peaks were hardly available, builders were glad to resort to small, broken pieces of rocks for the piling of rockeries.

Of course, in the construction of large and small scenic areas, not only was variety of themes much sought after, but the proper foil effects of the surroundings as well as harmony in the shapes and heights and sizes of the buildings were needed before beauty and variety could be attained in garden scenery.

In order to fit in well with the different requirements for the different halls, pavilions, studios, and with the different scenic objects in different scenic areas, there should be variety in the arrangement of garden space, variety in size, in height, in the proportion between light and shade, and in the dimensions of scenic objects.

Generally speaking, before entering upon a fairly large scenic area, there should be a transitional stage of some smaller space that is tortuous, narrow, and dark, in order first to contrast one's vision and feeling of dimension; then, when one enters into a broader space, one can have the impression of a sudden broadening of vision. Based on this principle, upon entering the garden gates, the common practice in most gardens is for one to go through winding corridors or small courtyards as a preliminary step that serves as a foil for the main view of the garden.

In Liu Yuan (Lingering-Here Garden) such an effect is achieved by going from the garden gate to Gumujiaoke (Old-Tree-Intertwining-One-Another) or by proceeding from the residence through the Hesuo (The Crane Hall) to the area around Wufeng Xianguan (Five-Peak Celestial House)(Figs. II-14, II-15, VII-13, and VII-17).

Another example of this foil effect is having the visitor proceed from Xiaoshanconggui Xuan (Litte-Hillock-and-Laurel-Grove Hall) through winding corridors and courtyards and then to arrive at the area in front of Zhuoying Shuige (Washing-Tassel Waterside Pavilion) in Wangshi Yuan (The Retired Fisherman's Garden). Still another example would be to go from Yanyu Tang (Famed-for-Swallow Hall) through small courts and winding corridors and then to reach the central area in Shizilin (The Forest of Lions Garden).

The device of entering upon broad open spaces by first passing through narrow areas is adopted frequently not only at the entrance to a garden, but also at other chosen places. In Liu Yuan (Lingering-Here Garden), there are some small and cleverly contrived pavilions and corridors between Quxi Lou (Winding-Creek Two-Storied Building) and Wufeng Xianguan (Five-Peak Celestial House), and there are several tortuous and gloomy courtyards that serve as a transitional stage between Wufeng Xianguan (Five-Peak Celestial

House) and Linquanqishuozhi Guan (The House for Aged Giants of Groves and Springs)(Fig. VIII-3).

In the classical gardens of Suzhou, the division of space into scenic areas is managed in several ways, including the use of walls, corridors, buildings, rockeries, trees and groves, and bridges, as elements for spatial articulation (Figs. II-16 through II-18). Of these devices, the use of rockeries and trees adds to the division of areas by producing an impression of orderliness and neatness. If the various devices are employed one after another, the scenery may sometimes represent broad and open space, or sometimes seem substantial and palpable.

Overlapping and intertwining the scenic areas can add to the perspective and the feeling of depth in the scenery. The central areas of Zhuozheng Yuan (The Humble Administrator's Garden) provide us with a typical example of the effect. It is not possible, however, for small-size gardens to make extensive use of rockeries and groves of trees for the division of spaces. One can only resort to the use of courtyard walls and covered ways for such purposes, or sometimes simply form enclosed courtyards with walls and corridors; but the closed-in space then would be completely isolated from the other parts of the garden.

To avoid this sense of complete segregation, gaps in a wall are sometimes provided or lattice doors are built to serve as walls, thus linking the indoor and outdoor area. The builder might even resort to the construction of open pavilions, open halls, open corridors, or "moon-gate" (i. e., leafless gate), casementless windows (otherwise known as *moon caves*) and tracery windows, so that the entire garden space would seem to be partly separated and partly joined together. Examples of such treatment of spaces may be found in Zhuwaiyizhi Xuan (A-Branch-from-Bamboo Lounge) in Wangshi Yuan (The Retired Fisherman's Garden) (Fig. II-20), or in courtyards adjacent to Shilin Xiaoyuan (Small Courtyard of Stone Forest) in Lin Yuan (Lingering-Here Garden) (Fig. VIII-18), or in Xiaocanglang Water Court (Little-Surging-Wave Water-Court) in Zhuozheng Yuan (The Humble Administrator's Garden) (Fig. V-3).

Trees and flowers are also sometimes planted and trimmed for specific purposes. When trees are not planted for the purpose of separating or concealing one area from others, tall trees or flowers and grass close to the earth usually are planted in a way that will not obstruct the view or block up the space. This is particularly true in front of halls and pavilions, or two-story halls and pavilions (Fig. II-21).

Observation Spots and Routes

The scenic objects in a garden should be linked into a series by one or several appropriate routes, so that they can have their due effect upon the observers; otherwise, even though the garden scenery on the whole is good, it cannot be fully appreciated. Therefore, in making sketches for the layout it is necessary to consider the proper locations of the observation spots in relation to the observation routes; then visitors on pleasure tours may successively see view after view of beautiful scenery unfolding before their eyes.

The halls in the gardens were the centers of activity for the garden owners, so inevitably they became the main observation spots in the gardens. They usually were placed in front of the main scenic objects, such as hillocks (or rockeries) and pools. In each garden, the arrangement with the main hall facing the rockery across the pool almost invariably was adopted. Other observation spots were located beside the pools or around hillocks. In Zhuozheng Yuan (The Humble Administrator's Garden), and in the central area of Wangshi Yuan (The Retired Fisherman's Garden), the observation spots were placed around the pools, while in Huanxiu Shanzhuang (Mountain Villa of Encircled

Elegance), they were located around the hillocks. In each case, the specific arrangement of observation spots was usually made in accordance with the topography, the relative height of the different areas, and the location of these areas in relation to the others; hence, one observation spot might be placed on top of a hillock and another beside a pool; one might be located in an open and bright place and another in a gloomy, deep, and tortuous area. The ultimate aim of all such arrangements is to introduce variety to the scenery. If an observation spot is placed somewhere high, the visitor has the advantage of observing the scenery from outside of the garden proper, and at the same time of looking down and having an overall view of the entire garden. If an an observation spot is placed somewhere low and close to the water, the observer has the advantage of commanding a pleasant view of the pool. Because of this, the ground level of landboats in almost all the gardens is level with or one or two steps below the surface of the ground, while efforts are made to build the ground floor of two-story water pavilions as low as possible. The various locations of the major observation spots at different heights in the central part of Zhuozheng Yuan (The Humble Administrator's Garden) are meant to produce the above-stated effect.[3]

In the classical gardens of Suzhou, the distance between an observation point and the scenic object to be observed generally is not great. Though this is a natural consequence of the space limitation of these gardens, it also is partly due to the usual height of a rockery, the main scenic object in contraposition to the main hall, which ordinarily does not exceed seven meters. If the distance between the rockery and the main hall is too great, the rocks would appear too small and insignificant. Therefore, the in-between distance was commonly set at between 12 and 35 meters.[4] Also, lake-stone peaks should be observed from a short distance and therefore are usually placed in a small area. As a rule, when rocky peaks serve as the main scenic object of a garden, the observation distance is generally within 20 meters.

With the main hall as the chief observation spot in the garden, one is meant to enjoy not only the main scenic object in front of it, but also other scenic objects, which should be placed on the other sides of the hall. When the halls face four sides, with doors and windows in all four directions, one can enjoy the scenery on all sides. For the so-called "mandarin-duck" halls, as well as halls in general, arrangements usually are made not only for observing scenic objects both in front of and behind the buildings, but also through the walls on the other two sides. A number of tracery windows may provide observation spots, or there might be hangings on the side doors and windows to provide "scenery-in-frames" views (Figs. II-23 and VII-24).

Observation routes are meant to guide the visitors on their tour through the gardens as they take in the scenic objects that unfold one after another. In the classical gardens of Suzhou, the observation routes generally are of two types: (a) to lead visitors through corridors, buildings, and paths along the hillocks (or rockeries) and beside the pools, and (b) to proceed through hilly paths, caves and caverns, and bridges, up and down the hillocks and over the pools or across the creeks. Both types of observation routes usually are employed in larger gardens.

The common arrangement is a circular route, the simplest of which would encircle the hillock and the pool. For instance, in Huanxiu Shanzhuang (Mountain Villa of Encircled Elegance), whether you go from the winding bridge on the southwest to inside the ravine, or proceed from the northeast and walk through the Buqiu Fang (Replenishing-Autumn Landboat) and then turn south and mount the hillock, you come round to the same spot (see Chap. XV). But in most gardens, several other pathways up the hillock or over the pool are inserted into the encircling route. Even with a small-size garden like Chang Yuan (Carefree Garden), there is not only the encircling route through corridors or covered ways but there is also a winding bridge over across the pool, so that one can go directly from Tonghua Shuwu (Parasol-Flower Studio) to Diwochenjin (Washing-My-Dusty-Clothing Pavilion) (see Chap. XVIII).

In a large garden like Shizilin (The Forest of Lions Garden), the encircling route of corridors and covered ways is interlaced with hilly paths over the hillocks (or rockeries) and bridges across the pools, so that the visitor can observe the garden scenery from different angles. The narrow paths over the hillocks are usually winding and zigzag, so the spaces in the garden seem to be expanded, and, the visitor is given more opportunities to observe garden scenery on his lengthened route. An encircling route on the outer circuit generally is placed as close as possible to the external walls of the garden, so that the fullest use is made of the garden space. Winding and zigzag covered ways of great length are built to enable the visitors to go on their tours unthreatened by rain, snow, or the hot sun. The winding covered paths also help to conceal certain views beyond external walls of the garden and thus avoid viewing everything in the garden at one glance from any specific spot on the observation route.

As visitors follow the observation route, at one moment they might go up to a height when they mount a hillock or climb up to the second story of a hall or pavilion, and at the next moment descend to a lower level when they cross a bridge or walk across a creek. Now, they might come to a broad and open space and then reach a narrow, enclosed area. Sometimes they can see far ahead in the distance and at another time look downward. Now they are indoors and the next moment out in the open. In other words, the observation route provides change and variety in the visitors' surroundings and in the scenery they observe, with differing characteristics for different scenic objects at different points of the tour.

Take, for instance, a rugged path on a rockery. Although the route on the rockery in Huanxiu Shanzhuang (Mountain Villa of Encircled Elegance) is much shorter than that at Shizilin (The Forest of Lions Garden), yet, because of the variety in the way they are arranged along the observation routes, scenes of deep ravines and impassible gorges, as well as views of steep cliffs and perilous peaks are visible to the eye in the former case; whereas in the case of Shizilin (The Forest of Lions Garden), though there are more than ten observation routes and over twenty caves in the hillocks, the lack of variety in its treatment of the scenic objects leads to monotony and a failure to arouse one's interest in nature and the landscape.

Contrast and Foil Effect

Contrast is a device that is indispensable to all artistic creations, and the art of garden building is no exception. In the classical gardens of Suzhou, there is concentration versus dispersion in the spacing of scenic objects, openness and brightness versus tortuousness and gloom in the treatment of space, the rough steepness of a rockery versus the bright smoothness of a pool, buildings contrived with ingenuity and artifice versus groves of trees in the wild state of nature, the feeling of palpable concreteness versus that of intangible unsubstantiality, brightness versus gloom in lighting effects, as well as the different textures of building materials, and the contrast in the shapes and dimensions of the scenic objects. All of these utilize the device of contrast (Figs. II-26 through II-29).

Thus, in the general layout of a garden, as one moves from one scenic area to another, the continual change in the arrangement of space and the scenic objects produces the effect of contrast, so that after visiting all parts of a garden, one feels one has encountered an infinite variety of scenes. If on one side of the main hall is a pool of water and on the other side are rocks (or rockeries), flowers and trees, an effect of contrast is produced. Such is the case with Zhuozheng Yuan (The Humble Administrator's Garden), Liu Yuan (Lingering-Here Garden), with Yi Yuan (Happy Garden) and others. In Wangshi Yuan (The Retired Fisherman's Garden), the small courtyards and rocks (or rockeries) in front of and behind the Xiaoshanconggui Xuan (Little Hillock and Laurel Grove Hall) contrast with the rocks and the pool in the central area.

Inside a scenic area, groves of trees and rocks and the pool often are arranged to contrast with the buildings; for instance, on one side of the pool would be rocks (or a rockery) and on the other side, buildings. An arrangement like this not only fully exploits the attractions of the scenic objects and displays them to the best advantage, but it also achieves the effect of contrast. A good example of this is the contrast between two emerald-green rockeries in the pool in the central area of Zhuozheng Yuan (The Humble Administrator's Garden) and in the environs of Yuanxian Tang (The Distant Fragrance Hall) and Xiang Zhou (Fragrant Isle Landboat) on the south bank of the pool. Another example is found in Liu Yuan (Lingering-Here Garden), where the pool and rockery in the central area set off the shades and reflections around Hanbi Shanfang (Encompassing Jade Mountain House) and Quxi Lou (Winding Creek Two-Storied Building).

The use of foils to thrust some scenic theme into prominence is also a common practice in the arrangement of scenic objects, so that the major scenic object is distinguished from the minor ones and one can "see a broad expanse in a small object." By using something low as a foil for a very high object, one can make scenes appear bigger and more grandiose that their actual size. By using something light-colored as foil for a dark object, or vice versa, one can make the contour of a scenic object more striking. By using something dark and gloomy as foil for a bright object, the bright spot can be made to appear more brilliant and resplendent. So the devices frequently employed in the classical gardens in Suzhou were: (a) the use of buildings and white walls as foils for flowers, trees, and rocky peaks, (b) the placement of smooth and deep blue water in a pool against rough and steep rocks on a rockery, and (c) the use of the low, winding banks of a pool, flat-surfaced, simple bridges, and open and dainty-looking pavilions to set off the open breadth of the level surface of the water in the pool.

Bluish-green rocky peaks need proper foils to show off their shapes and contours. We cannot say that there are no good rocky peaks on the rockery in Shizilin (The Forest of Lions Garden), but all the peaks there are covered up by small, broken-up hilly areas, and the total effect hardly amounts to anything. A simple and clear background is best for rocky peaks, and the arrangement of "making the white-washed wall serve as paper and using the rocks to draw pictures"[5] is commonly adopted in the gardens of Suzhou to form numerous miniature scenes for appreciation (Figs. VI-26, VI-27, and VI-31).

Another possibility is the use of dark-colored doors, windows and roofs, as in Guanyun Lou (Cloud-Topping Two-Storied Building) in Liu Yuan (Lingering-Here Garden) as foils for Guanyuan Feng (Cloud-Topping Peak), to give striking brilliance to the peak's contour (Fig. IV-20). At other places, deep-toned bamboo trees are used to set off some rocky peak, with a similar desirable effect. Beautiful flowers and greenish bamboos also require proper surroundings to serve as foils; either something light-colored is used to set off the dark-colored flowers or bamboos, or something dark-colored is placed alongside the light-colored flowers or bamboos, in order to show off the color tones and the striking features of the plants.

The use of clear, crystalline water of a pool to encircle a lake stone or yellow-stone rockery at the base can set off the rockery's steepness and precipitousness. The clear winding creek beneath the rockery at Huanxiu Shanzhuang (Mountain Villa of Encircled Elegance) is an example. The rockery south of the pool in Yi Pu (Art Orchard) not only is set off to advantage by the water in the pool but the stony path and the winding bridge along the pool also serve as foils. This is another successful attempt at foil effect. The shores of the pool as well as the buildings, flowers, and trees surrounding the watery area in the central part of Wangshi Yuan (The Retired Fisherman's Garden) serve well as foils for the pool, so that although the pool is a small one, one gets the feeling of broad expansion (Fig. V-1). All this shows that the prerequisite for foil effect is the choice of the main scenic theme to be set off by secondary scenic objects; of course the foil effect works both ways: in other words, it is necessary to arrange the major and minor scenic objects in proper relation to each other, and thus to achieve the desired foil effect for both.

In the arrangements for contrast and foil effect, it is important to have a scene of proper dimensions. In a small-size garden, this is especially necessary. There the dimensions of the buildings should not be too large, if you want to create the feeling of a broad expanse of space. Even though the main hall is the chief building in the garden, it must not be so prominent as to overshadow all the other scenic objects and be out of proportion what the rockery and the pool. The size of the hall must fit in well with the space around it. The 36-Yuanyan Guan (Thirty-Six-Mandarin-Duck Hall) in the west part of Zhuozheng Yuan (The Humble Administrator's Garden) is oversized in proportion to the rockery and pool, so the whole area seems too cramped and overcrowded. A better arrangement is that of the main hall in Wangshi Yuan (The Retired Fisherman's Garden), which is placed far behind the rockery.

A hall or pavilion placed right next to a pool should also be small and slight, as in the case of the Zhengguan Lou (Clearly-Viewing Two-Storied Building) in Zhuozheng Yuan (The Humble Administrator's Garden) and that of Mingse Lou (Bright-Zither-Two-Storied Building) in Liu Yuan (Lingering-Here Garden); or the hall should be placed in one corner of the garden as with the Quxi Lou (The Winding-Creek Two-Storied Building) in Liu Yuan (Lingering-Here Garden); or the hall should have a small, low, and open building in front of it as an intermediary edifice, as with Jixu Zhai (Gathering-the-Void Study) in Wangshi Yuan (The Retired Fisherman's Garden).

If the hall is located in the middle of a pool, however, as with Jianshan Lou (Seeing-the-Hill Two-Storied Building) in Zhuozheng Yuan (The Humble Administrator's Garden), the pavilion is placed in the northwestern corner of the pool, and the ground base, as well as the height of the building, is kept as low as possible.[6] Generally speaking, all the structures in the environs of the rockery and the pool, whether they be halls, pavilions, or waterside pavilions, covered paths or corridors, bridges, or even the embankment of the pool, should not assume oblong shapes, but should appear tortuous and undulating and be scattered about rather than crowded together, so that none of these scenic objects seems to vie with the pool or the rockery for prominence.

The pavilion on top of a rockery particularly should appear small and slight, or the rockery would seem like merely the groundwork for the pavilion and fail to create an impression of towering majesty. So the Luoji Ting (The Snail-Shaped Coiled-Hair Pavilion) in Yi Yuan (Happy Garden) measures only two meters in diameter, while the dimensions of Ke Ting (Just-Right Pavilion) in Liu Yuan (Lingering-Here Garden) and those of the several pavilions on the rockeries in Zhuozheng Yuan (The Humble Administrator's Garden) are just right for their purposes, because these pavilions are analogous to "inserting the eye-pupil in painting a dragon," and they light up all the scenery around the rockery (Fig. II-30).

Just as the gardens vary in size, the sizes of the buildings should vary as well. The dimensions of the halls and pavilions in Wangshi Yuan (The Retired Fisherman's Garden), for instance, generally are smaller than the buildings in Zhuozheng Yuan (The Humble Administrator's Garden), thus demonstrating the keen sensitivity of architects in ancient China to the sizes and proportions of buildings in gardens.

In choosing the trees to be planted, the emphasis usually is on single trees planted for appreciation; trees of slow growth usually are planted at the corners of a courtyard or beside a pavilion to serve decorative purposes. Large-sized miniature landscape and flower arrangements in basins also are used for scenic effect in courtyards. All these are based on considerations of proper dimension for the scenic objects in the gardens. Other examples of such considerations are: (a) the use of a dwarfish bamboo grove as the central theme in the earthen hillock amid the pool in Zhuozheng Yuan (The Humble Administrator's Garden), and (b) the use of broad leaved bamboos to blanket the entire rockery in Canglang Ting (The Surging-Wave Pavilion Garden).

Scenic Objects in Contraposition and Borrowed Distant Scenery

In the classical gardens of Suzhou it is a common practice to consciously place certain scenic objects in contraposition to each other, near important observation spots. But the Chinese practice is different from that in Western garden design, where scenic objects are placed in contraposition on an axis. In classical Chinese gardens the scenic objects in contraposition unfold gradually as visitors follow a tortuous path on the same ground level; new vistas appear along the path as the visitor walks on, step by step. Such scenes in contraposition are most striking and attractive when they are encountered (a) as one walks forward on a path or along some covered way, (b) as one passes through a gate or takes a turn, or (c) as one views the scene through the aperture of a door or the latticework of a window.

It is most common for a visitor to meet scenes in contraposition in the above-mentioned circumstances. For instance, in the central area of Zhuozheng Yuan (The Humble Administrator's Garden) through the Wancui (Evening Green) moon-gate, one can see from the Pipa Yuan (Loquat Orchard), the Xuexiangyuanwei Ting (The Pavilion of Fragrant-Snow-and-Colorful-Clouds) north of the pool, even though the pavilion is somewhat concealed among a grove of trees. Similarly, from Shanmian Ting (Fan-Shaped Pavilion) in the western part of Zhuozheng (The Humble Administrator's Garden), one can observe the Daoying Lou (Inverted-Image Two-Storied Building) beyond the moon-gate (Figs. II-31 and II-32). In addition to the scenes in contraposition that you encounter directly in front of you, sometimes a number of window apertures or circular doors that open on the sidewalls of some covered path may serve to frame the scenic views, and a continuous series of pictures may unfold before you as you walk along the path flanked by tracery windows and circular doors. An example of this device may be found in the environs of Hesuo (Crane Hall) in Liu Yuan (Lingering-Here Garden). When halls, two-story halls, and pavilions are the main spots for observing the scenery, it is important to arrange the contrapositional scenes by placing in front of the halls or pavilions a pool or rockery, a bamboo grove, or rocks, flowers, and trees, or pavilions and water pavilions.

Of course, scenes in contraposition generally have a mutual effect, so the buildings in the gardens are both observation spots and, at the same time, scenic objects to be observed; together with the pools and rockeries and the flowers and trees, they serve as contrapositional scenic objects in an intricate and complex way.

Borrowing distant scenery constitutes one of the traditional devices for enriching garden scenery. Examples of borrowing are many, as can be seen from our illustrations:

1. Fig. II-33. Viewing westward at a distance the Beisi Ta (North-Temple Pagoda) from Xiuqi Ting (Embroidered-Silk Pavilion) and the environs of Wuzhuyouju (Pavilion amid-Secluded-Wutong-and-Bamboo) in Zhuozheng Yuan (The Humble Administrator's Garden).
2. Gazing from Kanshan Lou (Looking-at-the-Hill Two-Storied Building) in Canglang Ting (Surging-Wave-Pavilion Garden) at the scenery of southwestern hills far away, or looking from the winding corridors and pavilions and water pavilions in the northern area of Canglang Ting (Surging-Wave-Pavilion Garden) at the scenery of the watery surface immediately outside the garden.
3. Fig. II-34. Looking from two pavilions atop the hill in the western part of Liu Yuan (Lingering-Here Garden) at the far-away view of Huqui (Tiger-Hill Park) and Xiyuan Si (Western-Garden Temple) and the distant hills to the southwest.
4. Fig. II-34. Looking from Guanyun Lou (Cloud-Topping Two-Storied Building) at Huqui (Tiger-Hill Park) nearby.

On the other hand, Yiliang Ting (Fit-to-Observe-Scenery-in-Two-Directions Pavilion), which used to be a subsidiary park itself but now belongs to the western park of Zhuozheng Yuan (The Humble Administrator's Garden) is a good place from which to view scenery; one may climb up to its second story which commands an overall view of all the scenes in the garden (Figs. II-35 and II-36).

Unfortunately, most of the gardens in Suzhou are located within the city limits, so that the alternatives are: (a) if there is good borrowed scenery available, it is used, but (b) if there are no scenic objects in sight, then the view must be blocked. For instance, the garden in Mayike Lane is located on a high mound and if one looks downward one sees the many undulating house roofs on all four sides. Therefore, a rockery is constructed on the southeastern corner, while corridors and halls have been put up on the other three sides to screen off the ugly sights. Also in this garden, the growth of lotus and sleeping lilies is controlled to prevent them from spreading out too far; this leaves plenty of water surface open to view to reflect the clouds and the inverting images of rockery, trees, halls, and pavilions. In this way extra space and scenic objects appear to be added to the garden as one gets the effect of "borrowed scenery" by looking downward into the pools.

Depth and Sequence

In many gardens in Suzhou emphasis is placed on depth and tortuosity. When one says, "Depth is essential to scenery, and no tortuosity means no depth," one is speaking of the device by which the tortuous arrangement adds to the feeling of depth in garden scenery while avoiding the none too gratifying impression of taking in all the sights at one glance. In gardens that contain naturally scenic "hills and rills," inevitably there will be uneven ground, irregular-shaped hillocks and pools, zigzag paths and corridors, and unconventional wavy-topped walls, all of which are winding and circuitous, and therefore are suitable for tortuous garden layouts. At the entrances of most gardens usually there are some rockeries, small courtyards, and tracery windows to serve as screens that conveniently restrict one's vision and make one see only indistinctly the scenery at one corner of the garden (Fig. VIII-14). Only after circling the observation route for some time will one finally have seen the garden including the rockery, the pool, and the halls and pavilions. Thus, whether you are on the move or remain still, the scenic objects in contraposition are not exposed to your view through direct approach or by some shortcut; they can be reached only by following a circuitous path for a while. The different areas in the garden usually are closely linked with one another as the halls and courtyards stretch out in sequence. All these are devices to create a feeling of depth in the general layout of the garden.

One garden area overlapping another is an essential arrangement for adding a sense of depth and sequence to garden scenery. Adjacent areas are thus half-closed from and half-open to each other, so that the buildings and the hillocks and pools serves as foils for one another and mutually act as borrowed scenic objects, thus contributing to the impression of sequence. The central area of Zhuozheng Yuan (The Humble Administrator's Garden) and that of Liu Yuan (Lingering-Here Garden) are good examples of this sequence stretching far into the distance: In the former case the garden areas are mostly open to one another and are only closed up in a few places (Figs. II-37 and II-38), while in the latter garden, the halls and courtyards are the main features but only a few of them are open (Fig. VIII-3). So the effect is totally different in the two different cases.

Other commonly adopted practices to add to the feeling of depth and sequence include: (a) corridors are sometimes constructed alongside a wall or on the corners of a courtyard, to form small separate courts which are dotted with a few trees and rocks here and there; and (b) sometimes banana trees, bamboo groves, or other trees and flowers, or lake stones may be seen through apertures in the doors and windows.

The irregular placement of tall trees, bamboo groves, a hall here, and a pavilion there to serve as background to the buildings and hillocks, can have the effect of pushing backward and upward the nearer buildings and hillocks; this gives one the sense of envisaging distant scenery far beyond the immediate sights. Therefore, when one looks westward from Hanbi Shanfang (Encompassing-Jade Mountain House) in the central area of Liu Yuan (Lingering-Here Garden), and views the earthen hill against its background of trees, rocks, pavilions and corridors, and at the farthest the maple grove, one seems to see a whole sequence of scenery stretching high into the distance. But when one looks northward from the same spot, although the main scenery of the garden comes into view, because there are no other objects behind the hillocks to serve as foils, the scenery appears near at hand and lacking in depth. Similarly, in Wangshui Yuan (The Retired Fisherman's Garden), in between Zhuwaiyizhi Xuan (A-Branch-from-Bamboo Lounge) and Jixu Zhai (Gathering-the-Void Study), the small courtyards and the bamboo groves add much to a feeling of a sequence in depth. On the lake-stone-piled terraces in front of the main hall in some gardens, the so-called "fish-scale-pits" arrangement is adopted;[7] this is the common practice in hilly orchards in Suzhou suburbs. According to such an arrangement, the flowers and trees are planted in tiers and pushed far upwards. This is an excellent way to create an impression of sequence in depth in flower terrace planting.

Several typical devices for the layout of Suzhou gardens have been analyzed and discussed in the preceding passages. Other devices, such as suiting the arrangement to specific locality, and considerations of variety and unity, will be discussed here.

Notes

1. Records are extant of the gardens of officials and landowners of the Song Dynasty that were open to the public at the time. (See *Collections of Books Ancient and Modern*, vol. 123, where records about Sima Guang's Enjoyment-in-Solitude Garden in Loyang are quoted from *Quotations from Yuan Cheng*.) This practice of opening gardens to the public became more common in Suzhou in the Qing Dynasty, as evidenced in a record about the enjoyment of springtime scenery in March found in *Qing Jia Records*, written by Gu Yiqing in the tenth year of the reign of Emperor Daoguan. The record reads:

   It is warm in the springtime, and a hundred flowers are in bloom in the gardens; the gatekeepers only ask for a few coins to pay for their labor in sweeping clean the fallen blossoms, and they open the gardens to visitors. Many men and women go there, and the gardens are full of people. Exotic birds and fowls are on display and rare species of flowers attract attention.

   Some verses on the Beautiful Sights in the City of Suzhou, by Yuan Xuelan, published in the third year of the reign of Emperor Tongzhi, was an anthology of his poems written after his springtime visits to the gardens of several families in Suzhou. In the preface to these verses there was the following passage:

   Aristocratic families and wealthy tribes compete with each other in constructing halls and pools for pleasure. Some remodel old gardens while others build new ones, all indulging in luxury and ease. The gardens are open to the public in the spring when visitors are admitted to enjoy the sights.... This usually lasts for more than a month.

2. See the "Biography of Dao-Gai" in *The History of the Southern Dynasties* and the "Biography of Niu Sengru" in *The History of the Tang Dynasty*. See also Li Deyu's Pingquan Zhuang in "Quotations from Mr. Jia," quoted in vol. 123 of *Collections of Books Ancient and Modern*. See also the "Biography of Mifu" in *The History of the Song Dynasty*. Also see the records about the great passion for quaint and bizarre-looking rocks as described by Li Deyu, Niu Sengru, Bai Juyi, Su Shi, Mi Fu, et al, in *Rocks Talk* by Yang Fuming, a modern writer.

3. The relative heights of the several major observation spots in the central area of Zhuozheng Yuan (The Humble Administrator's Garden) are given below in meters. Each of the heights is marked +0.00 meter to show its distance above or below the water surface level in the garden on a specified day in 1962:

   Inside the Yuanxiang Tang (The Distant-Fragrance Hall) 1.91 meters
   Terrace outside the hall 1.60 meters
   Terrace in front of Xiang Zhou (Fragrant-Isle Landboat) 0.96 meters
   Ground level of Jianshan Lou (Seeing-the-Hill Two-Storied Building) 0.91 meters
   Xiaocanglang (Little-Surging-Wave Pavilion) 1.10 meters
   Xiban Ting (West Half Pavilion) 1.15 meters
   Ground level in front of Xuexiangyunwei Ting (The Pavilion of Fragrant-Snow-and-Colorful Clouds) 4.63 meters
   Ground level in front of Daishuang Ting (The Waiting-for-the-Frost Pavilion) 4.47 meters
   Wuzhuyouju (Pavilion amid-Secluded-Wutong-and-Bamboo) 1.71 meters
   Hefeng Simian Ting (Breeze-from-the-Lotus-in-Four-Directions Pavilion) 1.50 meters
   Xiuqi Ting (Embroidered-Silk Pavilion) 4.51 meters

4. The distance between the chief observation spots and the chief scenic objects in the gardens in Suzhou (in meters):

From Yuanxiang Tang (The Distant-Fragrance Hall) to Xuexiangyunwei Ting (The Pavilion of Fragrant-Snow-and-Colorful Clouds) in Zhuozheng Yuan (The Humble Administrator's Garden): 34 meters

from Hanbi Shanfang (Encompassing-Jade Mountain House) to Ke Ting (Just-Right Pavilion) in Liu Yuan (Lingering-Here Garden): 35 meters

from Ouxiang Xie (Lotus-Root-Fragrance Waterside Pavilion) to Xiaocanglang (Little-Surging-Wave Pavilion) in Yi Yuan (Happy Garden): 32 meters

from Hehua Ting (Lotus Hall) to the rockery in Shizilin (The Forest of Lions Garden): 28 meters

from Kansongduhua Xuan (Looking-at-the-Pine-and-Painting Hall) to Zhuoying Shuige (Washing-Tassel Waterside Pavilion) and Huangshi Shan (Yellow-Stone Hill) in Wangshi Yuan (The Retired Fisherman's Garden): 31 meters

from Mingdao Tang (Comprehending-the-Doctrine Hall) to Canglang Ting (Surging-Wave Pavilion): 13 meters

from the path on the west to the main peak in Huanxiu Shanzhuang (Mountain Villa of Encircled Elegance): 12 meters.

5. Taken from the entries "Embellishing Hills" and "Steep-Cliff Hills," in sec. viii of *Yuan-Ye (Garden Building)*, by Ji Cheng.

6. The height of the ground level is the lowest here of all the buildings in the central area of the garden; the height of the ground floor is 2.63 meters and of the eaves on the second floor is 2.20 meters.

7. Fruit growers in the environs of East Bongting Hill in the suburb of Suzhou build along the irregularly shaped hill-slope terraced fields, which appear like fish scales and are called Yulinkan (Fish-Scale Pits) by the residents there.

III
Water

In the natural world, rivers and lakes, brooks, ravines, and waterfalls have their different shapes and characteristics; this became the basis for the treatment of water areas in traditional Chinese gardens. Chinese artisans in the past, engaged in their lifelong efforts in imitation of nature, piled the rocks and channeled the waters to create gardens of natural beauty; they accumulated much experience in abstracting the characteristic features of natural hills and in making natural phenomena appear in their essence in the gardens. As Suzhou is located on the plains south of the Changjiang (Yangtse) River, with crisscrossing rivulets and havens and a relatively high level of underground water, it is comparatively easy to channel the water into pools; so in most of the Suzhou gardens the zigzag-shaped natural pool becomes the focal point of the major scenic area (Figs. III-1 and III-2). In addition, there is plenty of rainfall in the Suzhou region. Digging pools not only takes care of accumulated rainwater, it also helps to adjust the temperature and humidity, purify the air in the gardens, and water the flowers and trees. Thus, the pool is a common feature in traditional Suzhou gardens.

The traditional way to construct a garden in China is to use a pool as the focal point, link it with brooks, ravines, and waterfalls, and ornament it with rocks and rockeries, flowers, trees, pavilions and two-story pavilions, thus producing beautiful scenery of all kinds. The brightness and clarity of the water surface creates an impression of expanded garden space, and gives one a feeling of calm, quietude, and good cheer. When the pool is placed beside gloomy and tortuous courtyards and small scenic areas, there are the contrasting effects of sparsity with density, or openness with confinement; these contrasts create attractive scenes against the background of hills, groves, and halls.

The inverted reflections in the pool, the sunlight and clouds, the fish swimming under the blue ripples, and the lotus flowers and sleeping lilies floating on the water all contribute to the beauty of the garden. Therefore, placing scenic objects and observation spots around a pool has long been the most commonly accepted practice in the layout of classical gardens in Suzhou (Figs. III-4, VIII-13, IX-1, and XI-1). In large gardens, the pool often branches out into small streams that are full of twists and turns, and form a number of smaller scenic areas; in some of the gardens there are also small brooks and creeks, ravines, and waterfalls.

The Surface of the Pool

The pool in a garden may be gathered into one big watery basin or be split into several smaller units, but in each case the arrangement should be fitting and proper. When it is gathered into one entity, the pool generally has a broad, extended surface and produces an impression of an expansive water country. Even though it was artificially constructed, it looks like a work of nature. For instance, the pool in Wangshi Yuan (The Retired Fisherman's Garden) is centered in one place, with the halls and water pavilions on its shores, all rather low and dwarfish, so that one gets a feeling of brightness and openness.

When a pool is split up into several areas, generally it twists and turns or sometimes seems to flow like a continuous stream; sometimes it appears broken up, so that occasionally it is concealed behind the shores and ravines, or amid the halls and pavilions, or flowers and trees, thus producing scenes of depth and gloom. For example, the surface of the pool in Zhuozheng Yuan (The Humble Administrator's Garden) seems broken up into several parts by the two hilly islets in its midst, and by halls and pavilions, winding bridges, bamboo groves, and clumps of trees. The main part of the pool is north of Yuanxiang Tang (Distant-Fragrance Hall) but the water winds back and forth in small streams and forms ponds here and there, so that small scenic areas follow one another in a row and scenic objects stretch far into the distance; you get the same effect whether you look westward from Wuzhuyouju (Pavilion amid-Secluded-Wutong-and-Bamboo) (Fig. VII-24) or northward from Xiaocanglang (Little-Surging-Wave Water-Court) (Fig. VII-25), or view Xiang Zhou (Fragrant-Isle Landboat) and Yiyu Xuan (Leaning-on-Jade Hall) from Hefengsimian Ting (Breeze-from-the-Lotus-in-Four-Directions Pavilion) (Fig. VII-26).

Of course, whether the pool is concentrated in one region or is dispersed, the arrangement depends largely upon the size of the garden. Usually, in a small garden the pool should be kept intact in one place, whereas in a large garden, although the pool may branch out into several minor units, there should always be one body of water with a broader expanse then the others to dominate as the major water scene.

The shape of the pool and its overall arrangement should be considered in light of the topography of its immediate environs, its size, and its surroundings in all directions. Generally, for small gardens or separate courtyards attached to private residences, the shape of the pool should be simple and natural, adorned with lake stones, flowers and trees, and wisteria along its shores; there should be fish and sleeping lilies in it, as in the case of Chang Yuan (Carefree Garden) and Hu Yuan (Kettle Garden) (see Chaps. XVIII and XIX). For medium-size gardens, a composite arrangement of the pool and the rockery, with due consideration for flowers and trees as well as halls and pavilions, is usually adopted. But because the garden space usually is not big enough, the concentrated treatment of water in one pool is still the common arrangement, with subsidiary watery areas here and there. That is, at one corner of the pool the water is channeled out through bridged-over creeks and streams, and is linked with small-size bays and coves; or else the water caverns are formed with piles of rocks to show the distant source of the water. Wangshi Yuan (The Retired Fisherman's Garden) contains a good example of this type.

A narrow but long pool is another kind commonly found in small and medium-size gardens, with different arrangements for different gardens. In the cases of Hu Yuan (Kettle Garden), Chang Yuan (Carefree Garden), He Yuan (Crane Garden), and Ban Yuan (Half Garden), a bridge is built over the pool near one end; it seems to divide the surface of the water into two parts, one major, the other lesser, to produce the effect of depth and variety.

In the case of Yi Yuan (Happy Garden), the pool is divided into three parts by means of a winding bridge and a brook outlet (Fig. III-6), so that the pool assumes a narrow, long, and zigzag shape, and the major and minor parts of the water area not only are distinctly shown, but different scenes are formed in accordance with the adjacent rocks, flowers, and trees against the background of the neighboring halls, pavilions, and landboats. But in the gardens where a hillock is the major scene, a long and narrow belt-shaped pool frequently is constructed to encircle the hillock and extend into a hilly gorge; it then serves as a foil to the steepness and depth of the hillock. The water area and the hilly region then complement each other to best advantage. Huanxiu Shanzhuang (Mountain Villa of Encircled Elegance) is a good example of this.

Large-size gardens such as Zhuozheng Yuan (The Humble Administrator's Garden) and Shizilin (The Forest of Lions Garden), each have several different scenic areas; the pool always assumes a shape of great variety so as to link up these areas into a unified entity with a number of major and minor scenic objects. In Zhuozheng Yuan (the Humble Administrator's Garden), not only is there the main pool, but the water is channeled into streams to encircle and wind about the halls, pavilions, hillocks, and groves; it is led to form separate watercourts, thus giving an impression of change and variety. The surface of the water in the pool at the central part of the garden takes up only two-fifths of the whole garden space, but because it is well arranged, it creates the feeling of a spacious lake country south of the Changjiang (Yangtse) River (Fig. III-2).

In rare cases, a pool is placed inside a hilly case, as in the Small-Wood-House Cave in Qiayin Yuan (Harmony-Hermitage Garden); there, water is stored up inside the cave, and a winding bridge extends far into it, so that a unique scene is created (Fig. IV-15). In Xiaolinyanshan Guan (Little-Linyan Hill-Lodge), there is another rare instance of two water caves, one big and one small, that are connected with the pool there on the north. The shapes of the pools are different in the different gardens of Suzhou (Fig. III-3), with the majority of them long and narrow, because a pool like that, seen from a distance vertically, not only shows the scenery sequentially in depth, but also makes the gardens appear remote and attractive, especially if one stands on a bridge at the outlet of the pool or upon one of its twists and turns and takes a near view at some scene in the middle distance.

In classical gardens in Suzhou, there are different ways to divide up the surface of a pool, depending on the size of the body of water. In a pool with a broad surface, islets may be used for partitioning, as with the small islets amid the pool in the central part of Zhuozheng Yuan (The Humble Administrator's Garden) or in Liu Yuan (Lingering-Here Garden). In the former case, there is only a narrow strait between the two islets, so the pool is at once separated, yet connected, at once concealing, yet revealing each other, and an effect of sequence in depth is achieved. Because the garden space for a private garden usually is small, the surface of the pool in it usually is divided by some bridges, except for the two above-mentioned gardens. The use of the bridge device separates one garden space from another and yet does not cut them apart. This is suitable for smaller water surfaces. The water surface may also be divided by means of a water outlet, as in Yi Yuan (Happy Garden), or with a pavilion, as in Shizilin (The Forest of Lions Garden); or it may be effected by means of a hall, as in the Xiaocanglang (The Little-Surging-Wave) and Xiaofeihong (Little-Flying-Rainbow) in Zhuozheng Yuan (The Humble Administrator's Garden); but such cases are few.

A bridge generally is vaulted over a pool at the narrower part of the water and usually takes the form of a stone pavement made of big slabs. The bridge may have only one or two twists but sometimes may extend to three or four

(Figs. III-8 and III-9). Such stone bridges usually are built horizontally, in conformity with the architectural style of gardens south of the Changjiang (Yangtse) River, but the height of these bridges above water level depends much upon the size of the pool. A number of bridges in Zhuozheng Yuan (The Humble Administrator's Garden) are built with low and open railings, so that the watery area seems to be immediately below; yet the water actually does not touch the bridge, so a feeling of depth is obtained, and inverted images are reflected in the water (Fig. III-5).

With smaller pools the bridges are built on the same level as the surface of the water, so that visitors can more easily appreciate the fish swimming back and forth and the floating water lilies; this also gives the impression of a wider expanse of pool than actually exists (Fig. XI-1). If there should be a rockery or a rocky cliff nearby, such a bridge can also serve as foil and accentuate the steepness of the rockery or a particular rocky cliff. The winding bridges in the pools in Yi Pu (Art Orchard), Wangshi Yuan (The Retired Fisherman's Garden) and Shizilin (The Forest of Lions Garden), as well as the zigzag bridge that links the Eight-Cornered-Pavilion with the pool in the Xi Yuan (West Garden), all built near the water level, belong to this category.

Stone strips are placed horizontally on top of the stone blocks to serve as railings on the bridges; the railings are flat and low, simple and clean, and light and lively, and therefore are more in harmony with the environment than iron railings (Figs. III-5 and III-8). In some cases lake stones are piled to serve as railings on stone-slab bridges, as in Mu Yuan (Adoration Garden) (Fig. III-9).

Wooden bridges are rarely to be found, one exception being the small stone slab bridge with wooden railings south of Xiang Zhou (The Fragrant-Isle Landboat) in Zhuozheng Yuan (The Humble Administrator's Garden), where Xiaofeihong (The Little Flying Rainbow) is the only "corridor-bridge" in all the gardens in Suzhou; it not only separates the space but also adds to the feeling of depth in garden scenery (Fig. III-10).

Round-arched bridges are rarely built, because the altitude of such a bridge would be unusually great and would not fit in well with the water surface of the pool. If it were built, such a bridge would be located in some obscure spot and limited to one arch only. The small-arched bridge in Wangshi Yuan (The Retired Fisherman's Garden) is placed at one corner of the pool, so the effect is not bad. A greatly arched stone bridge possibly was traditional in the Ming Dynasty, and the only example of it may now be found in the Yi Pu (The Art Orchard).

Where the pool is especially narrow, it is also possible to provide a flight of stone steps in lieu of a bridge. The only extant example of this may be found in the ravine in Huanxiu Shanzhuang (Mountain Villa of Encircled Elegance).

Aside from the above-mentioned ways, it is also possible to pile up an arched bridge with yellow stones or lake stones, with creepers planted around it. This gives on the impression of a small rockery as well as a bridge. Xiaochibi (The stone-piled arched bridge, Little Red Cliff) in Shizilin (The Forest of Lions Garden) (Fig. III-2), shaped like a water gorge or rocky cave, is a case in point.

Lake stones and yellow stones are described in detail in Chap. IV.

The Shores of the Pool

The natural shores of a pool usually take the form of gentle earthen slopes, in the plainland, while the running brooks and deep ponds are generally lined by stone precipices, projecting rocks, crumbling cliffs, or scattered shoals. In classical gardens in Suzhou, there are earthen shores for a pool and there are stone shores, depending on the natural surroundings. We can gather from the painting of Zhuozheng Yuan (The Humble Administrator's Garden) by Wen Zhengming of the Ming Dynasty (Fig. VII-2), that there were more earthen than stone shores along the pools in that garden when it was built during the Ming Dynasty. However, earthen shores collapse more easily when drenched with rain, so there are few earthen shores for the pools in Suzhou gardens today; in most cases, stones are piled to serve as shores, and occasionally stone slabs, stone cliffs, or level, low stone shores are built. Sometimes, to avoid monotony and create variety in the shores beside the pool, pavilions or corridors are constructed right next to the water.

Shores Piled with Stone

Placing stones alongside the pool prevents the shores from collapsing and enables visitors to go very close to the pool to enjoy the scenery. However, artistic effects must be considered if such an arrangement is made. Whether they are piled with lake stones or yellow stones, the stone-piled shores in the Suzhou gardens are successful only when the builder has shown a good knowledge of the characteristics of the different veins and shapes of the stones; the big and small stones must be happily mixed up, the veins of the stones placed in harmony, the convex and concave pieces alternated, and there must be a general impression of proper arrangement of the protruding with the receding, and the rise with the fall; furthermore, there must be plenty of earth between the stones so that flowers, trees, and creepers can be planted there (Figs. III-14, III-15).

In Wangshi Yuan (The Retired Fisherman's Garden), along the stone shores south and northwest of the pool, stones are piled up to form a number of concave caverns, into which the water extends and appears to have come a long way from the fountainhead of the pool. The shores there rise and fall, sometimes lower than the surface of the footpath and immediately above the water level, sometimes rising to a height, where one may find a seat and take a rest. This is an example of a successful arrangement of the yellow-stone shores of a pool (Fig. III-16).

In Huanxiu Shanzhuang (Mountain Villa of Encircled Elegance), huge lake stones shoot forth at the foot of the rockery immediately beside the pool, appearing much like a natural water cave. This is another example of a successful arrangement for the shores of a pool in a garden (Fig. III-17).

In short, the stone-piled shores of a pool should not be entirely straight; still less should they be too high; otherwise, with the shores high and the water low, it would almost be like leaning on a railing to look into a well, and this is contrary to the original purpose of having pools dug for scenery.

To facilitate the watering of flowers and trees near the surface of the water, natural stone steps down to the water level generally are provided for from the stone-piled shores of the pool. Such stone steps are also useful in introducing more variety to the shape of the shores of the pool.

Rocks Projecting above the Water

Rocks projecting above the water are often found along the shores of pools in both large and small gardens in Suzhou (Fig. III-18). The smaller type consists only of horizontal stone slabs protruding above the water, as in Canli Yuan (Remnant-Grain Garden) in Zhuangjiajiao Lane, in the north shore of the pool in the Wangshi Yuan (The Retired Fisherman's Garden) (Fig. III-16), and in one corner of Hefengsimian Ting (Breeze-from-the-Lotus-in-Four-Directions Pavilion) in Zhuozheng Yuan (The Humble Administrator's Garden) (Fig. III-18).

The larger type of protruding rocks usually use the shore wall and the stone steps as a background, with the rocks piled to form a terrace facing the water. In this way the horizontal terrace contrasts with the shore wall and serves as the natural transitional stage from the pool to its shore. The protruding rocks south of the Xuexiangyunwei Ting (The Pavilion of Fragrant-Snow-and-Colorful Clouds) in Zhuozheng Yuan (The Humble Administrator's Garden), are a good example of this.

Low Stone Shores

Low stone shores are simple in structure, but often are not used, because no matter whether they are constructed with long, narrow stone strips, unshapely stones, or with black, spotted stones, and are neatly built in layers, they can hardly harmonize with the garden scenery. However, in most cases where a hall or terrace is built immediately beside the water, usually stone shores are needed. They become almost indispensable when the commonly adopted way of piling up stones to form the shores of a pool in a way that imitates nature requires a very large number of lake stones or yellow stones and entails a rather complicated construction process.

In constructing stone shores the proper shapes of the stones and the appropriate treatment for gaps between the stones usually have a great effect on the garden scenery. From the point of view of the shapes of stones, the gaps between long, narrow stones are horizontal and therefore harmonize better with the surface of the water and with the buildings, so they are naturally better than shores piled with odd-shaped or black, spotted stones. Of course they require more labor to construct. In constructing the stone shores for the Buqiu Fang (Replenishing-Autumn Landboat) in Huanxiu Shanzhuang (Mountain Villa of Encircled Elegance), a certain number of lake stones are inserted into the gaps of long, narrow strips of stones, in order to harmonize with the stone shores on both the left and the right. This device adds liveliness to the scene.

Earthen Shores

In order to prevent the earth from collapsing, earthen shores of a pool must not be too steep, so they usually take up much space. For this reason, earthen shores are seldom used in smaller gardens. If the garden is large, earth shores result in a good effect if they are well arranged.

In the central part of Zhuozheng Yuan (The Humble Administrator's Garden), on two sides of the earthen hillock amidst the pool are rank growing reeds, while on the north is a dense grove of trees, so that the whole scene appears to closely resemble nature and possesses the peculiar characteristics of the area south of the Changjiang (Yangtse) River. This rare example of a well-arranged earthen-shore pool is unique among all the classical gardens in Suzhou.

IV
Rockeries

In Chinese gardens, where natural landscape has ever been the thing to strive for, the device of piling rocks to form rockeries can be traced back to the early period of the Western Han Dynasty.[1] Technical advances in that field continued through the Eastern Han Dynasty to the era of the Three Kingdoms. According to a record in The History of Later Han Dynasty, a man named Liang Ji

> "built many gardens and parks, in which earth was piled up for the construction of hillocks, and within a distance of ten li nine hillocks were amassed to resemble the two Yao hills, where thick groves and seemingly inaccessible ravines gave the visitors an impression of finding themselves amidst wild nature."[2]

Then, during the years of the Wei Kingdom in the era of the Three Kingdoms, Fangling Yuan (The Fragrant Grove Garden) was described as containing the wonders of "nine ravines and eight brooks."[3] These records show that Chinese gardens built in the Han Dynasty and the Wei Kingdom were no longer constructed simply in imitation of nature, but that, within limited space, artificial specimens modeled after natural hills were created to suit the fancies of the garden owners.

Then, in the Western Jin and Eastern Jin Dynasties, and later in the Northern and Southern Dynasties, high officials and intellectuals became absorbed in the study of metaphysics, and they strove for artifice and freedom from all restraints, in order to find "escape from the realities of life." They adored strange-shaped rocks and considered it "refinement" to give free rein to their sentiments in the surroundings of gardens and hills and rills. As a result, in the gardens built at the time, finding delight in fanciful reproductions of wild nature became the vogue.[4] Thus, this synthesis and abstraction of natural hills and rills gradually evolved upon the groundwork of gardening in the Han Dynasty and Wei Kingdom period. Then, later in the Tang and the Song Dynasties as further advances were made in the country's economic and cultural development, not only were more gardens built, but more experience was gained in the art of garden building, both in theory and in practice.

At the same time, with the impact made by paintings, the heaping of rocks to pile up hillocks gradually acquired a peculiar resemblance to the hills and rills in classical Chinese watercolor paintings. This became an important architectural feature in the art of gardening in China through the centuries. Such rockeries, constructed in a great variety of highly creative shapes, rarely find their parallels in the gardens of other countries of the world. This was possible because the Chinese garden-building artisans of the past, from their frequent contacts with various phenomena in wild nature, had gained indelible impressions of the external appearances of hills and precipices, as well as caves and ravines; they also had a knowledge of the composition of various kinds of rocks and the special features of earth compounded with stones. Only after they had gained such comprehensive knowledge of gardening and had repeated practice in actual construction were they able to create garden scenery that was at once majestic and grotesque, towering and steep, dim and deep, on the same plane and in perspective.

Suzhou gardens are located mostly within the city limits. Owing to the limited garden space and other restricting circumstances, different ways are adopted for the piling of rockeries in different gardens. For the very small-size gardens, a few peaked rocks usually are placed in the courtyards either behind or in front of the parlor or study of the family residence; rocks are heaped up to form hillocks, stone precipices are built to project from the walls, or a few lake stones are embedded beside some small pool.

In a slightly larger but still fairly small garden, the compound attached to the residence may be bigger in size, but the arrangement of rocks still cannot be very complicated. There, a pool generally serves as the center of attraction, while rocks are placed as foils either for the pool or for the halls, flowers, and trees; or an earthen mound of a natural hill slope is utilized to plant trees and flowers in the garden; or an artificial rockery is piled to serve as the major scenery.

In a medium-size garden, usually there are both a hillock and a pool, used to form several scenic areas, together with the halls and pavilions and flowers and trees; but within the major scenic area some hilly range and caves and ravines are constructed in imitation of natural hills (Fig. IV-1). Beside the pools some gardens have steep precipices and overhanging cliffs, or wavy embankments that rise and fall in uneven heights, while down below are placed projecting rocks and fishing nooks so as to bring the water in the pools closer to the hillocks.

When there are large-size rockeries, in order to provide the observer with a wider field of vision, one or two story pavilions generally are built atop them, so that the scenic objects both within the garden and beyond can be viewed. It is common to build a rockery and plant a grove of trees on one side of a pool, while on the other side are randomly placed halls and lounges, pavilions, and waterside pavilions; then, whether you stand on the hill and look beyond the clear water in the pool to the buildings of irregular heights in the distance, or you stay in a hall or pavilion and watch the rocky precipices, flowers, and trees on the other side of the pool, you get the wonderful effect of opposite scenes vis-à-vis each other; you can also enjoy the contrast between the buildings and the hillock that face each other at a distance.

In the really big gardens, the piling of rockeries, rocky peaks or precipices, or of just a few rocks, depends on the size of the scenic area or courtyard in which it is located. It is possible to construct several rockeries in a scenic area, and place them near one another to look like a chain of hilly ranges, and thus to divide the garden into several parts; this makes the garden scenery seem at once separable and merged, and gives one the feeling of tortuosity and depth in all the scenery.

The Relationship Between Earth and Stones in Rockeries

All the garden rockeries are built of rocks and earth, but the proper proportion of earth and rocks is an essential factor that not only has an effect upon the style of each rockery, but is closely concerned with the materials chosen and the labor required to build it.

From the viewpoint of rockery construction, different kinds of earth have different degrees of friction. If the friction is too great, the piled rockery may crumble. So a rockery built of earth must not be too high, for then it would sprawl and in consequence occupy a very large area and be too bulky to assume an elegant shape or an appearance of majesty or intricacy. Therefore, the mixed use of earth and rocks is technically inevitable. In the construction of caves, ravines or precipices, and cliffs, or in the piling of a fairly high rockery within a small area, more rocks should be used than when building ordinary rockeries. On the other hand, using more rocks requires more human labor, more money, and more time for buying, transporting, and heaping the rocks; thus, it leads to the lavish consumption of human labor and material. Hence, using the proper proportions of rocks and earth is essential.

From the Han Dynasty onward, although there were plenty of records on artificially constructed rockeries, specific detailed descriptions were wanting. Beginning in the Wei, the Jin, and the Northern and Southern Dynasties, large-scale peaks, hilly ranges, and caverns and ravines were often constructed in the gardens of the top rulers. For instance, in the Taiqing Years of the Liang Dynasty (547–549 A.D.), in the Xiangdong Yuan built by Xiao Yi (alias Emperor Yuan) in the city of Jiangling, the rocky cavern extended up the hillock for more than 200 steps.[5] In the Northern Song Dynasty, Zhao Ji (alias Emperor Huizong), built Genyue Garden, which contained lofty hills and spacious ravines; in addition, complicated combinations of banks and gorges, and caverns and caves, were scattered about.[6]

Also in the Northern Song Dynasty, in the gardens in Loyang, earthen hillocks, pools, and bamboos were the major features,[7] whereas in the Southern Song Dynasty, the gardens in Wuxing usually made the fullest use of the natural surroundings, while rocks were not very extensively employed.[8] In the Late Ming Dynasty, according to *Records of Several Gardens Visited in Jinling* and *Accounts of Gardens in Loudong*, both written by Wang Shizhen, most hillocks were piled with rocks; there were caves and caverns underneath and odd-shaped rocks on top.

In the last years of the Ming Dynasty, the book *Garden Building*, by Ji Cheng, gave a special chapter to details on the choice of rocks, and devoted separate sections to the peculiar characteristics of different hilly scenes, including:

- Hillock-inside-the-garden
- Hillock-beside-the-hall
- Hillock-beside-a-two-story building
- Hillock-beside-a-study
- Hillock-beside-a-pool
- Steep-precipiced hillocks
- Peaks
- Hilly ranges
- Cliff's caverns
- Waterfalls

These descriptions reflected the specific conditions of hillock construction south of the Changjiang (Yangtse) River at that time.

However, no matter whether more rocks or more earth is used in the construction, the piling of rocks to form a hillock should bear a close resemblance to a hill in wild nature. This is the fundamental principle to be observed. One passage in *Leisurely Sentiments Jotted Down* by Li Yu in the Qing Dynasty says:

> I have wandered far and wide in my life and visited many famous gardens, yet I have never come across any rockery either filling only one [hectare] of land or extending to more than several hundred [meters] in length where no traces of artificial tricks or unnatural devices are visible or which really looks like a hill in the distance.

In *Annals of Jiaxing*, written during the reign of Emperor Kangxi in the Qing Dynasty, it is also stated: "In the past it was considered truly artistic for the rocks to be heaped up into lofty piles, and few people liked to see much earth in a hillock." This seems to indicate that in the early period of the Qing Dynasty, overuse of rocks in hillock construction led to artificiality and unnaturalness. Besides, it resulted in the consumption of too much labor, expense, and time in selecting, purchasing, transporting, and piling the rocks. Therefore, Li Yu proposed the use either of chiefly earth and a few rocks or of equal proportions of earth and rocks in hillock construction.

Another rockery-piler, Zhang Lian (alias Nanyuan), who was Li Yu's contemporary, also suggested:

> Instead of constructing several rocky peaks that reach up to the sky, it would be better to build flat mounds with gentle slopes, to form continuous hilly ranges, and to employ odd-shaped rocks as decorations.[9]

The gardens that are still preserved south of the Changjiang (Yangtse) River that date back to a time before Li Yu and Zhang Lian include the rockery in Yu Yuan (Comfort Garden) in Shanghai built by Zhang Nanyuan in the last years of Emperor Wanli in the Ming Dynasty, the rockery in Qiuxiapu Garden (Autumn Sunset Clouds Garden) in the county of Jiading, the rockeries in Yi Pu (Art Orchard) and Wufeng Yuan (Five-Peak Garden) in Suzhou, and the waterfall rockery in Qiaying Yuan (Harmony-Hermitage Garden) (as piled by Zhou Bingzhong), also in Suzhou. The rockeries, possibly contemporaneous with those by Li Yu and Zhang Lian, include the rockery on the eastern part of Ou Yuan (Twin Garden) in Suzhou and the Bayingjian (Eight-Tone Ravine) in Jichang Yuan (Expressing Delight Garden) in the city of Wuxi. Of a little later date then these were the rockery in Huanxiu Shanzhuang (Mountain Villa of Encircled Elegance) in Suzhou and the yellow-stone rockery in Yan Yuan (Swallow Garden) in the county of Changshu. The last two were both designed by a man named Ge Yuliang during the reign of Emperor Qianlong in the Qing Dynasty. The largest-sized rockery among all these is in Yu Yuan, where no earth was used in its construction, while the stone walls, caverns, and ravines in all the other rockeries of the period, as mentioned above, were built almost entirely of stone, with only a little earth on the top areas of the hillocks for planting flowers and trees.

As for the rockeries in the other preserved gardens in Suzhou, most were built after the Taiping Uprising, while only a few were reconstructed on the foundations of old rockeries, and they also were built almost entirely of rocks. This shows that when the rockeries were built south of the Changjiang (Yangtse) River in the four hundred years since the reign of the Emperor Wanli in the Ming Dynasty, the tendency was to use much stone and little earth. Of course, this does not mean that this tendency achieved perfection and excluded the use of other methods. On the contrary, there were still a number of very admirable rockeries that did not follow this tendency. For instance, only one of the rockeries in Zhuozheng Yuan (The Humble Administrator's Garden) was constructed with much stone and little earth, while the other three rockeries in the same garden were built with little stone and much earth, so that they could harmonize with the pool and the trees there and produce scenery that appeared more natural.

The General Layout

The Relationship Between Hillock Construction and the Surroundings

In hillock construction, the decisions on the location of the hillock and its shape, as well as its height and size, must be made first in accordance with the requirements of the garden and with due consideration of the suitability of it surroundings. In small-size gardens, because of their limited space, the hillock generally serves as the major scenery opposite the main hall; flowers and trees are planted to add liveliness to the scene, and sometimes to make up for the absence of a pool. The flowers and trees are usually few but carefully chosen, and their size and height should be designed to produce a sense of depth; the shape of the hillock should fit in with these arrangements. Therefore, the size of the hillock should be in keeping with the available space. Its frontal part should be lower than its rear portion, and its contours should be irregular. The highest point of the hillock should not directly face the center bay of the hall opposite, nor should a pavilion be built atop the hillock. In constructing the hillock, not too many rocks should be used, but those used should be used appropriately.

For a large or medium-sized garden, deciding whether the hillock or the pool is the main item in it is the major consideration in determining the size and shape of the hillock. In a garden where the hillock is the main entity, the emphasis on the hillock often leads to its over-bulkiness, so that it does not fit in well with its surroundings. This defect appears to a certain extent in Canglang Ting (The Surging-Wave-Pavilion Garden). However, although the rockery in Huanxiu Shanzhuang (Mountain Villa of Encircled Elegance) measures 7.2 meters in height from the surface of the pool to the topmost peak, and is the second highest hillock in Suzhou gardens, still it does not appear to be overencumbered, because there is so much empty space to its south and west. In a garden where the pool is the major entity, the hillock is relegated to secondary importance; yet it should be sized in proportion to the pool.

It is perhaps unnecessary to say much about the importance of matching well in the case of a fairly large rockery that faces the pool on two or three sides. Even in the case of a hillock that faces the pool on one side, it is necessary to consider whether the shape of the hillock and the size of the planted flowers and trees when fully grown would be in proportion to the size of the pool; also, whether the shape and size of the hillock would fit in well with the size and contours of buildings such as halls, pavilions, and two-story mansions that may be put up on the shores opposite the pool.

A tall hillock should not be constructed by the side of a high building, for that would make that particular part of the garden appear too huge and unwieldy, as is the case of the northwestern corner of Shizilin (The Forest of Lions Garden). High buildings built on mountains exert a bad influence upon the spacial composition of gardens even if the buildings are beautifully designed.

Sometimes the contours of the buildings may appear too high, pointed, and stiff, such as we find in Fucui Ge (The Floating-Jade Two-Storied Pavilion) in the western part of Zhuozheng Yuan (The Humble Administrator's Garden).

The Form and Contour of the Hillock

There may be from one to three or four rockeries in any one of the classical gardens of Suzhou, but in most cases there is only one. From the point of view of architectural design, there are only a few truly excellent examples among the many rockeries constructed in about one century of late Qing Dynasty and Minguo (the Republic of China) in Suzhou. Most of the rockeries either have too few component parts or the parts are not properly arranged, so there is insufficient variety in the shape and body of the hillock, and its contours appear too simple and monotonous. Such a phenomenon is most obvious in the gardens that have only one hillock.

The component parts of the rockeries built from the last years of the Ming to the middle of the Qing Dynasty consisted chiefly of precipices and peaks, hilly ridges, gorges and ravines, caves, footpaths, bridges, terraces, and waterfalls. One common way of assembling and arranging these component parts was to construct precipices right next to the pool, to build a footpath under the precipices that goes through a valley, spirals upward, and comes to a bridge over the ravines, and then to set up a terrace on the top of the rockery to provide a view of the distant scenery.

The decision on the number of peaks and hilly ridges to be built, and on their different locations, should depend on the size and shape of the hillock or rockery. In each hillock there generally is only one or two caves, concealed at the foot of the hillock and inside some gully; in some cases there may be a waterfall down the hillock in the form of small streams. In Huanxiu Shanzhuang (Mountain Villa of Encircled Elegance), gullies divide the rockery into three parts, so the separate parts, left and right, front and rear, serve as foils for each other, with the major scenes predominant; a feeling of layers and depth is thereby created. At the same time, since the hillock is a solid body, whereas the gully is insubstantial, the contrast between the two is between substance and insubstantiality; thus, the hillock appears lively and full of variety (Figs. IV-1, XV-5, and XV-7).

In the last decades of the Qing Dynasty, the hillock was mostly low and flat; horizontally, there was seldom a combination of deep gullies and ravines with fairly large hilly ridges and peaks; vertically there was only a footpath of stone steps representing different horizontal levels. The result is that the hillock appears flat and stiff, and lacks variety. One exception may be found in the rockery in Yi Yuan (Happy Garden). There, above the precipice at the northwestern corner of the garden are a cave and a peak that recede some distance from the precipice. This produces a distinct feeling of depth, and there is variety in the contours of the hillock (Fig. IV-9).

Regardless of its size, a hillock should have clear contours at the low and high points, and at the rises and falls; to avoid symmetry and monotony, the highest spot need not be located in the central part. In this respect the arrangement is excellent in Huanxiu Shanzhuang (Mountain Villa of Encircled Elegance), and in Yi Yuan (Happy Garden). In some other gardens, in addition to the lack of variety in shape and contours is the further defect of too many disjointed items on the hillocks. The rockeries in the central parts of Shizilin (The Forest of Lions Garden), and Liu Yuan (Lingering-Here Garden) are examples of this kind. In contrast, in Yi Pu (Art Orchard) a pavilion is built on the eastern tip of the rockery and is flanked by trees, in order to make up for the flat terrain of the hillock. This certainly is neatly done.

If a rockery is constructed beside the pool, not only should its height be in proportion to the size of the pool, but the water surface in the pool and the height level on the terrain on the opposite shore should also be taken into consideration. The last two factors are often neglected, especially the one of the highest water level in the pool, so that when the water in the pool reaches its high level, one gets the feeling that the hillock is too low and dwarfish.

The discussion above is limited to the cases where there is only one rockery in the garden. Should there be several hillocks in a garden, they must not be constructed or arranged in an artificially assembled pattern. It would not be proper to have hillocks on three sides of a pool, for that would give one the feeling of overcrowded space. For instance, in Shizilin (The Forest of Lions Garden), the stone precipices on the south and the east of the rockery form a 90 degree angle and therefore appear to be somewhat artificially joined together; on the two flanks of the precipices there are earthen hillocks, and the buildings on top of these hillocks are also too high, so the whole place seems too crowded. Fortunately, at the southwestern corner there is an opening through which one can see far into the distance. In Zhuozheng Yuan (The Humble Administrator's Garden), where the rockeries are most numerous, the arrangement of the hillocks is relatively successful. The two rockeries located inside the pool are separated by a ravine and a valley, yet they are still linked into one entity, so that they appear like natural hillocks and also give one a feeling of depth. Two other rockeries are more distant from each other, while the earthen hillock on the eastern flank serves well in linking the northern with the southern parts of the garden. The arrangement of the pool and the rockeries in the central part of the garden produce the effect of brightness and expansiveness.

Devices for Foil Effect

To achieve foil effect for a hillock, it is essential to make the component parts of the hillock, such as precipices, peaks and hilly ridges, gorges and gullies, terraces, footpaths, bridges, and waterfalls, serve as foils for the main peak; the different locations, different heights, and different sizes of the component parts can be made to serve as foil for each other; then one sees the contrast between the solid and the insubstantial, and gets a sense of layers and depths as well as an impression of the infinite variety of the hillock and its three-dimensional presence. In a hillock of a fairly large size, such as the rockery in Yu Yuan (Comfort Garden) in Shanghai, the main peak is placed at the rear, while at the front is the tortuous footpath of stone steps and a curious mixture of terraces, gorges, brooks, waterfalls, and precipices that extend from the ground level to the highest points in tiers of complicated structure; as a result, the main peak appears towering and steep.

On the other hand, on a small hillock such as we find in Huanxiu Shanzhuang (Mountain Villa of Encircled Elegance), the main peak is placed in the foreground, while the gullies, bridges, lower peaks, and ridges to the left and right serve as foils; this also serves to create an impression of the majesty and grandeur of the main peak.

But whatever the device employed, the location of the main peak should not be right in the middle but should be inclined slightly to one side, especially when the hillock stretches far lengthwise. The highest point of the rockery in the central part of Liu Yuan (Lingering-Here Garden) is concealed on the west side among the laurel grove; this constitutes an effective device for foil effect.

In gardens of the Ming Dynasty, underneath the precipices, were winding bridges that stood barely above the surface of the water; or low rocky seats that almost touched the top level of the pool; both were used to show by contrast the towering, steep precipices (Fig. XIV-1).

Usually it is taboo to put up tall pavilions or two-story halls on top of a hillock, but if a pavilion or hall is put up there, at least it should be in proportion with the size and shape of the hillock. For instance, in Zhuozheng Yuan (The Humble Administrator's Garden), the hillock west of the pool in the central part looks flat and low, so the pavilion of Xuexiangyunwei Ting (Pavilion of Fragrant-Snow-and-Colorful Clouds) that is built on top of the hillock is oblong-shaped. If the hillock is steep and majestic, it is better to build a pavilion at a lower site than at the top; the main peak would serve as its background, as in the case of Yu Yuan (Comfort Garden) in Shanghai.

In planting trees on a hillock, it is necessary to consider the locations of the trees, the rate of density in their planting, their shapes, and their rate of growth, so that they can produce the desired foil effect. Generally, along gentle slopes, it is proper to plant long and straight-boughed deciduous trees but not to plant them too densely. In large, hilly regions, evergreens and deciduous trees should be planted alternately, and more densely. On top of steep precipices and deep gorges it is better to plant bending, tortuous pines than tall deciduous trees, so that the pines can grow aslant and reach beyond their bounds. Some few finely-shaped trees and flowers of slow growth are planted nearby to match, with the result that the ancient and clumsily-shaped are placed side by side with the comely and elegant, to produce a lovely combination. In Huanxiu Shanzhuang (Mountain Villa of Encircled Elegance), however, only an evergreen cypress, a maple with its comely leaves, and a crape myrtle with its beautiful flowers, are planted on the rockery, with the large-sized maple placed in the middle, the crape myrtle growing aslant beyond the precipice, and the cypress serving as background. Here we have an admirable arrangement.

Basic Conditions for the Piling of Rocks

A good knowledge of the features of a natural hillock and of the shapes, veins, and hues of the rocks is a basic prerequisite for the piling of rocks.

If a hillock built of natural limestones borders on water, the stones at the foot of the hill may erode with the buffetings of the waves, and a number of small holes and horizontal concave troughs would be formed in them, with convex portions bulging like nasal bridges and eddying cavities appearing on the surface. These stones are called lake stones. The better type of lake stones would have the peculiar features of eddying circles, small cavities and wrinkled veins. The eddying circles may be large or small, but generally are rather shallow, and they often enclose one another in irregular patterns.

In some cases there are cavities within the eddying circle but not all eddying circles contain cavities. There is a great variety of shapes for these cavities, but because they are formed by centuries of waves lashing at them, their surface is generally smooth, glossy, and slippery. The borders of the cavities are almost all round. In addition to the larger cavities usually there are one or two smaller ones which not infrequently are linked by small cavities concealed beneath the surface.

The wrinkly veins are in some cases rather broad and shallow, lying aslant, but in other cases may be deep and numerous, and generally restricted to one part of a stone; most are aslant but in some few cases are nearly vertical. Between the wrinkly veins usually there are lengthwise-shaped cavities that are different from the other cavities. Most of the wrinkly veins have smooth, glossy surfaces; only a few are rough-surfaced or have small crevices of all kinds.

During the reign of Emperor Qianlong in the Qing Dynasty a man named Ge Yuliang knew about all these factual details, so in the Huanxiu Shanzhuang (Mountain Villa of Encircled Elegance), which was constructed under his direction, most of the stones have eddying circles in them, some few have wrinkly veins, and some with small cavities are found among them; because of these features the hillock very much resembles an actual hill in the world of nature (Fig. IV-10).

Like other limestones, yellow stones fall under the climatic influence of the changing seasons and the erosions caused by wind, so in the course of time they split and break up from big pieces into small ones, and finally into tiny bits of earth. During the breaking up process, the pieces of stones that split from the rock stratum are of different shapes—vertical, horizontal, or oblique—and of different sizes, and they are intertwined with each other, overlapping, uneven, and irregular.

The precipices of the rockery in Ou Yuan (Twin Garden) in Suzhou well illustrate the above descriptions of the rock formations, so the rockery there appears like a naturally formed hillock (Figs. IV-11 and IV-13). Also, low areas at the bend of a hill are much drenched and scoured by rain, so some pieces of stone there are exposed to view; if footpaths are built beside the hillocks, such small stones would also appear. Therefore, the stones piled to form stone steps going up the rockery in the eastern part of Ou Yuan (Twin Garden) are built in imitation of nature. But it would be absurd to pile up yellow stones in the way the "tiger-skin" stony walls are built, or use yellow stones in place of lake stones and pile them into caves of different shapes, as in the case of the pool embankment in Canglang Ting Garden (The Surging-Wave Pavilion Garden).

Large cobbles may be about a meter in length and in width. Cobbles were mixed with yellow stones in Liu Yuan (Lingering-Here Garden), and recently, in Hu Qiu (Tiger-Hill Park) in Suzhou, cobbles were piled up for slope protection, with excellent results.

Detailed Descriptions of Different Construction Devices

Stone Cliffs

Stone cliffs built with lake stones are made in the following ways:

1. The cliffs are piled with pieces of cavityless grey stones, with the lowest layer almost touching the water level and appearing rather uneven on the surface, so that when viewed from a distance the concave parts appear to be full of shadows that suggest the presence of cavities. This is the case in Yi Pu (Art Orchard) (Figs. IV-3 and IV-4), and seems to be an old-fashioned device.

2. If the surface of the rock on the cliff does not hunch up like the nasal bridge, or contain vertical concave troughs, and the large pieces of rock have several small cavities, the stone cliff appears majestic and imposing (Fig. IV-9). Such a cliff may be found above the northwestern corner of the pool at Yi Yuan (Happy Garden).

3. Most of the cliffs in Huanxiu Shanzhuang (Mountain Villa of Encircled Elegance) imitate the intertwining eddying caves made of Tai-Lake stones, with the occasional presence of big and small cavities in the eddying caves; the surface of the stone is glossy and slippery, and the borders of the caves are round and naturally shaped. Stone cliffs in the southwestern corner of this hillock project outward obliquely, for in piling these stone cliffs, instead of using horizontal stones that jut out artificially, stones are rolled into an oblique, eddying shape and made to bear the weight of the cliffs above. This device may have been invented by Ge Yuliang (Figs. IV-10 and XV-5).

4. The stone cliffs in the southeastern corner of Huanxiu Shanzhuang (Mountain Villa of Encircled Elegance), to the south of the maple trees on

the hillock, employ the device of using vertical concave troughs matched with small cavities, with the convex parts appearing uneven like stalactite. This seems to be an innovative development from the wrinkly veins of the Tai-Lake Stones.

5. The stone cliffs in Shizilin (The Forest of Lions Garden) contain neither wrinkly veins nor eddying circles, and the stone caves are rather large, with sharp, pointed borders. Besides those, there are quite a number of horizontal stones projecting out of the cliffs, some pointing upwards and others slanting downwards, thus producing an odd and somewhat disorderly impression. In recent times this device has exerted much bad influence on the way stones are piled.

A good example of stone cliffs piled with yellow stones is found in the rockery facing the pool in the eastern part of Ou Yuan (Twin Garden). Here the vertical and horizontal stones are fairly even in size, so the convex and concave parts alternate with and overlap each other, closely resembling real hillocks (Figs. IV-11 through IV-13). Next in excellence in piled stone cliffs are "Yungang" (Cloudy Heights) south of the pool in Wangshi Yuan (The Retired Fisherman's Garden) and the stone cliff south of Xiuqi Ting (Embroidered-Silk Pavilion) in Zhuozheng Yuan (The Humble Administrator's Garden). A worse instance would be the stone cliffs facing the pool in Canglang Ting (The Surging-Wave-Pavilion Garden).

Stone Caves

Judging from those that are preserved today, there are two main kinds of stone caves: one kind is an ordinary cave, and may be subdivided into dry caves and water caves. Usually there is just one cave in a rockery, the only exception being the one in Qiaying Yuan (Harmony-Hermitage Garden), where a water cave is linked to a dry cave (Fig. IV-15). The other kind of stone cave winds along like a tunnel, and is common in the gardens in Suzhou. In some gardens' caves, the latter type is linked up with those of the first type, as can be seen in most of the caves in the rockery at Shizilin (The Forest of Lions Garden). But these caves are too elaborate and artificial, and do not resemble natural caves.[10]

The stones lining the two sides of the gate of a cave sometimes are placed vertically but in most cases they are piled horizontally in layers (Fig. IV-16). There may be different types of structures on top of the cave's gate. The simplest type would be a horizontal, rectangular shaped stone slab, or several pieces of lake stone placed on such a stone slab. Another type is a large, irregular-shaped stone structured like a roof beam placed on top of the cave gate. Still another type is made of stones piled roughly layer by layer. As for the arched cave gate, usually it is built with stones of varying shapes, but sometimes the inside of the arched cave gate is reinforced by horizontal stone slabs. The arched kind of cave gate in Huanxiu Shanzhuang (Mountain Villa of Encircled Elegance) may either consist of two layers, one upper and one lower, or of several arched tops of different sizes overlapping each other, with eddying veins and small cavities on the surface, so as to appear natural and at the same time function to reinforce the structure (Fig. IV-17).

To keep the structure firm and durable, regardless of the historical period in which it was built, the walls of the caves are piled up with horizontal stone slabs. To provide light in the cave, fairly large cave windows are set in the walls of the water cave in Qiaying Yuan (Harmony-Hermitage Garden), while in Huanxiu Shanzhuang (Mountain Villa of Encircled Elegance) light is admitted through a number of small caves.

As for the top of the cave, it is usually covered with stone slabs, except in

Qiaying Yuan (Harmony-Hermitage Garden) where the water cave is covered with rough-surfaced, horizontal stones which jut out downward in layers; at midpoint, thick, long stone slabs are added for reinforcement, while small stones hang downward in the shapes of stalactite. This is rather unusual. In Huanxiu Shanzhuang (Mountain Villa of Encircled Elegance) a number of irregular-shaped stones form the top of the cave, in round, arched-top fashion, closely resembling a real hillock.

Gullies

In Suzhou, the gully in Huanxiu Shanzhuang (Mountain Villa of Encircled Elegance) garden lies close between two tall stone cliffs, with an opening to the sky as narrow as a thread (Fig. IV-1). It winds along in quietude and seclusion, like a real mountain ravine. In the rockery in the eastern part of Ou Yuan (Twin Garden), there is also a short, narrow passage, called "Deep Ravine," but the two opposite precipices are rather low, so that this can be regarded as an ordinary mountain pass (Fig. IV-12). South of the earthen hillock in the western part of Liu Yuan (Lingering-Here Garden), the arrangement is somewhat similar, except that the opposite cliffs are even lower than those in Ou Yuan (Twin Garden); still, as an ordinary mountain path it is a bit too high. This is not so well planned.

Stone Steps

Whether the rockery is high or low, in order to produce contrast on two sides of the stone steps at the starting point, two vertical-shaped stones usually are placed there, one very tall and the other dwarfish. The vertical stones should be neither too thin nor pointed, but should have a thick, roundish contour (Fig. IV-18). Where the stone steps turn, the same device is applied to the corner on the inside. If the stone steps lead up to a terrace that leans against a tall, hilly region in the rear, stones should be piled up there to serve as a screen wall. In the rockery in the central part of Liu Yuan (Lingering-Here Garden) there is a stretch of stone steps paved with oblique-shaped lake stones that looks very lively.

Stony Peaks

The most famous of the stony peaks piled with lake stones in Suzhou is the Ruiyun Feng (Auspicious-Cloud Peak) (Fig. IV-4) on the original site of Zhizao Fu (Weaving Prefect's Mansion). Besides those constructed in a group on a hillock or rockery, stone peaks may be placed singly, in front of a hall, inside a courtyard, beside a footpath or a covered way, or arranged together with other combinations of lake stones (Fig. IV-20). The above-mentioned Ruiyun Feng (Auspicious-Cloud Peak), being placed in the midst of a small pool and surrounded by a rockery piled with lake stones, flowers, and trees, shows the shape of the rocks to best advantage. This is an example of an effective arrangement for a stony peak.

As for artificially piled stony peaks, the two now preserved in Xiaolingyanshan Guan (Little-Lingyan Hill-Lodge), which was built during the reign of Emperor Qianlong in the Qing Dynasty, are the most majestic and lively. But in constructing stony peaks in the last decades of the Qing Dynasty, usually not enough attention was paid to the contour, but much effort was made in determining the number and the size of the cave in these peaks. This is an example of neglecting the fundamental problems by thinking too much about the details.

Stones Piled on Earthen Slopes of Hillocks

One way to place stones on the earthen slopes of a hillock is to lay them scattered about. The only example of this is found in Sui Yuan (Satisfactory

Garden). Another way is to place the stones at random and to make them serve as a screen-wall. A good instance of this is found on the earthen hill in the western part of Liu Yuan (Lingering-Here Garden) (Fig. IV-6). A third way is to place the stones horizontally in an irregular pattern. In this case, although some stones are placed obliquely and some straight, in a complicated and overlapping fashion, attention is still paid to the proper arrangement and combination. Representative examples of this are found south of Xuexiangyunwei Ting (Pavilion of Fragrant-Snow-and-Colorful Clouds) in Zhuozheng Yuan (The Humble Administrator's Garden) and in the northeast of Huanxiu Shanzhuang (Mountain Villa of Encircled Elegance). A fourth way is to build three parallel layers of stone embankment on the earthen hillock, as was done in the western part of Shizilin (The Forest of Lions Garden). In all of the above examples except the last, the piled stones harmonize with the shape of the hillock.

Construction

A draft sketch should be made before construction begins. In the past the artisans engaged in piling stones first drew sketches, then used earth and mud to make molds. In piling stones, it is necessary to pay attention to the shapes, veins, and colors of the stones so that the best and most attractive parts of the stones are fully shown. Of course, during the course of construction, adjustments inevitably must be made. For instance, the same stone may appear more proper and appropriate when placed in a different way or direction, or when an end which faces upward in the original plan is made to face downward. Stones must be pieced together naturally, so it is necessary to observe the stones carefully before they are used; then the construction work can proceed smoothly and successfully. The project is most successful if there is no visible trace of the stones that were pieced together or the slits between the stones that were patched up. One example of this is the stone cliff leaning against the wall in the southeastern corner of Huanxiu Shanzhuang (Mountain Villa of Encircled Elegance).

In piling stones, it should be determined whether the foundation is firm and solid. In the past, in piling stones beside a body of water it was the common practice first to drive piles, then to lay a tier of stone slabs, and finally to pile the stone embankments or precipices. For instance, at the pool embankment west of Taying Ting (Pagoda-Shadow Pavilion) in the western part of Zhuozheng Yuan (The Humble Administrator's Garden), this process of piling stones step by step is easily visible, especially when the water in the pool dries up or is low. In piling stony peaks and stone caves it is also necessary first to pound the earth hard, then to pave the large foundation stones, and finally to pile stones up, layer by layer.

The specific steps in piling stones include the following:

- Piling
- Erecting
- Placing something under something else for cushioning
- Piecing together
- Picking out
- Pressing down
- Hooking up
- Hanging down
- Propping up

"Piling" means piling up horizontal-shaped stones, and that is the safest and the most commonly employed method. Of course it is necessary to pay attention to the veins of the stones, so that stones in that shape do not point in the same direction; they should not be piled up together in layers.

"Erecting" means setting upright the vertically placed stones that are used to build stone cliffs, stone caves and stony peaks. Because of the great weight they must sustain and because of their own great height, it is important to make them stand on solid and stable foundations so they will hold their balance. Generally speaking, in constructing stone cliffs, piling horizontal-shape stones and setting up vertical-shape ones usually go together; however for tall and broad stone cliffs one should use not only large horizontal and vertical stones, but should set smaller stones between the large ones for a natural effect; this device is "placing something underneath the bigger stones for a cushioning effect." It is often the practice to place smaller stones underneath large stones that jut outward, in order to strengthen the structure and make it look more natural.

"Piecing together" means using a number of smaller stones and placing them together to form a bigger body. Of course, if there are too many small stones placed together, they will not be strong or stable enough, so it is necessary to place some bigger ones among them or to lay large stones on top of smaller ones.

"Picking out" applies to the projecting portions of stone cliffs, stone caves, and stony peaks, and it goes hand in hand with the device of "pressing down." In picking out stones that project outward, it is necessary first to observe if the stone is firm and strong enough, and then to see whether the tips of the stones answer the need. If one wants a stone to be pointed at both tips, one has to pick and choose particularly carefully, and finally to consider the length and surface area of the rear tips of the chosen stone that take the pressure from above. In piling stony peaks, frequently two or three sides of the stones project outward; in that case, the surface of the rear parts of the stone that bears the weight and pressure should be made to conform to mechanical principles.

As for the use of iron hooks to strengthen the structure (i.e., "hooking"), it is resorted to only occasionally, when necessary. In constructing stone caves, when the middle portion of a stone slab seems to curve upward and the two tips of the slab look like hooks, the tips are hooked up to the vertical stones on the two sides. This is used mostly for smaller stone caves. For larger caves, the two tips of a stone slab need to have large, flat surfaces before they can be safely and firmly hooked on to the vertical stones.

"Hanging" means hanging a piece of stone from above. The only examples of this can be found in the stalactite at the water cave in Qiaying Yuan (Harmony-Hermitage Garden). It rarely is seen elsewhere.

"Propping up" means providing side support in the case of an arch-top stone cave, where support is provided on two sides to prop up the stone above. The surface of the stone cliffs, as well as the eddying stone cave on its top, in Huanxiu Shanzhuang (Mountain Villa of Encircled Elegance) are propped up not only with large stones but even with smaller ones, thus making the fullest use of side supports. In the past, for the rockeries that were built with fastidious care, the juice from glutinous rice was mixed with limestone in proper proportions to serve as cementing material that glued together the lake stones while piling them. Usually, after the bottom of a stone is made flat and even with thin pieces of iron placed under it, the slits in the stones on the outside are cemented together with this material. In recent years thin pieces of stone were used instead of thin iron pieces. In the past, the material used for cementing was either limestone mixed with tung oil, or limestone mixed with hempen fiber plus soot (or peat), but in both cases the great defect was that the material dried up rather slowly so that gluing together took time. Then, following applying this glue material, one generally brushed on bittern and iron scraps, so that the embedded slits of stones glued together would not be too clearly visible. To cement together yellow stones, pure glue and soot (or peat) were used, together with yellowish earth brought from Yixing.

Nowadays, no matter whether it is for lake stones or yellow stones, cement mixed with color tints is used, because it dries very quickly and is therefore convenient to use. The slits between the lake stones should be cemented closely together, but in the case of yellow stones, traces of the stone slits should be left visible so that the stones may resemble natural rocks. Therefore, in both cases the material for gluing together stone slits should best be concealed within the slits.

Notes

1. See *Random Records of the Western Capital*, vol. ii and iii; *San-Fu-Huang Map*, vol. iii, a geographic manual of ancient China, about three districts of Changan, ancient Chinese capital, in 6 volumes.
2. See *History of Later Han Dynasty, Biography xxiv, Life of Liang Qi*. See *Shui Jing Zhu*, a Chinese book on geography, especially on rivers in China, vol. xvi, article on "Fanglin Garden on River Gu."
3. See *Shui Jing Zhu*, a Chinese book on geography, especially on rivers in China, vol. xvi, article on "Fanglin Garden on River Gu."
4. See *Shui Jing Zhu*, vol. xvi, article on "Fanglin Garden on River Gu"; *Book of Wei Kingdom*, vol. xciii, "Life on Ru Hao," in *Records of Buddhist Temples in Loyang*, vol. ii, *Residence of Zheng Lun*.
5. See *Tain Ping Yu Lan*, an encyclopaedic work of one thousand volumes compiled in the early Song Dynasty (977–985 A.D.), vol. 196, articles on Xiangdong Yuan or Xiangdong Imperial Garden.
6. See *History of Song Dynasty*, vol. 85, *District History*; *Fang Chuang Xiao Du (Correspondence inside the Window by the Maple Tree)*, by Yuan Geng, vol. i; *Chronicle of Genyue (Records on Northeastern Mountain)*, by Zhao Ji (the Emperor Huizong of the Song Dynasty); *Chronicle of Huayang Palace*, by Zu Xiu; *Chronicle of Genyue (Records of Northeastern Mountain)*, by Zhang Hao.
7. See *Chronicle of Famous Gardens in Loyang*, by Li Gefei.
8. See *Chronicle of Gardens in Wuxing*, by Zhou Mi.
9. See quotations from "Biography of Zhang Nanyuan," by Huang Zongxi and "Biography of Zhang Nanyuan," by Wu Weiye, given in *Zhe Jiang Lu (Records of Skilled Craftsmen)*, in the combined 3rd and 4th issue of vol. iv, of *Zhongguo Yingzao Xueshe Huikan (Proceedings of the Chinese Association of Architects)*.
10. The cave south of Duhua Lang (Picture Gallery) in Beihai (North See Park), Beijing, piled with granite and looking very majestic, must have been constructed not later than the Ming Dynasty. The long caves on both flanks of Duhua Lang (Picture Gallery) are also rather magnificent and may be considered among the better rockery caves.

V
Buildings

In the classical gardens in Suzhou, buildings are put up to serve the dual functions of habitation and appreciation. Together with hillocks, pools, flowers, and trees, they contribute to the composite garden scenery. In certain scenic areas, they sometimes constitute major scenic themes. Hillocks and pools are the main elements in classical gardens, but their scenic beauty is usually viewed from the inside of buildings. Buildings, therefore, are not only places for rest but also observation postrs for scenic appreciation. The different types of buildings and their relation to each other to a great extent depend on the life styles of the garden owners, and the number of buildings in proportion to other elements in the gardens. These factors have become an outstanding feature in garden construction in China.

In small and medium-size gardens, the total space occupied by buildings would take up 30 percent of the total garden space, as in the cases of Hu Yuan (Kettle Garden), Chang Yuan (Carefree Garden), and Yongcui Shanzhuang (Mountain Villa of Embracing Emerald). In most of the larger gardens, all the buildings together would occupy more than 15 percent of the entire garden space, as in the cases of Canglang Ting (Surging-Wave-Pavilion Garden), Liu Yuan (Lingering-Here Garden), and Shizilin (The Forest of Lions Garden). Because of this, the architectural design of buildings and their artistic arrangement in relation to each other are of special importance in planning each garden as a whole.

The buildings in the classical gardens in Suzhou not only are differently shaped and located, but also vary as to type, decoration, and adaptation to the surroundings. The basic types of buildings designed for gardens usually include:

- Halls (*Ting* or *Tang*)
- Lounges surrounded by windows (*Xuan*)
- Guest houses (*Guan*)
- Two- or three-story buildings (*Lou*)
- Two-story pavilions (*Ge*)
- Waterside pavilions (*Xie*)
- Landboats (*Fang*)

- Pavilions (*Ting*)

- Corridors or covered ways (*Lang*)

Except for a few pavilions and two-story pavilions, most of the buildings are placed around or beside hillocks and pools. Covered corridors generally are used to link up buildings and to map out the routes for observing and enjoying garden scenery. Besides their practical functions, buildings of different types also serve as scenic objects themselves. The variety of building shapes and types creates a spatial experience of diversity and irregularity, with an intricate interplay of solids and voids in the garden.

Because buildings serve different functions, different artistic considerations come into play when they are planned. Lounges and halls, the principal edifices in garden architecture, generally are placed in the central part of gardens, and are surrounded by walls, corridors, and other secondary buildings, which form courtyards or compounds around them. Lounges and halls usually are tall and spacious, majestic and open, and often fitted with gorgeous ornaments and furniture for comfort and luxury. The Wufeng Xianguan (The Five-Peak Celestial House) in Liu Yuan (Lingering-Here Garden) (Fig. V-11), and the Yanyu Tang (Famed-for-Swallow Hall) in Shizilin (The Forest of Lions Garden)(Fig. V-124) are good examples.

Halls with openings on all four sides generally are built amid spacious surroundings and at spots where a variety of scenes are visible. Doors and windows open on four sides, and the building is surrounded by a veranda under the eaves, so that it is possible to observe the scenery either by sitting inside the hall or walking along the veranda. Yuanxian Tang (Distant-Fragrance Hall) (Fig. V-13) in Zhuozheng Yuan (The Humble Administrator's Garden) is an example.

A study, a studio, or a parlor requires quiet surroundings and therefore is frequently separated from the main scenic area. Designed in a peculiar architectural style, usually it is placed within a small courtyard or compound of its own. For example, Huanwodushu Chu (The Restored-to-Me Study)[1] in Liu Yuan (Lingering-Here Garden) and Yulan Tang (Magnolia Hall) in Zhuozheng Yuan (The Humble Administrator's Garden) are situated in small compounds where only a few flowers, trees, and some scattering stone peaks make up a scene in miniature.

Pavilions, water pavilions, and winding corridors, are chiefly places for rest, observation, and the enjoyment of scenery. At the same time they constitute part of the scenery themselves, since they usually are placed on the summit of a hillock, by the side of a pool, or in one of the four corners of a garden. "Water-pavilions are hidden among the flowers, and pavilions are built beside the water," is a saying that describes the skillful employment of such architectural features.

The shape and arrangement of the buildings in gardens are usually designed to make these edifices appear light and delicate, small and lovely, and full of variety. Yet there are no rigid conventions about their form. In Chinese architecture, ordinary living quarters usually require three to five rooms, but for the buildings in gardens, one room or even half a room should suffice, as long as it is deemed suitable and proper. Square wooden blocks to support beams and girders rarely are used, and buildings generally are not fitted with carvings of phoenixes or gold leaves. Efforts are made to attain simplicity and good taste.

In the treatment of space in garden buildings, openness and good air circulation are generally the aim. This applies to the free arrangement of courtyards and compounds and to such devices as open corridors, cave openings, open windows, tracery windows, transparent screens, and paper or wooden partitions for rooms. The more skillfully designed Suzhou gardens achieve and maintain both desirable separation of space, and continuity of space between buildings, and between buildings and other scenic objects. For instance, in the case of Gumujiaoke (Old-Trees-Interwining-One-Another) and Shilin Xiaoyuan (Small Courtyard of Stone Forest) (Figs. V-6 and V-7) in Liu Yuan (Lingering-Here Garden), the space inside the compound seems to overlap with that outside of it. This sense of free space gives the observer a feeling of infinite depth in the scenery.

Wide stretches of whitewashed walls matched with black-grey tile roofs and chestnut-brown pillars, railings, and overhanging ornaments, generally are the keynote colors for the garden buildings. The interior fittings usually are light brown with natural wood graining. With the white walls as their foil, the grey door and window frames made of water-polished bricks appear simple, elegant, and bright. The white walls not only serve as foils for flowers and trees but, more interestingly, are screens of innumerable and ever-changing scenes when the sun hits the ensemble from different directions and in varying intensity.

Buildings also play their roles in the creation of garden scenery. They may bring about a diversity of contrapositional and borrowed scenes as well as changes in and combinations of scenic objects.

Various devices are employed to use buildings as elements in contrapositional scenery. For instance, Yuanxiang Tang (Distant-Fragrance Hall) in Zhuozheng Yuan (The Humble Administrator's Garden) faces Xuexiangyunwei Ting (The Pavilion of Fragrant-Snow-and-Colorful Clouds), directly to the north, and faces Xiuyi Ting (The Embroidered-Silk Pavilion) to the east. From Xuexiangyunwei Ting (The Pavilion of Fragrant-Snow-and-Colorful Clouds) one may look southward and enjoy a panoramic scene of Yuanxiang Tang (Distant-Fragrance Hall) and Yiyu Xuan (Leaning-on-Jade Hall) in the distance. This technique of interweaving and merging one entity with another is an excellent device in the art of classical gardens in Suzhou.

There are different ways for buildings to "borrow" scenery:

• Borrowing from afar

• Borrowing from adjacent objects

• Borrowing from scenery underneath

• Borrowing in different seasons.

The space within the window frame or a door frame, and the pillars of a veranda can also serve as a frame through which to view scenery, and there are a number of admirable examples of such devices.

The climate in different seasons can also be used to good advantage in constructing buildings. For instance, 36-Yuanyang Guan (The 36-Mandarin-Duck Hall) (Fig. V-19 through V-21) in Zhuozheng Yuan (The Humble Administrator's Garden) was built with winter and summer in mind, while Tingyu Xuan (Listening-to-the-Rain Hall) was constructed chiefly for enjoying rainy-day scenery.

Synthesizing buildings, hillocks, pools, flowers, and trees into an organic whole is critically important in the art of gardening. When a pavilion or a two-story pavilion is built atop a hillock, it should be relatively small and delicately shaped. With trees and plants as foil, it would look natural and lively. Moreover, due to its high elevation, it can always serve as an important spot for observing scenery, whether one gazes downward at the scenery inside the garden or looks afar at the scenic objects beyond the garden limits. Xuexiangyunwei Ting (The Frangrant-Snow-and-Colorful Clouds),

Daishuang Ting (The Waiting-for-the-Frost Pavilion), and Xiuyi Ting (The Embroidered-Silk Pavilion) in Zhuozheng Yuan (The Humble Administrator's Garden) may be regarded as buildings of this kind (Figs. V-62 and V-63). These pavilions atop hillocks not only are shapely and delicate in themselves, each with a different feature of its own, they also fit in very well with their surroundings and add to the beauty of the garden scenery. Buildings are the main attraction in a garden, and hillocks and rocks as secondary scenic objects, may be seen in Ting Shan (Hall Hill); e.g., the compounds in front of and behind the Wufeng Xiangguan (The Five-Peak Celestial House), in Liu Yuan (Lingering-Here Garden), Lou Shan (Two-Storied Building Hill), east of Guanyun Lou (Cloud-Topping Two-Storied Building); other examples are in Liu Yuan (Lingering-Here Garden) and Shufang Shan (Study Hill) in the residence at No. 7 Wangxima Lane.

To attain harmony with the water surface, a building beside a pool usually is spacious and low. Fitted with white walls and tracery windows, and surrounded by one or two tall trees, the building's inverted image is vividly reflected in the water.

There are sevrval ways to relate a building to the surface of a pool. One way is to place the building astride the water as in the case of Xiaochanglang (Little-Surging-Wave Watercourt) (Fig. V-4), in Zhuozheng Yuan (The Humble Administrator's Garden), Zhuoying Shuige (Washing-Tassel Waterside Pavilion) (Fig. V-38) in Wangshi Yuan (The Retired Fisherman's Garden), and Sanshuijian Shuige (Waterside Pavilion amid-the-Hillock-and-Pool) in Ou Yuan (Twin Garden) (Fig. XIII-6).

Another way is to place the building immediately beside the pool, as in the case of Xiang Zhou (Fragrant-Isle Landboat) and Yiyu Xuan (Leaning-on-Jade Hall) in Zhuozheng Yuan (The Humble Administrator's Garden) (Fig. V-43), and LÜyin Xuan (Green-Shade Lounge) and Qingfengchi Guan (Fresh-Breeze-Pool House) in Liu Yuan (Lingering-Here Garden).

Still another way is to build a terrace as a transitional stage between the hall and the pool, as in the case of Yuanxiang Tang (Distant-Fragrance Hall) in Zhuozheng Yuan (The Humble Administrator's Garden) (Fig. VII-23), Hanbi Shanfang (Encompassing-Jade Mountain House) in Liu Yuan (Lingering-Here Garden) (Fig. V-22), and Ouxiang Xie (Lotus-Root-Fragrance Waterside Pavilion) in Yi Yuan (Happy Garden) (Fig. V-12).

Buildings in gardens are also designed to match the flowers and trees. Not only can flowers and trees form scenery in a small courtyard, but their shapes and locations can play an important part in a building's overall design. There are many examples of buildings planned to match delightful garden scenery or flowers and trees, especially trees having many long years' growth. Including old trees in garden planning is traditional. Many examples can be found in Liu Yuan (Lingering-Here Garden), Zhuozheng Yuan (The Humble Administrator's Garden), Wangshi Yuan (The Retired Fisherman's Garden), Canglang Ting (Surging-Wave-Pavilion Garden), and other famous gardens.

Compounds or Courtyards

Compounds (or courtyards) constitute one of the architectural units in the classical gardens in Suzhou. The total area of each garden usually is small, so it is necessary to create a number of separate environments within the limited space, or to insert transitional scenic areas between buildings to bring change and variety to the garden scenery. It became common to use separate compounds (or courtyards) to carve the garden space into various scenic areas (Fig. V-1).

According to the components included, compounds in gardens may be categorized into three types: courtyards, small courts, and large compounds.

Courtyards

Courtyards generally are located in front of or behind halls or lounges, and form regular or irregular patterns with walls and buildings. Inside a courtyard usually there is a flower terrace, some trees, and rocks with pointed peaks. The assemblage is placed against a background of white walls, and provides the front view of the main building in the garden. Examples of this are found in the courtyards in front of Yulan Tang (Magnolia Hall) in Zhuozheng Yuan (The Humble Administrator's Garden) (Fig. VII-21), Yanyu Tang (Famed-for-Swallow Hall) in Shizilin (The Forest of Lions Garden) (Fig. IX-3), and Wufeng Xianguan (Five-Peak Celestial House) in Liu Yuan (Lingering-Here Garden) (Fig. VIII-16).

Small Courts

A small court usually is placed to the left or right of a building or by the side of a corridor (or a covered way). It takes up little space but allows much variety and flexibility in planning. The function of a small court is to provide ventilation, lighting, and embellishment for a small building (or a row of buildings and corridors), and to reduce the monotony of long corridors; at the same time it may serve as a contrapositional scene or foil for minor scenic objects.

In a small courtyard, usually there are only one or two arbor trees, or Tianzhu (heavenly bamboos, a kind of Chinese bamboo), wintersweets, banana trees, or a bamboo grove; when these are matched with a few lake stones, the place appears very much like a miniatured landscape. Such small courts are very common in the garden; for example, the courts at Gumujiaoke and Huabuxiaozhu (Fig. VIII-12).

Liu Yuan (Lingering-Here Garden), and the side court at Xiaoshanconggui Xuan (Little-Hillock-and-Laurel-Grove Hall) in Wangshi Yuan (The Retired Fisherman's Garden). Similar small courts may be found in many other gardens, often at the turn of a winding corridor or covered way.

Large Compounds

A large compound usually consists of a group of buildings. It is an area of great complexity and irregularity, consisting of encircling walls, buildings, corridors, a hillock and a rockery, and flowers and trees. Such a compound apparently is cut off from the space outside; yet, its inside and outside areas seem to overlap and merge, thus adding to the depth and variety of the scenery. The whole of Pipa Yuan (Loguat Orchard) (Fig. V-2) is a good illustration, as it contains Linglong Guan (Exquisite Hall) which is the main building, and other components in Zhuozheng Yuan (The Humble Administrator's Garden). The harmony and variation in the arrangement of scenic objects create a refreshing and delightful atmosphere. On the north, the earthen hill serves as a screen wall; yet the compound is separated but not isolated from other parts of the garden; it is linked to them in a way that seems natural.

The space in a compound may be treated in either of two ways, closed or open. A closed compound (or courtyard) produces a quiet and independent environment of its own. In the cases of Huanwodushu Chu (The Restored-to-Me Study) in Liu Yuan (Lingering-Here Garden), and the courtyard in front of Xiyuan Cangshuchu (West Garden Library) in Ou Yuan (Twin Garden), the compound is closed off on all sides by buildings and corridors and is surrounded by whitewashed walls. This creates a quiet environment at the front of the main building.

Open compounds (or courtyards) are also quite common in Suzhou gardens, whether they are in the forms of courtyards, small courts, or large compounds. Open corridors, cavelike doors on walls, open and tracery windows are built in an open compound to provide contact with the outside and link up the areas within and without; not only do they provide communication between the inside and outside to avoid a feeling of enclosure in a cramped area, but they also make it possible to "borrow" scenic objects from within and without the compound. A good example of an open compound can be seen in Xiaochanglang Suiyuan (Little-Surging-Wave Watercourt) in Zhuozheng Yuan (The Humble Administrator's Garden) (Figs. V-3 through V-5) .

A compound group made up of several courtyards is another type of courtyard. In some of the gardens, a main courtyard, which is the focal point, is surrounded by several smaller courtyards. They provide more variety in the division of garden space and the unfolding of scenic areas. A typical example of such a combination of courtyards is the Shilin Xiaoyuan (Small Courtyard of Stone Forest) in Liu Yuan (Lingering-Here Garden) (Figs. V-6 and V-7). Here, in the environs of the central area are placed six small courts of various shapes and sizes; each has its own peculiar characteristics. In order to echo and give prominence to the major scenic theme, the stone peak in the Small Courtyard of Stone Forest, lake stones are placed in each of the small courts as the common denominator. In the space around Haitangchunwu (Spring-Begonia-Cove House) in Zhuozheng Yuan (The Humble Administrator's Garden) (Figs. V-8 through V-10), the major scenic theme is the courtyard in front of the hall, and there is a small court on each side of the hall. This arrangement provides observation points on all four sides of the hall; in addition the two small sidecourts, by contrast, effectively draw attention to the spaciousness of the front courtyard. This is an example of a successful scenic arrangement.

Types of Buildings

Although different names have been given to different types of garden architecture according to their functions and shapes, these names are often ambiguous and confusing and are not used consistently. The following is an attempt to clarify some of the confusion and to standardize several types of major buildings often found in Suzhou gardens:

Ting (Lobbies or Lounges), Tang (Halls), Xuan (Lounges)[3] and Guan (Guest Houses) (Figs. V-11 through V-21)

The Ting (or lobby) and Tang (or hall) in the gardens were the main places where garden owners carried out their various social activities. They were interchangeably called Da Ting (big lobby), Si-Mian-Ting (lobby open on four sides), Yuanyan Ting (twin lobbies, because mandarin ducks always appear in pairs), Hua Ting (flower lobby), Hehua Ting (lotus lobby) and Hualan Ting (flower-basket lobby). Moreover, a "Ting" or "Tang" (lobby or hall) may sometimes serve several functions and their practical use cannot be strictly defined.

A "Ting" and a "Tang" may be distinguished from each other according to their design structure: A "Ting" is built with flat wood (i.e., rectangular-shaped timber is used for the beams or framework), while a "Tang" is built with round timber.

A Da Ting (big lobby or main hall) is the main building in a garden, varying from three to five bays in width. On the facade that faces the courtyard, lattice doors (or paper or wooden partitions) stretch all the way across between pillars; there may be windows on the two sidewalls for ventilation and light. A typical example of this is Wufeng Xianguan (The Five-Peak Celestial House) in Liu Yuan (Lingering-Here Garden).

A Da Ting (big lobby) may assume the shape of a Si Mian Ting (a lobby open on four sides) to facilitate the observation of scenery in four directions. Surrounded on four sides by corridors, its width also ranges from three to five bays. Lattice doors (or paper or wooden partitions), in place of walls, are placed between pillars. Between the pillars along the corridor and under the eaves, usually wooden carvings hang down to serve as partial partitions; balustrades with railings are built up from the floor to serve as seats for resting. Examples of this may be found in Yuanxiang Tang (Distant-Fragrance Hall) in Zhuozheng Yuan (The Humble Administrator's Garden).

A Yuanyan Ting (mandarin-duck hall) is another type of Da-Ting (or big lobby), in which a screen or curtain is used to partition it into two parts, the front and the rear. With the roof beams in one of the two parts made of flat timber and those in the other part made of round timber, the building appears to contain a front and a back room. The southern half of the hall is more suitable for use in the winter and spring, and the northern half for summer and autumn. The hall is named "Yuanyan Ting" because Yuanyan, mandarin ducks, usually swim in pairs. Linquanjishuozhi Guan (House for the Aged Giants of Groves and Springs) in Liu Yuan (Lingering-Here Garden) and Yanyu Tang (Famed-for-Swallow Hall) in Shizilin (The Forest of Lions Garden) belong to this building type. The 36-Yuanyang Guan (The 36-Mandarin-Duck Hall) in Zhuozheng Yuan (The Humble Administrator's Garden) also is a kind of mandarin duck hall. But the roof beams for all four parts of its ceiling are joined together and are known as the Whole Ceiling (Fig. V-20).

A Hua Ting (flower hall) serves both as a living room and a parlor, and generally is located near the residential quarters of a garden. In the courtyard in front of a flower hall, usually there are flowers and trees as well as rocky peaks, together forming an environment of secluded quietude. Yulan Tang (Magnolia Hall) in Zhuozheng Yuan (The Humble Administrator's Garden) is such an example.

A Hehua Ting (lotus hall) is built right next to the pool, for viewing water scenery; generally there is a spacious terrace in front of the hall, as in the cases of Ouxiang Xie (Lotus-Root-Fragrance Waterside Pavilion) in Yi Yuan (Happy Garden), and Hanbi Shanfang (Encompassing-Jade Mountain House) in Liu Yuan (Lingering-Here Garden).

Huiding (i.e., bent rafters, otherwise called Juanpeng), generally serve as roof framework for a Hua Ting (flower hall) or a Hehua Ting (lotus hall). In some cases, Hua Ting (flower halls) are built into a Hualan Ting (flower-basket hall) or constructed with "gong"-shaped roof framework. In the case of Hualan Ting, the pillar in the middle does not reach down to the ground. It is shaped like a pendent lotus, and its richly ornamented capital resembles a flower basket. The roof framework of Hualan Ting (flower-basket halls) may take any shape, but flat timber rather than round timber is used. The Hualan Ting in the residence at No. 7 Wangxima Lane is an example (Fig. V-15). Flat timber is used for the "gong"-shaped roof framework, and is made to look round by digging into the base of the timber and shaping the wood like a soft carved belt. A good example of this can be found in Xihua Ting (West Flower Hall) in a residence along Tieping Lane (Iron-Bottle Lane).

The ceilings in a hall (lounge) generally are made in the traditional Chinese way known as Xuan. This is also a special feature in the Suzhou gardens. On those ceilings, the beams or rafters are formed into different shapes such as the handle of a teapot, a bow, a stick of incense, the mat roofing of a boat, a water chestnut, or a crane's shin bone (Fig. V-99). Also, beams on top of the rafters may allow the ceiling to assume various different shapes that correspond to the plan of the hall.

There are two types of hall rooftops: the gable and hip roof (Xieshan); and the flush gable roof (Yingshan). The former is used in halls that face four sides, and occasionally in mandarin duck halls; the latter may be used for all halls other than those that face four sides. The height of the eaves for a hall is usually eight-tenths the width of the main room, and is the same as the width of the adjacent room.

Xuan (lounges) and Guan (guest houses) also are halls, but sometimes are placed in locations of secondary importance. They are smaller buildings designed for observation and enjoyment, such as Zhuwaiyizhi Xuan (A-Branch-from-Bamboo Lounge) in Wangshi Yuan (The Retired Fisherman's Garden), and Qingfengchi Guan (Fresh-Breeze-Pool House) in Liu Yuan (Lingering-Here Garden).

Lou (Two-Story Buildings) and Ge (Two-Story Pavilions)

Lou and Ge generally are located at the periphery of a garden or by the side of a hill or pool. Usually they have two stories, with the height of the upper story equal to about seven-tenths of the lower one. If a two-story building or two-story pavilion is the major scenery in a garden, it is placed in a prominent location. If, on the other hand, it serves only as a foil or secondary scenic object, it is placed in a secluded and somewhat obscure spot. Examples of the former are Jianshan Lou (Seeing-the-Hill Two-Storied Building) and Fucui Ge (Floating-Jade Two-Storied Pavilion) in Zhuozheng Yuan (The Humble Administrator's Garden); examples of the latter are Kanshan Lou (Looking-at-the-Hill Two-Storied Building) in Canglang Ting (Surging-Wave-Pavilion Garden) (Fig. V-27) and Yuancui Ge (Distant-Green Two-Storied Pavilion) (Fig. V-30). Xi Lou (West Two-Storied Building) and Huanwodushu Chu (The Restored-to-Me Study) in Liu Yuan (Lingering-Here Garden).

The width of a two-story building generally stretches out to three or five bays. Occasionally it comes in four bays, three-and-a-half bays, or even one bay with an attached corridor. The depth of each room may extend to six roof-spans, and usually it has a gable and hip roof (Xieshan) or a flush gable roof (Yingshan).

Two-story buildings in gardens are very varied in structure; the half-railings and eave-hangings may be designed at will. The side of a two-story building that faces a garden, usually has lattice doors[4] and winding balustrades on the outside, piled gables, or moon-gates, open windows, and brick-framed tracery windows on both sides.

The stairway may be built indoors or outdoors on top of a rockery that may reach up to the second floor. Examples of indoor staircases are Jixuzhai (Gathering-the-Void Study) and Wufeng Shuwu (Five-Peak Study). Examples of outdoor staircases are Jianshan Lou (Seeing-the-Hill Two-Storied Building) in Zhuozheng Yuan (The Humble Administrator's Garden) and Mingse Lou (Bright-Zither Two-Storied Building) (Fig. V-23), and Guanyuan Lou (Cloud-Topping Two-Storied Building) in Liu Yuan (Lingering-Here Garden). If a two-story building is built alongside a pool, the size of the hall building should be in proportion to the surface area of the pool. Quxi Lou (Winding-Creek Two-Storied Building) in Liu Yuan (Lingering-Here Garden) (Fig. V-26), and Daoying Lou (Inverted Image Two-Storied Building) in the western part of Zhuozheng Yuan (The Humble Administrator's Garden) (Fig. V-24) are good examples. In one case, the hall is larger, while in the other it is smaller than the pool. They serve as good examples of a hall that matches the pool well.

To be sure that a two-story hall harmonizes with the surface of the pool, the hall's upper story usually is smaller than the lower. Between the two stories there usually are eave-hangings made of horizontally laid bricks. The lower story is surrounded by whitewashed walls, while the upper story is made of wood. The whole structure therefore appears light and lively.

A two-story pavilion is similar to a two-story hall in that under the eaves it is open on all four sides. But the two-story pavilion is lighter and more delicate in structure. Usually it is square-shaped or multi-sided with a gable-and-hip or pointed-top roof. A Ge may have one story only when it is built on top of a hill or beside a pool. Fucui Ge (Floating-Jade Two-Storied Pavilion) in Zhuozheng Yuan (The Humble Administrator's Garden) and Yuancui Ge (Distant-Green Two-Storied Pavilion) (Fig. V-30) in Liu Yuan (Lingering-Here Garden) are examples of two-story pavilions, whereas Xiuzhu Ge (Tall-Bamboo Pavilion) in Shizilin (The Forest of Lions Garden) and Liuting Ge (Lingering-to-Listen Pavilion) of Zhuozheng Yuan (The Humble Administrator's Garden) (Fig. V-35) are one-storied Ge constructed beside the pool and against the hillock.

Xie (Waterside Pavilions) and Fang (Landboats)

A Xie (waterside pavilion) or a Fang (landboat) invariably is built next to a pool. In order that its shape and size harmonize with the water surface, the entire contour of its structure as well as its doors, windows, balustrades, railings, and even the goose-neck chairs inside, are constructed with horizontal lines as its design emphasis. A Xie usually is a waterside pavilion, placed beside a pool; its shape and size vary, depending on its surroundings. The foundations of a Xie are partly under water and partly on shore, with its structure of stone pillars and beams above the water. The front of a Xie that faces the pool is open and spacious and has railings around it. Its roof is usually of the gable-and-hip type that winds around. Examples of this include Zhuoying Shuige (Washing-Tassel Waterside Pavilion) (Fig. V-38) in Wangshi Yuan (The Retired Fisherman's Garden), Furong Xie (Lotus Waterside Pavilion) (Fig. V-36) in Zhuozheng Yuan (The Humble Administrator's Garden), and Sanshuijian Shuige (Waterside Pavilion amid-the-Hillock-and-Pool) in Ou Yuan (Twin Garden) (Fig. XIII-6).

A Fang, also called a dryboat or landboat, is shaped like a boat and is almost always built at the side of a pool. Its front generally faces water on three sides, and there is a flat bridge, resembling a gangplank, on one side of the bow which links the boat to the shore. The plan of a landboat has three parts: front, middle, and rear. The front of the cabin is slightly higher than the middle part, whereas its rear, in two stories, is usually the highest. The high position is designed to facilitate the observation of distant scenery, a set-up which is somewhat similar to Hua Fang (i.e., Painting Landboat) of Suzhou. The staircase in the landboat is placed between its rear and middle parts, with a cabin door at the lower entrance to the stairway. The front side of the boat's prow is open, and on both sides of the front and middle cabins are low walls with lattice doors. The rear cabin is walled in with whitewashed walls, which serve to contrast it with the front and middle cabins—the solid pitted against the insubstantial. A gable-and-hip roof usually is used for the front and rear parts of a fang, while in the middle part the roof generally slopes on both sides. Typical examples are Xiang Zhou (Fragrant-Isle Landboat) (Figs. V-39 through V-43) in Zhuozheng Yuan (The Humble Administrator's Garden) and Huafangzhai (Painting Landboat Study) (Figs. V-44 through V-47) in Yi Yuan (Happy Garden). In these two cases, not only is the structure properly designed with appropriate proportions, but also, the ornamental fittings are exquisite.

A landboat (or dryboat) that is not built immediately beside a pool is called a boat lounge. It has an oblong shape. Lattice doors are usually constructed on the shorter sides of the oblong structure, while windows are built on the longer sides. A gable-and-hip roof with bent rafters is used on a boat lounge. Tonghua Shuwu (Parasol-Flower Studio) in Chang Yuan (Carefree Garden) is an example of one of those with only one story. In some cases, an alley links the second floor of the rear cabin of a dryboat to an adjacent two-story building. This practice is not common, and the only example available today is found in the garden of a residence on Nanshizi Street.

Ting (Pavilions)

A pavilion is a place to rest and observe scenery, and is also an important structure in a garden scene. A pavilion may be built atop a hill, amid a grove, beside a path, or at the side of a pool, with its form, shape and size adapted to its surroundings. There are two kinds of pavilions: a half-pavilion and a whole one. Usually, the former is built against a wall and linked with a corridor, as in the cases of East Half-Pavilion (otherwise known as Yihong Ting, or Leaning-on-the-Rainbow Pavilion) (Figs. V-49 and V-50) and West Half-Pavilion (Bieyoudongtian, or Unique-Beauty Pavilion) (Figs. V-51 and V-52) in Zhuozheng Yuan (The Humble Administrator's Garden).

A whole pavilion usually is located beside a pool, on top of a hill, or in the midst of a grove of flowers and trees. For example, Xuexiangyunwei Ting (Pavilion of Fragrant-Snow-and-Colorful Clouds) (Fig. V-62) in the central part of Zhuozheng Yuan (The Humble Administrator's Garden) is built on top of a hill. Because the hill is flat and narrow, the pavilion is given an oblong shape. Shanmian Ting (Fan-Shaped Pavilion) (Figs. V-74 and V-75) in the western part of Zhuozheng Yuan (The Humble Administrator's Garden) is located on the shore of a pool, where it bends toward the water, so the pavilion is convex-shaped where it faces the pool. Shanzi Ting (The Fan Pavilion) (Figs. V-76 and V-77) in Shizilin (The Forest of Lions Garden) is built on a higher site at the southwest corner of the garden; to facilitate observing the scenery by leaning against the railings, the pavilion is also convex-shaped.

A pavilion may take different shapes: square, oblong, hexagonal, octagonal, round, plum-shaped, begonia-shaped, and fan-shaped (Fig. V-48). Examples of square-shaped pavilions include Wuzhuyouju Ting (Pavilion amid-Secluded-Wutong-and-Bamboo) in Zhuozheng Yuan (The Humble Administrator's Garden) and Jinsu Ting (Golden-Millet Pavilion) in Yi Yuan (Happy Garden). Rectangular pavilions include Xuexiangyunwei Ting (The Pavilion of Fragrant-Snow-and-Colorful-Clouds) and Xiuyi Ting (Embroidered-Silk Pavilion) (Figs. V-62 through V-65) in Zhuozheng Yuan (The Humble Administrator's Garden).

Then, there are the hexagonal pavilions, such as Hefengsimian Ting (Breeze-from-the-Lotus-in-Four-Directions Pavilion) in Zhuozheng Yuan (The Humble Administrator's Garden), Ke Ting (Just-Right Pavilion) in Liu Yuan (Lingering-Here Garden) and Xiaocanglang Ting (Little-Surging-Wave Pavilion) in Yi Yuan (Happy Garden) (Figs. V-67 and V-68).

Octogonal pavilions are also common, such as Taying Ting (Pagoda-Shadow Pavilion) in Zhuozheng Yuan (The Humble Administrator's Garden) and Huxin Ting (Heart-of-the-Lake Pavilion) in Xi Yuan (West Garden).

Round pavilions include Li Ting (Bamboo-Hat Pavilion) in Zhuozheng Yuan (The Humble Administrator's Garden) (Figs. V-71 and V-72). Then there is an example of a hexagonal pavilion with a round roof in Shuxiao Ting (Comfortable-Whistle Pavilion) in Liu Yuan (Lingering-Here Garden). A pavilion shaped like a "sharp-jade-corner" may be found in Zhile Ting (Supreme-Happiness Pavilion) in Liu Yuan (Lingering-Here Garden) and in Sixian Ting (Four-Immortals Pavilion) at Tianping Mountain (Fig. V-73). Fan-shaped pavilions are not uncommon; examples include Yushuitongzuo Xuan (With-Whom-to-Sit Lounge) in Zhuozheng Yuan (The Humble Administrator's Garden), and Shanzi Ting (The Fan Pavilion) in Shizilin (The Forest of Lions Garden).

An example of a begonia-shaped pavilion is the recently built Haitang Ting (Begonia Pavilion) in Huanxiu Shanzhuang (Mountain Villa of Encircled Elegance). There is also a pavilion made up of two square-shaped structures, named Baiyun Ting (White-Cloud Pavilion), at Tianping Mountain (Fig. V-78).

The ceiling of a pavilion may be single-eaved or double-eaved with the former being the common type. The roof of a pavilion usually is gable-and-hip, pyramidal, (Zuanjian Ding), or pagoda-shaped. The structure of a pavilion is determined by its design and elevation. A single-eaved square pavilion usually has either four or twelve pillars; a hexagonal pavilion usually has six pillars; while an octagonal one has eight. A double-eaved square pavilion may have as many as sixteen pillars, whereas a hexagonal or octagonal double-eaved pavilion often has twice as many pillars as a single-eaved hexagonal or octagonal one.

The height of the pillars in a square pavilion is eight-tenths the width of the pavilion, while the diameter of a pillar is one-tenth its height. The height of the pillars in a hexagonal pavilion is about 1.5 times its width, whereas the height of the pillars in an octagonal pavilion is 1.6 times its width. Generally there are no doors or windows between the pillars, but usually there are half-walls or balustrades between them. A half-wall usually is about 50 centimeters high, and balustrades may be placed on it to serve as seats. Goose-neck chairs are also positioned to serve as resting places, and hangings generally are suspended from above.

Lang (Corridors or Covered Pathways)

Corridors serve as the arteries and veins of gardens. They link up the buildings and mark the routes for visitors. Corridors usually wind around and turn about in accordance with the placement of buildings and the terrain of the environs, so they may be tortuous or circular, and full of variety. They may also be used to divide up the garden space and add to the feeling of depth in garden scenery.

There are four types of corridors classified by their shape: straight, winding, wavelike, and double. But if classified by their locations, they may be categorized as:

• Corridors along walls

• Open corridors

• Tortuous corridors

• Two-story corridors

• Hill-ascending corridors

• Waterside corridors (see Figs. V-79 and V-80)

Corridors are built not only to encircle pools, hillocks and forests, sometimes they climb and pass over hill slopes, wind through groves of trees, or pass over pools and brooks, linking buildings with hillocks and pools into a single scenic entity.

A winding corridor is usually tortuous and labyrinthian, some parts of it built against the wall, and some extending to the open space, so that small courts of various shapes are formed between the corridor and the wall for flowers and rocks. This is one of the frequently used devices in Suzhou gardens (Fig. V-81).

A double corridor is a combination of two corridors separated by a wall in which tracery windows may be installed. With the adoption of this device in a garden, it is possible not only to separate scenic areas from one another, but also to link them by the tracery windows. Using a double corridor adds to the feeling of depth in garden scenery and reveals different scenic views that unfold as the observer walks through the corridor. This kind of double corridor may also serve to reveal alternative scenic objects on both sides in a very natural way. Examples of the double corridor may be found in Yi Yuan (Happy Garden), in Canglang Ting (Surging-Wave-Pavilion Garden), and in Shizilin (The Forest of Lions Garden).

A two-story corridor is sometimes called a border building. It is usually built near a two-story building or is used to link a rockery with the building. Examples of these may be found beside Jianshan Lou (Seeing-the-Hill Two-Storied Building) in Zhuozheng Yuan (The Humble Administrator's Garden), at the east of the library in the western part of Ou Yuan (Twin Garden), and at a residence in Nanshizi Street.

An ascending corridor usually is built on a hill slope. It not only serves to link up buildings at different levels along the slope, but also enriches the garden scenery with its undulating shape. Examples of this type of corridor may be found in the stretch from the west of Hanbi Shanfang (Encompassing-Jade Mountain House) to Wenmuxixiang Xuan (Smelling-the-Frangrance-of-Osmanthus Lounge) in Liu Yuan (Lingering-Here Garden) (Fig. VIII-6) and in the hill-ascending corridor west of Jianshan Lou (Seeing-the-Hill Two-Storied Building) in Zhuozheng Yuan (The Humble Administrator's Garden).

A waterside corridor often passes over the surface of the water. It can make the watershed seem half-separated and half-connected and thus add to an impression of the depth of the water and the spaciousness of the pool. The Chinese saying, "The floating corridor seems like a ferry," expresses the symbolic significance of a corridor in relation to the water. An example of such a type is Boxing Lang (The Wave-like Corridor) in the western part of Zhuozheng Yuan (The Humble Administrator's Garden) (Figs. V-82 and V-83).

A corridor is at its best when it is light and small; it usually is unpleasant for a corridor to be too high or too wide. In common practice, the appropriate dimensions are: the net width between 1.2 and 1.5 meters; the distance between pillars 3 meters; the diameter of the pillar 15 centimeters, and the height of the pillars 2.5 meters. The top of a corridor usually is open, but sometimes walls with open or tracery windows are used. Along the corridor between pillars, checkers are formed at the lower part with bricks polished with water stones; or, low walls are piled and covered with slabs of brick where one may sit and rest. The roof frames of the corridor generally are simple. They are mostly two or three-span or roof frames of bent rafters.

The roof of a corridor built along a wall is single-sloped while that of circular corridors around halls or lounges usually is similar to the roof of the hall or lounge, with a traditional Chinese ceiling underneath. The roof of a double corridor is entirely double-sloped along the line of the partition wall; the ceiling may be built in a variety of traditional Chinese designs. The two-story corridors, waterside corridors, hill-ascending corridors, and wave-like corridors are constructed in ways appropriate to their settings, and permit much flexibility. But their design usually falls into one of the various types described above.

Elements of Construction

The Roof (Figs. V-90 through V-97)

The roof is the liveliest part of artistic expression in classical garden architecture. With its light wings and pointed corners, and its varied ways of construction, it constitutes one of the elements that exhibit the delicate and beautiful style of classical garden-building in Suzhou.

The commonly adopted types of roofs include the full-gable roof (Yingshan), the gable-and-hip roof (Xieshan), and the pyramidal roof (Zuanjian), with the gable-and-hip roof supported by bent rafters as the type most frequently employed. However, in order to adapt itself to the surroundings, only the pointed tip of the roof at the front of the building bends over backwards; the one at the rear does not. Sometimes the pointed tip of the roof on the east side bends over backwards, while its counterpart on the west side does not. Although the methods of roof construction are manifold, the commonly practiced ones are as follows:

Roofing and Ti-Zhan[5].   Since the climate in Suzhou is mild and the wind is gentle, the roofing tiles are applied directly on top of roof bricks and roof boards. Plaster is used only on the roof ridge and at the ends of the eaves. The tiles used on pyramidal roofs (Zuanjian) are cylindrical, with the smaller tiles placed above the bigger ones.

The roof slope usually is gentle. As the difference in height between purlins (horizontal members) gradually increases, the slope of the roofing becomes correspondingly greater, thus making the roofline a curve. This kind of construction by the craftsmen in Suzhou is called "Ti-Zhan" (Fig. V-87).

The Ridge of the roof.   In addition to the "Hui-Ding" (winding-top) and "Juan-Peng" (rolled-tent), the main ridge of the roof usually is one of the following types:

- You-Ji (floating ridge)

- Ganze-Ji (sugar-cane ridge)

- Wentou-Ji (fret ridge)

- Cimao-Ji (female-bird-feather ridge)

- Buji-Ji (hen ridge)

See Fig. V-96 for illustrations. The first three types are comparatively simple and are commonly used for ordinary one-story buildings. The last two are employed primarily for halls and lounges. An outstanding example is the main ridge of the roof of Yuanxiang Tang (Distant-Fragrance Hall) in Zhuozheng Yuan (The Humble Administrator's Garden). The height of the roof ridge ranges from 36 to 60 centimeters depending on the roof's size. The construction of a Chui-Ji (perpendicular ridge) is relatively simple: at the end of the ridge is sometimes placed I-shaped or fret designs. The types of "Qiang-Ji" (prop ridge) are numerous, and they may assume many different shapes.

The point tip of the roof.   If the roof is a gable-and-hip or a pyramidal type, the pointed tip generally bends up backwards in one of two ways: Either it starts to bend from the branch prop-beam, Nen-Qiang Fa-Qiang, which is perpendicular to the ridge prop-beam, Shui-Qiang Fa-Qiang, (i.e., the former starts to bend up backwards from the smaller beam, and the latter starts to bend up backwards from the large beam that serves as the ridge) (Figs. V-90 through V-94).

The structure of Shui-Qiang is relatively simple as it involves only the oblique ridge beam (that is, the big prop-beam) and not the branch prop-beam (that is, the smaller prop-beam perpendicular to the prop-beam). The wooden structure itself does not bend up backwards; only the tip of the ridge beam points upwards. The structure of Nen-Qiang (the branch perpendicular to the ridge beam) is more complicated, because a branch prop-beam is placed at the lower end somewhat perpendicularly, so the two ends of the eaves rise very high upwards.

The angle at which the ridge prop-beam meets the branch prop-beam should be almost equal to the sum of the two acute angles formed by the ridge beam and the branch beam with the horizontal line; the angle formed by the ridge beam and the horizontal line depends on the roof's degree of slope. Therefore, when the roof's precise degree of slope is determined, the extent to which the pointed tip of the roof should bend up is determined also. This is because when the slope of the roof is very steep, the pointed tip of the roof would bend up less; if the slope of the roof is very gentle, the pointed tip of the roof would bend up rather high. Either case would give the impression of discord or incongruity.

In Sishixiaosa Ting (Spirited-and-Unrestrained-through-the-Four-Seasons Pavilion) and Huafangzhai (Painting Landboat Study) in Yi Yuan (Happy Garden), only a ridge beam is used; yet its lower end curves upward and looks as though a branch beam is there also. This constitutes a hybrid type.

Although the wooden structure allows the corner roof beam to bend up backwards in either of two ways (i.e., the pointed tip of the corner of the roof generally assumes different shapes), the ridge beams (i.e., the ridge for the prop) usually are similar in structure. In some cases the ridge beam is straight and forceful, while in others it is gentle and relaxed. But architecturally it appears light and lively. The height and curvature of the ridge beam generally is proportionate to the roof's size and slope.

When choosing one of the two ways to bend up the roof corner, aside from considering the curve's relationship to the roof's slope, attention should be paid to how it relates to the surroundings, and its artistic effect. For instance, although the branch beam is used for the pointed tip of the roof in both Yuanxiang Tang (Distant-Fragrance Hall) and Yiyu Xuan (Leaning-on-Jade Hall) in the central part of Zhuozheng Yuan (The Humble Administrator's Garden), there is a striking difference between the two. In the two examples, one roofline bends up gently, and the other steeply. The choice between the two is that between a sense of lightness, or a feeling of flight.

The Roof Framework (Figs. V-85, V-86, and V-89)

Accommodating and reflecting differing architectural styles, the structure of the roof frame varies a good deal, but the common approach is how to make the best use of Cao-Jia (the highest part of the roof framework) and Fushui-Chuan (obliquely placed rafters to help support the roof). (Neither can be seen from down below.) The latter device is adopted in practically all the halls, lounges, verandas, and waterside halls with extended structures in both the front and rear, as well as in the Hui-Ding inside mandarin-duck halls. When viewed from inside, there appear to be several roofs joined together, but viewed from outside, the whole structure is unified.

Most of the Cao-Jia may freely assume different forms in accordance with the external appearance of the roof and the ceiling arrangement inside; they are not restricted by the number of bays. The craftsmanship in the construction of these Cao-Jia may be crude as long as it does not harm to the artistic effect of the interior.

Fushui-Chuan (oblique rafters) and Wang-Zhuan (a kind of bricks) may frequently be used in place of the ceiling. They are placed above the rafters to hold tiles and keep away dust, and also to keep out the heat during the summer and the cold air in the winter months. Beams and pillars are made to look light and airy, graceful and elegant. Between pillars and under beams are ornamental flowery-patterned panels* of all sorts, an architectural feature of southern China.

In accordance with the different roof shapes, the roof frame generally is one

---

* Ornamental netlike patterned wooden board hanging down from the beam between the pillars.

of three kinds: the flush-gable roof, the overhaning-gable roof, and the gable-and-hip roof.

Framework. The framework for the flush gable roof and the overhanding gable roof is composed of "tie" (the craftsmen in Suzhou called it a piece of framework), while "Hui-Ding" (winding top) is commonly used for the ceiling because the curves formed at the tip-top appear soft and supple and fit in well with the juan-peng. The timber used for the truss of the juan-peng may be flat in shape, or may be round or cylindrical. The same is true for pavilions with the gable-and-hip roof, as in the cases of Xiban Ting (West Half-Pavilion) (Figs. V-51 and V-52) in Zhuozheng Yuan (The Humble Administrator's Garden) and Youyicun Ting (Just-Another-Village Pavilion) in Liu Yuan (Lingering-Here Garden).

Although various patterns of "tie" may be used, its construction principle is similar in all situations; that is, the beams are placed crossways on top of pillars; atop the beams are mini-pillars (also called "gua-zhu," i.e., melon pillars), otherwise known as "dou." The there are crossbeams again, and pillars again, as supports for the purlin.

Pyramidal roof framework. The framework for a pyramidal roof is usually built in one of three ways, as follows:

1. The oblique ridge-beam can be used to support a round central column, under which it is possible to construct a traditional Chinese ceiling for ornamental purposes as in the case of the Hexagonal Pavilion in a residence on Jingde Street. But this type of structure gives little support and is suitable only for a small pavilion. Li Ting (Bamboo-Hat Pavilion) in Zhuozheng Yuan (The Humble Administrator's Garden) is constructed this way, except that here the solid prop-beam juts out beyond the cross-beam under the eaves.

2. A girder may be used to supp[ort the round central column. Usually one girder is sufficient structurally. But if the pavilion is fairly large, two girders are used, placed either parallel to each other or with one perpendicular to the other. But because the truss may appear disorderly, a ceiling should be constructed to cover it up, as in the case of Xiaochanglang Ting (Little-Surging-Wave Pavilion) in Yi Yuan (Happy Garden) (Fig. V-91).

3. The third way is to use overlapping corner-beams. For a square pavilion, the structure would be fairly simple: that is, simply place a mini-pillar on the lower, overlapping corner-beam, and on top of the pillar place another square, overlapping corner-beam that is set at a 45-degree angle to it. For a hexagonal or an octagonal pavilion, the overlapping corner-beam on the top should be correspondingly hexagonal so that the sold ridge-prop may be placed on it. A traditional Chinese ceiling may be constructed under the framework, or the space may be left open, as in the case of Taying Ting (Pagoda-Shadow Pavilion) in Zhuozheng Yuan (The Humble Administrator's Garden) (Fig. V-95).

In Ruyu Ting (Breeding-Fish Pavilion) in Yi Pu (Art Orchard), the roof framework is somewhat unusual. It has a square, pyramidal roof with an overlapping corner-beam which is placed on top of cup-shaped solid wooden blocks under the eaves. Then, on top of the overlapping corner-beam is another cup-shaped solid wooden block, on which is again placed a solid prop-ridge-beam. The tail of this ridge-beam juts out quite a bit; on it, the purlins form a #-shaped ceiling (Fig. V-97).

Using framework for a mixed-type roof allows many variations in the external appearance of the roof. Such a framework is generally used to accommodate architecturally unusual plans. Examples of this are found in Shanmian Ting

(Fan-Shaped Pavilion) in Zhuozheng Yuan (The Humble Administrator's Garden) (Fig. V-75), in Baiyun Ting (White-Cloud Pavilion) (Fig. V-78), and in Sixian Ting (Four-Immortals Pavilion) (Fig. V-73) at Tianping Mountain.

Paints

The materials for painting the buildings in Suzhou gardens and the process for painting them generally follow the old local traditions and are different from those for ordinary house painting. The following are four commonly adopted methods of painting the buidings in gardens:

1. The method used for pillars, beams, and rafters is "to fully cover the surface with paint and to varnish it once with raw lacquer from Hunan and Hubei."[6] With this method, surface paint is first applied to the timber as a base, a layer of diluted pig's blood is then added to mix the colors well, and, finally, the raw laquer from Hunan and Hubei is spread over it as varnish. Chestnut-colored paint is usually used, but other colors are available as well.

2. Another method is "to fully cover the surface with paint and then apply two coats of raw lacquer from Hunan and Hubei." This is used on doors, windows, and other ornamental structures both inside and outside the building. Instead, the raw lacquer from Hunan and Hubei is used on the surface as a base and is followed by another application of raw lacquer from Hunan and Hubei to blend the colors. The paint and the timber are thus thoroughly blended and the painted surface can better withstand the test of time. Again, chestnut is the commonly chosen color, but other colors are also used.

3. The third method is "to fully cover the surface with surface paint and then varnish it once with black raw lacquer from Hunan and Hubei." Black has a high surface-luster so it is often used on the pillars and front gates of halls and lounges.

4. A more luxurious way of painting than the one above is "to use grey cloth...covered with black varnish from Hunan and Hubei." It is a process of "covering flax to catch the dust" in the official architectural style of the Qing Dynasty. This method of painting is used on the pillars in Yuanxiang Tang (Distant-Fragrance Hall) in Zhuozheng Yuan (The Humble Administrator's Garden) and in Wufeng Xianguang (Five-Peak Celestial House) in Liu Yuan (Lingering-Here Garden).

Decorative Devices

The decorative devices in garden architecture have the traditional characteristics of subtlety and pliancy, as handed down from ancient Chinese architecture. The elegant shapes of these ornaments, their exquisite carvings, and their appropriateness in embellishment and foil effect not only respond to the functional requirements of spatial partitioning but also bring harmony to the artistic style of gardening, so that the minutiae fit in well with the size and shape of buildings and thus achieve the desired artistic effect. Therefore, the various designs of doors and windows, the great variety of patterns of "Gualuo,"* lattice doors and screen partitions, "Xinzai" (i.e., window latticework), carvings and engravings, and lacquer work, all enhance the delicate and graceful appearance of garden architecture and add charming diversity to the art of garden building.

Varying the arrangements and highlighting certain decorations are common

---

* "Guoluo," decorative devices that hang down from the beam (in some cases all the way down to the ground level) in the form of fretwork or tracery of all sorts of patterns.

decorative devices in classical Suzhou gardens. The object is to achieve artistic effects by making clear distinctions between major and minor scenic objects, creating a wealth of artistic patterns, and gaining liveliness and vigor. The decorative devices in each of the different buildings of the same garden often acquire peculiar characteristics of their own. For instance, in halls, lattice doors generally are constructed for the center bay; and windows above balustrade are built for the side bays. On all sides of a building with corridors around it, from the cross-beam, and between the pillars hang exquisitely carved decorative panellings. Inside the rooms, on the gauze partitions there are paintings, calligraphic writings, or colored, spun fabric. A hall that opens out on all four sides has bright, framed windows that reach down to the ground. They are fitted from top to bottom with glass instead of decorative boards to facilitate the observation of scenery.

Small open halls usually are three bays wide, with lattice doors for the center bay and windows for the side bays. The elevations on the other two sides are gables or screenlike walls, while lattice doors with simple carvings make up the rear facade. In pavilions and waterside pavilions there are panelings with flowery patterns hung; balustrades or goose-neck chairs are provided beneath for sitting and resting. In two-story halls or pavilions, the upper story usually is fitted with upward-folding windows, while at the lower level there are whitewashed walls with open gates.

Emphasizing different decorative devices in each building is a common practice in gardens. For instance, numerous decorative devices may be found in the interior of Liuting Ge (Lingering-to-Listen Pavilion) in the western part of Zhuozheng Yuan (The Humble Administrator's Garden), where the infinite variety of flying panels and lattice doors achieve wonders. The floral pattern of the balustrades on the south and north sides of the 36-Yuanyang Guan (36-Mandarin-Duck Hall) and the carvings on the decorative boards in Cuilinlong (The Delicate-Emerald Hall) in Canglang Ting (Surging-Wave-Pavilion Garden) are all different from one another in detail. Again, in order to mark the importance of the bright bay in a hall or lounge, the decorative devices there usually are exquisite and luxurious, in contrast to the simple and plain furnishings of the bays next to it.

The wood selected for intricate decorative carvings is primarily fine hardwood of superior quality such as "nanmu," mahogany, rosewood, boxwood, and ginkgo, while that for ordinary use includes pine and Chinese fir. In timber of superior quality the wood grains generally are visible. When it is painted dark chestnut, drooping date, dark black, or yellowish brown, and set against a background of white walls and grey door frames, it achieves a soft, sober tone. There are two kinds of decorative devices: those for interior decoration and those for exterior decoration.

Exterior Decoration (Figs. V-100 through V-113)
Decorative devices for the exterior of a building include:

- Lattice doors

- Windows

- Windows-above-balustrades

- Transom windows (for ventilation)

- "Heng-pi" (horizontal transoms)

- Oblong upper windows that open upward or downward

- Brick-framed lattice windows

In addition, there are all sorts of "gualuo" (decorative devices in the form of floral-patterned panels that hang from the beams), and balustrades. Each of these is described below:

Lattice doors. Constructed primarily for a bright bay and occasionally for a whole suite of rooms, lattice doors (screen partitions) usually reach down to the ground. Depending on the size of the room, there may be four, six, or eight lattice doors in a room, with six being the number most common. The "Neixinzai," or central part of the lattice door, traditionally was decorated with oyster shells, and only recently glass has been used in its place.

There are numerous patterns for the central part of the window, of which some ten patterns are commonly used. Each pattern has a diverse arrangement. On the lattice doors for the "Jiatang" (i.e., horizontal boards in the upper part of the lattice doors) and the "Qunban" (i.e., the wooden boards in the lower part of the lattice doors), long wooden boards are usually used.

On these boards are carvings and engravings with contrasting decorative effects; i.e., darkness interplays with brightness, and convex patterns with concave ones. The decorative patterns are generally of "Ruyi,"* still life, flowers, and plants. If the lattice door consists only of the central parts within the window frame, and with no wooden boards at the bottom, it is entirely transparent. It appears delicate and bright and is called "Luodi Mingzhao" (i.e., clear screen that stretches all the way to the ground). An example of this is the lattice door at Yuanxiang Tang (Distant-Fragrance Hall) in Zhuozheng Yuan (The Humble Administrator's Garden).

There are several kinds of architraves on the vertical and horizontal wooden frames of the lattice doors. These are:

- Yamian (concave and round)

- Hunmian (convex and half-round)

- Wenwumian ("ya-mian" and "hun-mian" joined together)

- Hextaoxian (small round threads in the middle and several round threads on two sides, in a pattern resembling a walnut shell)

The architraves on the vertical and horizontal wooden frames of the lattice doors, (called Bianting and Hengtouliao), are joined together at the four corners.

Windows. Windows are usually built between the pillars in the side bay, in the passageway, and in the pavilions and two-story pavilions. A semi-wall is about 50 centimeters high; on top of it are windows and balustrades with seats. If there are windows in a pavilion or a two-story pavilion, goose-neck chairs may be installed in addition to the balustrade with seats. The width of the window depends on the size of the room, and generally is about the same as that of the lattice door, i.e., about 70 centimeters.

Windows-above-balustrades. This type of window usually is built between the corridor pillars in the side bay of a hall or lounge. Usually, there are six windows of this kind built in a bay. Their shape and structure are similar to those of the lattice door, but their height is equal only to that of the hengtou-liao, the horizontal lower wooden frame and the upper board of the lattice door, at the top of the door. Beneath the window are the railings. The flower patterns on the rail-

---

* "Ruyi"—an S-shaped decorative object usually made of jade, formerly a symbol of good luck.

ings and the windows all face inside. Outside the railings are boards that are used to give shelter from wind and rain; they may be put on and taken off at will.

Hengfengchuang (transom windows). These are found in taller buildings, and are built between the upper and middle transom bars. They are narrow and oblong.

Hehechuang (upward folding windows). These windows are peculiar in construction and different form all the above-mentioned types in the way they open and close. The upper and lower parts of the windows are fixed and movable only in a certain way, while the middle part may be lifted up from the inside and held open by hooks. In northern China, these are also called supported-by-hooks windows.

Brick-framed lattice windows. These are constructed on the gable of a building. The brick frames are made of water-polished bricks and may be square, oblong, or hexagonal; however, the brick-framed windows cannot be opened or closed. Larger ones are covered by window curtains, which serve both as decoration and protection from the rain and wind.

The decorative patterns on the above-mentioned windows are generally the same as those on the lattice doors, and so are the types of the architraves.

Railings. Usually, railings are placed between two pillars of a corridor, but they can also be placed beneath an upward-folding window or a window-above-balustrade to serve as a semi-wall. The railings can be either high or low. The low ones, also called semi-railings, measure from 50 to 73 centimeters in height. They may have sitting balustrades on top of them, and usually are placed in a corridor. The high railings usually are one-third the height of lattice doors. The decorative patterns should be beautiful and harmonize with the surroundings. There are only three types of architrave railings: Hunmian (convex and half-round), Yamian (concave and round), and Mujiaomian (wooden corner) (i.e., with two small round threads joined at right angles at the turning corner). They are all plain and in good taste.

Goose-neck chairs. The chairs generally used in pavilions, waterside pavilions, two-story halls, and two-story pavilions that face a pool. They are so named because their backs bend like the necks of geese. At the lower parts of both ends of the side frames, there are tenons joined to the wooden seats, which are fixed to the pillars with iron hooks. These chairs are used for sitting and resting in a leaning position.

Gualuo (decorative devices that hang down from the beam). Gualuo are made up of long wooden strips joined together and hung from the wooden beams between corridor pillars. The popular pattern is shaped like the Buddhist cross or "III"; rarely, it is shaped like rattan veins or ice cracks. Gualuo is framed on three sides, with the lower ends of the two side-border frames shaped like hooks carved into an S-shaped pattern (Ruyi pattern). The border frames are fastened to the pillars with tenons. Gualuo are then joined to the border frames with tenons on one side and bamboo pins on the other. The tenons and bamboo pins may be put on or removed.

Interior Decoration (Figs. V-114 through V-123)

Decorative devices for the interior consist mainly of various types and shapes of screen partitions (or gauze screen) and screen shades. They may be placed anywhere to help distinguish different areas that are intended for different purposes.

They are also used to distinguish one building from another. In a hall or a lounge, a screen partition or screen shade is often used to divide the front and back parts of a room. The arrangements for a twin hall can demonstrate the interior function of these decorative devices: In the hall, the ridge pillars reach down to the ground level. A screen partition generally is placed between the pillars in the hall's bright bay, while in the two side bays, a flying screen is hung between the pillars; thus the front and back parts of the room are divided to serve different purposes.

To give variety and depth to an interior space, not only can a screen partition or a flying screen divide a spacious room into several small, exquisite, and well-ventilated spheres of activity, but also the furniture in either area is available for use where needed. The different areas of the room are rendered separable but capable of being combined into one flexible space.

Screens. There are three kinds of screens in popular use: flying screens, screens that reach down to the ground, and flying screens of the panel pendent type, that hangs from the beam (Figs. V-115 through V-123).

Flying curtains are similar to gualuo, which hang down from the beam, except that their two ends hang down to form a sort of arched doorway, and that they are placed between the ridge pillar and the screen partition. A screen that reaches down to the ground is actually a flying screen with its two ends touching the grounds, with the inner fringe assuming a square, a round, or an octagonal shape. The flying screen of the panel pendent type that hangs from the beam resembles the gualuo, except that its two hanging ends are shorter than those of a flying screen. The size and shape of a screen generally depends on the size of the interior space.

The patterns of screen fall into the following types:

- Rattan stem patterns
- Irregular patterns
- Plum-shaped patterns
- Squirrel and walnut patterns
- Whole patterns
- Peach rattan patterns

The construction of the screen is similar to that of the gualuo that hangs from the beam. But a flying screen and a screen that reaches down to the ground are sometimes made of a whole piece, or two or three pieces of carved timber of superior quality, such as ginkgo and rosewood.

An excellent example of a screen is the Yuanguang-zhao (the round luster screen) in Linquanjishuozhi Guan (The House for the Aged Giants of Groves and Springs) in Liu Yuan (Lingering-Here Garden). As the screen is fairly large, both the inside and outside frames are made round, so that the border frames do not appear too thin and slender. Within the border frames, there are rather large leaf-shaped patterns, which are highly concentrated in some places but are quite evenly distributed in most areas, and which are linked together with slender and twisted branch-shaped patterns that serve as foils. The pattern designs are free and full of variety, and the carvings and engravings are carefully pieced together on the screen.

Another striking example of a flying screen is found in Liuting Ge (Lingering-to-Listen Pavilion) in Zhuozheng Yuan (The Humble Administrator's Garden). There, tree-root-shaped oblong patterns are everywhere on the screen, while in the middle and in two corners are scattered a few pine-shaped, sparrow-shaped, and plum-shaped patterns to serve as embellishment. The screen is delicate, and beautiful, and harmoniously fits in with the building.

The shape of the palm-leaf screen in Guwusong Yuan (Five-Old-Pine Park) in Shizilin (The Forest of Lions Garden) is rarely seen elsewhere, and the carvings there are more realistic. The screen that reaches to the ground in Sanshuijian Shuige (Waterside Pavilion amid-the-Hillock-and-Pool) in Ou Yuan (Twin Garden) is rather large and has exquisite carvings. It is also an outstanding example.

Screen partitions. A screen partition is similar in shape to a lattice door, but either a green gauze or a wooden board with mounted calligraphic writings and paintings is nailed to the back of the screen's middle section. The central portion normally is divided into three sections: in the middle there is an oblong framework around which are inlaid fret decorations called Chajiao (inserted cape), and around it are carved floral knots in a series. In some cases, ice-crack-patterned color glass is set in the framework, and around it are inlaid floral knots. A screen partition is light, delicate, and beautiful. On its wooden boards above and below the central window area are carvings of flowers and shrubs or representations of sacrificial offerings to be placed on the table. In some cases boxwood is used for the decorative carvings and the glued-on calligraphic writings; Chajiao (or inserted capes of floral knots), may also be carved on boxwood or ginkgo.

Furniture and Articles for Display

Furniture and articles for display are indispensable for the interior of a garden building. They not only provide for the needs of everyday life, such as entertaining guests, vacationing, and relaxing, but they also serve as ornaments and decoration. In the interior of a hall or a lounge, the furniture arrangement sets the tone for the major and subordinate parts of the room; furniture is also needed to fill up the space to avoid the feeling of emptiness (Figs. V-11, V-124, and V-125).

A great variety of furniture is used indoors and the most frequently used articles include tables and desks, other tables, chairs, and stools.

Tables and Desks

Among tables and desks, there are tea tables (or teapoys), flower tables (flower shelves), natural shape wooden tables, an altar or a table for sacrificial offerings, and a table for musical instruments. Tea tables are either square or rectangular. Since a tea table is placed with chairs as a set, its form and decorations, the inlay on its surface, the material used, and its color are determined by those of the chairs.

Flower tables (flower shelves). These are used for flowers in pots. Usually they are set on both sides of a natural shape wooden table in front of a screen partition or at a corner of a room. The tables are usually about 1.5 meters high. The carvings and decorations on them are relatively simple.

Natural shaped wooden tables. These are generally about 2 to 2.5 meters long, more than 33 centimeters wide, and about one-half meter higher than an ordinary table. The corners at the two top ends jut upwards and the two legs end in flat pieces. The decorations used are S-shaped carvings on jade, thunderbolt patterns, and Buddhist-cross-shaped flower patterns.

Tables for offerings (or altars), tables for musical instruments. The former is similar to a natural shape wooden table, but there are no corners jutting upward at the two ends. There are, however, four legs underneath. Their height is the same as that of square tables, and they are placed in front of natural shape wooden tables. Tables for musical instruments are similar to those for offerings, but are shorter, narrower, and smaller, and usually are placed against walls. They are used only for display, and their carvings and decorations are the same as those on natural shape wooden tables.

Other tables. Tables are square, round, or of other shapes. A large, round table has six legs; a smaller one has five. The surface of a table commonly is changeable. In the summer months, marble generally is used on the surface, while in the winter different wooden boards of superior quality are used to replace the marble. In addition, there are also oblong and semiround tables that may be taken apart and then reassembled; there is a great variety in shape and type.

Chairs

A taishiyi (as old-fashioned wooden armchair) has been the most dignified of all chairs since feudal times. The middle part of the chair's back is slightly higher, while the two sides are lower, thus forming a convex shape. The back of the chair generally is inlaid with round pieces of marble, set in patterns of the bottle gourd and the palm leaf.

A single-backed chair has a back but no armrests. Its shape is simple, and it usually is made of ordinary wood. Two chairs of this kind, with a small table between, are placed against the side walls or in some other inconspicuous location.

An "official-hat" type of chair is single-backed with an armrest on each side. Its shape and decorations are simple in some and complicated in others. These chairs usually are matched with small tables to form sets. Four such chairs and two small tables arranged in two sets may be placed at the side of the bright bay of a hall or lounge for display as a pair of sets.

Stools

There are many types of stools, and their sizes and surfaces vary greatly. Square stools usually are used in a hall or lounge either to form sets with square tables or be placed independently. Round stools, some shaped like crabapples or begonias, plums, pears, and fans, usually are matched with round tables. The stool surfaces are sometimes inlaid with marble and rosewood.

Among round stools, there are some shaped like drums; these are called small mounds. Some are made of wood and some of porcelain, with their surfaces about 33 centimeters in diameter. In olden days people used to cover the mounds with embroidery, so they are called embroidered mounds. Generally, they are used in pavilions, waterside pavilions, studies, and bedrooms.

A "ji," or a wooden bench, also called "manji," is another type of stool, which may be round or square. Usually measuring about two square meters, a ji's top is larger than a stool's. It has four legs that touch the ground and sprawl outward slightly.

Couches, or beds. In addition to the above-mentioned furniture, there is the couch (bed) which is as large as a bed and has leaning screens on three sides. It is placed at the back of the parlor's bright bay. This is a piece of furniture the garden owner used to reserve for respected guests. The couch is divided in the middle by a very low tea table on which is placed implements for tea-drinking. Because the couch usually is quite large and high, two small, narrow, oblong-shaped footstools are placed underneath. Sometimes, square bricks (also called golden bricks) are provided on which miscellaneous articles of daily use may be placed temporarily. Hollow bricks similar to those in the tombs of the Han Dynasty sometimes are placed atop a support for a stringed musical instrument. When the instrument is played, the bricks add to its resonance; but more often that not the bricks merely serve as decoration. Also, ancient rattans or old trees with twisting roots and intercrossing branches may be trimmed a bit and polished to serve as tables and stools. Though their fantastic shapes may arrest one's attention, they really are not practical and are only striking and outlandish.

Ever since the Ming Dynasty, the wood used for making furniture has included mahogany, "nanmu," rosewood, and other tropical woods. Such wood is hard, fine-grained, and lustrous, and may be cut into fairly small sections, delicate architrave patterns, and precise mortise and tenons. In Suzhou gardens today there are a few pieces of furniture that date from the Ming Dynasty; their characteristics are simplicity and good taste in structure, meticulous care in the choice of woods used, and the use of round sections for the components. There are few decorations but when they are used they are used in concentration. They are painted in simple and quiet colors and have carefully and precisely fitted mortise-and-tenon joints. Since the years of the Emperor Yongzheng in the Qing Dynasty, large, heavy timber has been used for furniture. Furthermore, decorative carvings and engravings have become more concentrated and numerous, and, in some cases, numerous mother-of-pearl inserts are closely inlaid. Since then, the furniture colors have included dark or dull brown, purplish date-red, and jet-black. Although the furniture is luxuriously made and carefully wrought, its structure and shape have been overly elaborate and rich in detail, in striking contrast to the furniture and architecture of the Ming Dynasty.

Indoors lamps are also very varied, the commonly seen being palace laterns (Gongdeng), flower-basket lamps, and assorted scenery lamsp (Shijingdeng). Palace lanterns use only candles, so they are simple and more widely used. Assorted scenery and flower-basket lamps are hung only for decorating pavilions, waterside pavilions, corridors, and open pavilions.

The articles for indoor display are also very varied. On the one hand, they serve everyday uses, while on the other they are decorative ornaments. The articles that may be independently displayed include screens, large standing mirrors, clocks, incense containers, and water jugs. Articles for display on table tops include Chinaware, cooperware, jadeware, and potted landscape plants, which serve only as decoration. Horizontal inscriptions and scrolls of poetic couplets are hung on the walls or pillars or hung from the roof-beams. Horizontal inscriptions usually are made of wood, while the scrolls of couplets may be made of bamboo, wood, paper, or silk. Chinese characters engraved on bamboo and wood may be either characters in relief, or characters engraved in the surface. Various colors are used for the horizontal inscriptions and scrolls. Those with black characters against a white background usually are found in halls or lounges. Other color schemes include green or white characters against a dark brown background, and green characters on a black background.

Walls and Tracery Windows, Moon Gates, and Casementless Windows

Garden walls are generally used to divide a garden space, serve as foil for scenic objects, and limit one's line of vision. Thus, they are an important element in garden design. Because the buildings in Suzhuo gardens are numerous and are crowded together, it is necessary to divide the limited garden space into many separate areas; courtyard walls are therefore built in great numbers. So many wall surfaces clustered so close together normally would seem abrupt or dull to garden visitors, but the ingenious treatment of architectural craftemen has made these walls a strikingly new and lively element in gardens. In fact, walls have become one of the most important features in Chinese gardening south of the Changjiang (Yangtse) River.

The garden walls usually are stacked with thin bricks alternately laid lengthwise and crosswise, to form a hollow space in the middle. They are variously described as cloudlike or wavelike walls, ladder-shaped walls, apertured walls, and ordinary walls. Most of them are white, but occasionally they are black or greenish-grey. White walls not only contrast with the grey roofs and dark chestnut doors and windows, they also can serve as foils for lake stones and bamboo groves, and for flowers, trees, and wisteria.

The unpredictable, infinite variety of shining water surfaces and tree shadows reflected upon a white wall is extremely fascinating and adds a great deal to the garden scenery. The garden walls have built-in tracery windows, leafless gates or moon gates, and leafless windows (kong-chuang), so that there are contrasts between void and solid, brightness and darkness, and various reflections on the wall surfaces.

Tracery windows (also called flower-wall-caves) not only can bring change to the otherwise flat, dull wall surfaces, but also can help to divide scenic areas by making the garden space appear separate but united, and rendering scenic objects seemingly hidden yet visible, thus creating a feeling of depth in the garden space. Also, the designs of the tracery windows themselves can subtly change the shadows in different lights, thereby making the garden scenery livelier.

The frames of the tracery windows in Suzhou gardens usually have only two rounds of architraves and are not inlaid with water-polished bricks. These windows are built in different shapes: square, horizontal oblong, vertical oblong, round, hexagonal, octagonal, fan-shaped, and other irregular shapes. Of the first three types, the corners generally are square but occasionally they are round or crabapple-shaped. Statistically, most of the tracery windows in Suzhou gardens are square or horizontally oblong. The lower window frames in the rows of tracery windows along the corridor are about 1.3 meters above ground level to facilitate viewing the scenery beyond. However, there are also tracery windows that serve only to illuminate, ventilate, or decorate; these are placed higher above the ground.

There are various kinds of pattern designs for tracery windows, numbering no less than several hundred in Suzhou (Figs. V-125 through V-129). The designs fall into two basic shapes: geometrical or natural; but the two may sometimes be mixed.

Geometrical designs generally consist of straight lines, arcs, and circles. Designs which consist of all straight lines include the folowing shapes:

- The Buddhist Cross

- Star or pentagon (dingsheng)

- Hexagonal

- Rhombohedron

- Long-paper-slip

- Silk-ring

- Olive

- Ice-cracks

Designs that consist of all arcs (or curves) include those shaped like:

- Fish scales
- Coins
- Balls
- Autumn leaves
- Crabapples
- Sunflowers
- S-shaped ("Ruyi"-shaped)
- Waves

Designs drawn from two or more of the above-mentioned types include patterns that are:

- Lizardlike
- Buddhist-Cross shaped
- Crabapple-shaped
- Hexagonal, plum-shaped
- Various scenic designs on lamps

There are also tracery windows with geometric designs on the four borders, and representations of lyres, chessmen, books, and paintings.

Designs based on the world of nature have a wider scope in their themes. Those based on the theme of flowers include patterns shaped like pines, cypresses, peonies, plums, bamboos, orchids, chrysanthemums, bananas, lotuses, fingered citrons, pears, and pomegranates. Those based on birds and beasts include patterns shaped like lions, tigers, dragons floating on clouds, bats, and phoenixes, as well as pictures of pines, cranes, cypresses, and deer. Those based on stories of human dramas include scenes taken from novels and romances, legends concerning Buddhism, and various plays and dramas.

Both geometric designs and those based on the patterns from the world of nature nevertheless closely depend upon the qualities and characteristics of the materials used in their construction. The chief materials used for goemetric designs are bricks, tiles, and wood. For short, straight-line designs, "Wang-Zhuan," a special kind of brick measuring 12.5 x 10.8 x 1.4 cm usually is used. But pieces of wood are used for the longer straight-line designs containing complicated brocade-like patterns. Wooden boards are indispensable for constructing horizontal oblong-shaped straight-line designs. Slab tiles of different lengths are used for arc-shaped or large circular designs. For smaller circular shapes, cylindrical tiles are used. The designs based on the world of nature traditionally are made of thin wooden boards or bamboo reinforcement. But because the thin boards lack strength, iron slabs and strips are later introduced. The ironwork is then covered with mortar or layers of hempen threads to form the various shapes.

Prefabricated tracery windows in geometric patterns are also available. They are made of glaze and are easier to install, and are more durable. But due to the limitations of the material and a lack of freedom in the construction process, the designs were monotonous and were rarely used in Suzhou gardens.

On the walls separating courtyards and along corridors, pavilions, and water-side pavilions, often there are leafless gates called "dong-men" (or moon gates), also called "di-xue" (leafless gates on walls), and "kong-chuang" (literally, leafless windows), also called "yue-dong" (literally, moon caves). Leafless gates serve as entrances and exits, while casementless windows are like picture frames for viewing scenery. They also provide light and air.

Stony peaks are often placed in small courtyards. Bamboos and banana plants are planted behind the leafless gates or casementless windows, to form beautiful miniature pictures. This has been a popular device in classical gardens in Suzhou. Such leafless gates and casementless windows link the open spaces on both sides of the wall and weave them together to achieve a sense of scenic depth and expansive garden space.

Dong-men (literally, leafless gates or moon gates) assume numerous shapes, as follows:

- Round
- Horizontally oblong
- Vertically oblong
- Shaped like elongated pointed jade tablets
- Elongated hexagons
- Regular hexagons
- Elongated octagons
- Dingsheng shaped (star shaped)
- Begonia shaped
- Pear shaped
- Bottle-gourd shaped
- Autumn-leaf shaped
- Shaped like the vases of the Han Dynasty

In addition, there are variations of any of these shapes (Figs. V-130 through V-133). For instance, the upper border of the oblong-shaped leafless gates may be horizontal, convex in the middle, or have four or five arcs or curves joined together. In the design of the upper corners of leafless gates, the simpler kind might have crabapple patterns, while the more complex type might be decorated with corner patterns shaped like beam supports, or may have fret or cloudlike patterns.

Casementless windows also come in different shapes (Figs. V-134 and V-135):

- Square
- Horizontally oblong
- Vertically oblong
- Hexagonal
- Round
- Fan shaped
- Bottle-gourd shaped
- Autumn-leaf shaped
- Shaped like the vases of the Han Dynasty

The shapes and sizes of leafless gates and casementless windows are determined by the character of the adjacent buildings, the wall surfaces, and the nature of their surroundings. For walls that separate two or more principal scenic areas in a courtyard, the leafless gates usually are simple rounds or hexagonals, and are large enough in diameter to enable visitors to pass through freely. Corridors and small courts usually have leafless gates and casementless windows that are long verticals, shaped like elongated, pointed jade tablets, elongated octagons , or other delicate and lively shapes. Generally, they are smaller, and their corner patterns have great variety.

The casementless windows of open halls, lodges, pavilions, and waterside pavilions usually are horizontally oblong or vertically oblong and rectangular with an emphasis on simplicity and plainness. Each of a continuous series of casementless windows along a corridor is usually small. They are varied in style, and sometimes placed close to each other, sometimes placed sparsely. To avoid repetition and monotony, they are sometimes closely placed in some locations and sparsely grouped in others, as in the case of the two-story corridor in Xiao Yuan (Smiling Garden) and the double corridor in Shizilin (The Forest of Lions Garden). Because a casementless window is constructed chiefly for observing scenery at a distance, its height is determined by the height of the observer's line of vision.

The border frames of leafless gates and casementless windows generally are made from greyish-green square bricks. The tops of the bricks are placed down to form straight and elegant architraves of all shapes, to match the white walls and produce a simple, bright, but quiet tone. This has become an important element in, and a peculiar characteristic of, classical garden architecture in Suzhou. The architraves commonly employed at the border frames of these leafless gates and casementless windows are shrunken rough ones, two round ones joined together (called Mujiaoxian*), convex-surfaced ones, concave-surfaced ones, and concave-convex-surfaced ones. These architraves all need special rough saws and planes; there are special planes for round-opening shapes, irregular shapes and level openings.

Then finally, these architraves must be polished and made glossy by convexround, concave-round, and flat sand-bricks. Dovetail-shaped mortises are needed on the backs of square bricks in which are inserted wooden tenons to support the weight; the rear ends of the wooden boards are pressed into the walls. After this is done, putty is forced into the slits, and brick dust mixed with pig's blood is used to fill the gaps and cavities on the surfaces of the bricks and the architraves. When all has dried, sand bricks are used to polish the architraves and make them smooth and shiny.

Ground Pavements and Light Architectural Elements

Ground Pavements

In classical Suzhou gardens the ground is paved in a variety of ways. In ordinary buildings, square bricks are generally used to pave indoor areas. Corridors often use bricks laid on edge to form simple geometric designs of all sorts; occasionally, square bricks are used. Outdoors, the ground is paved in accordance with the surroundings. In the cases of footpaths, courtyards, roads, and stone steps on hill slopes, regular oblong-shaped stones and bricks laid edgewise are used. In other cases, irregular shaped lake stones, stone slabs, and cobbles are fitted together with waste material (such as broken bricks, broken tiles, and pieces of broken porcelain and jars), to form ground patterns in exquisite, richly colored designs. These demonstrate the great creative talent and inventiveness of Suzhou garden builders. These ground patterns, with the exception of the oblong-shaped

---

*Mujiaoxiao, meaning two round architraves joined together.

stones, are commonly known as the "pavement of flowery lane" (Huajie Pudi) (Figs. V-136 and V-137).

Indoor pavement made with square bricks may be solid or hollow. Solid pavement is made by first packing down the earth and then spreading a layer of sand, and then placing square bricks on it. After that, putty is poured into the crevices and, finally, the cavities are filled and all the surfaces are polished. Hollow pavement is made by building a barrier to seepage of humidity from below the ground. First, blocks of bricks, or sleeper walls, are piled under the square bricks and then the square bricks are set on the top. Such a pavement requires more material and labor, and cannot bear a heavy load. Therefore, hollow pavement is rarely used.

The courtyards generally are paved with bricks, tiles, and stones. Harmony in colors and form is a prime consideration in choosing the type of pavement. The designs fall into the following types:

- Designs for pavement with only bricks and tiles include mat-like patterns, those patterned after the Chinese character, ren*, checkered square patterns, and those patterned after "dou"-shaped blocks of wood.

- Bricks and tiles are used as lines of demarcation for the designs inlaid with cobbles and broken pieces of porcelain in all colors. The patterns are shaped in hexagonals, linked hexagonals, linked six-squares, and linked eight-squares.

- Pavements made with a mixture of bricks, tiles, stone slabs, and cobbles are patterned after crabapples, cross-shaped scenes on lamps, and ice cracks.

- Pavements made with a mixture of cobbles and tiles are patterned after linked coins, football goals, and orchids.

- In most cases the ground is paved with cobbles of all colors and patterned after silk brocades. Sometimes bright-colored pieces of broken porcelain and broken jars are used to pave the ground in patterns resembling animals and plants, but this requires much difficult labor.

The old way of paving the ground was first to tamp down the earth until it was firm, then spread a layer of 5 cm of fine earth on it, and finally lay bricks and stones of different patterns on top.

Light Architectural Items

The light architectural items commonly found in gardens include railings on terraces, flower shelves, stone tables and stone seats, engravings on bricks, upright stone tablets, and upright oblong-shaped stones for calligraphic writing (Figs. V-138 through V-142).

Railings on terraces usually are found beside halls, lounges, waterside pavilions, and landboats that face water. Occasionally, they are also found in front of pavilions and two-story pavilions atop the hills. The size of the terraces and the height and style of the railings depend upon the type of buildings and pools in the environs. Low, horizontal stone railings are built on the terrace north of Yuanxiang Tang (Distant-Fragrance Hall) in Zhuozheng Yuan (The Humble Administrator's Garden); there they not only serve as foils for the hall but also harmonize with the spacious, bright surface of the pool. The railings on the terrace in front of Xiang Zhou (Fragrant-Isle Landboat) are light and delicate, to match the exquisitely painted landboat.

Most flower shelves are made of wood or iron. Bamboo shelves may look nat-

---

*ren means human being.

ural, but they are not durable. At the east side of the pool in Wangshi Yuan (The Retired Fisherman's Garden), however, a rockery is made to support Chinese wisteria in place of flower shelves, thus creating a new style.

There are two kinds of stone tables and seats for use outdoors. One is made of stone slabs and pieces molded into square or round shapes, as found in Canglang Ting (The Surging-Wave-Pavilion Garden) and little Canglang Ting (Little-Surging-Wave Pavilion) in Yi Yuan (Happy Garden). Another kind is stacked with natural lake stones and yellow stones, as in the case of the stone tables and seats in one corner of the east garden in Liu Yuan (Lingering-Here Garden) and inside the rockery caves in Huanxiu Shanzhuang (Mountain Villa of Encircled Elegance). These are all stacked with natural lake stones and are constructed in a natural and unaffected way.

Engravings on bricks are one of the most common decorative devices in Suzhou's garden architecture. Aside from the engravings on the architraves on water-polished bricks on the border frames of doors and windows, the more prominent examples are engravings on the bricks of gate towers, on both ends of gables, and the horizontal brick tablets over leafless gates. Among the most typical ones are the engravings on the gate towers in front of the main hall in Wangshi Yuan (The Retired Fisherman's Garden). Finely engraved and exquisitely shaped, they reflect the high level of technique attained by the Suzhou craftsmen.

Upright stone tablets and upright oblong-shaped stones for calligraphic writings are often found in Suzhou gardens. On the walls of corridors where no windows are installed, stone engravings of calligraphic writings by famous scholars (known as "Fati") are inlaid to make up for the paucity of scenic views. Yi Yuan (Happy Garden) and Liu Yuan (The Lingering-Here Garden) provide typical examples of these.

Stone engravings showing chronicles and pictures of gardens are also sometimes inlaid on wall surfaces. Upright stone tablets generally are displayed inside pavilions, such as the pavilions for imperial stone tablets in Canglang Ting (The Surging-Wave-Pavilion Garden) and Shizilin (The Forest of Lions Garden). On rock screens, rock hills, and rock bridges, it is also a common practice to use as decorations inscriptions in the ancient Chinese scripts of Li and Zhuang.

Notes

1. Originally the name of the study was "Still-Reading-My-Book Study."
2. Ji Cheng of the Ming Dynasty wrote in his *Garden Building*:

   Trees of many years' growth hinder the construction of eaves and walls. Retreating one step will allow a tree to take root; cutting off several forks [branches] will not prevent the construction of roofs. That is, it is easier to carve on the beams and build the eaves, but it is more difficult for scholar trees [young trees] to shoot up high and provide shade.

   This explains that when constructing building in gardens, utilizing big trees to create garden scenery was a traditional device in China.
3. "Xuan" is the name for a building, and also is a name sometimes used to refer to the ceiling of a room.
4. To be discussed in greater detail under "Decorative Devices."
5. "Ti-Zhan" means "Ju-Jia" (raising-the-frame) in the official construction method of the Qing Dynasty, or "Ju-Zhe" (raising-the-fold) in *Yinzaofashi* (*Building Standards*), a book on architectural construction, written in the Song Dynasty.
6. "Guang-Qi" means the raw lacquer from "Hu-Guang," which included, in olden days, the two Chinese provinces of Hunan and Hubei.

VI

Flowers and Trees

Flowers and trees are indispensable elements of garden scenery. In the classical gardens of Suzhou, the chief guiding principle in choosing and planting flowers and trees is the respect for and attainment of a natural irregular and asymmetrical arrangement. Its process involves either direct imitation of nature or indirect suggestions derived from traditional Chinese landscape paintings. The shapes and contours of flowers and trees should be a well-matched blend of majesty and delicacy, so that they imperceptibly merge with the rocks on the neighboring hillock, the propinquant surface of the pool, and the adjacent architectural elements; the result is a style peculiar to classical Chinese gardens in the area south of the Changjiang (Yangtse) River (Figs. VI-1 through VI-3).

In mixed plantings of large patches of deciduous trees and evergreens, one can use different sizes, shapes, densities and colors to create the varied and ever-changing landscape of nature. For instance, on the two islets in the central part of Zhuozheng Yuan (The Humble Administrator's Garden), numerous deciduous trees are combined with a selected group of evergreens. Next to these trees is a dense bamboo grove on a hill-slope and lush reeds beside a neighboring pool. A desirable effect is achieved when the composition of mixed plants is reflected in the broad expanse of the pool.

Flowers and trees are integral parts of garden scenery, but frequently they can become the chief objects of observation and appreciation. Buildings in gardens are often named after the flowers and trees in their environs to indicate the special features of the surrounding scenery. Using several buildings of Zhuozheng Yuan as examples: Yuanxiang Tang is literally translated as the Hall of Distant Fragrance (Fig. VI-4); Wuzhuyouju Ting means a pavilion amid secluded wutong and bamboo (Fig. VI-5); Songfeng Ting means the Wind-from-Pine Pavilion; and Liuyinluqu means the winding path under willow shades.[1] Similar names for buildings are frequently found in other gardens.

Using the seasonal differences of the flowers and trees to vary the effects in each of the four seasons was a common practice in classical Suzhou gardens. For instance, the magnolia in front of halls and lounges and the peony on flower terraces create beautiful springtime scenery (Fig. VI-6); the grove of crape myrtle in Yi Yuan (Happy Garden) and the lotuses in Zhuozheng Yuan (The

Humble Administrator's Garden) and in Shizilin (The Forest of Lions Garden) are for summer-season pleasure (Fig. VI-7); the maple grove on the earthen hill-slope in the western part of Liu Yuan (Lingering-Here Garden) and the laurels and chrysanthemums in various gardens offer autumn scenery (Fig. VI-8); the camellias in front of the 18-Mantuoluo Huaguan (The 18-Datura Hall)[2] in the western part of Zhuozheng Yuan (The Humble Administrator's Garden) and the Tianzhu (literally, heavy bamboo), and the wintersweet planted in the small courts of gardens are for winter scenery (Fig. VI-9).

Special attention is paid to the mixed plantings of flowers and trees in the gardens as well. For instance, in the front court of Xiaoshanconggui Xuan (Little-Hillock-and-Laurel-Grove Hall) in Wangshi Yuan (The Retired Fisherman's Garden) and in the courtyard around Guanyun Feng (The Cloud-Topping Peak) in Liu Yuan (Lingering-Here Garden), different kinds of flowers and trees are planted for the visitors' appreciation in different seasons. Since the blossoming days of certain flowers alternate and sometimes overlap, there is a good deal of variety and change of scenery in the four seasons.

In planting flowers and trees in the Suzhou gardens, one generally takes into account the topography in which they are planted, the direction they face, the degree of humidity in the locality, and the growing habits of the different flowers and trees. For instance, the flowers and trees such as the laurel, camellia, boxwood, Tianzhu (heavenly bamboo), holly, and glossy privet, which can flourish in the shade, are usually planted under the shade of a wall of at the corner of a building; those plants that can bear the drought, such as the pines, cypresses, elms, date trees, and Silan (silken orchid), are planted mostly on the hills; the weeping willows, poplars, and pomegranates, and other trees that flourish in dampness, generally are planted beside a pool. However, one does not simply plant the trees and flowers wherever conditions agree with their peculiar habits; one chooses them with due consideration to their shapes, contours, structure, colors, and fragrances. All these factors are considered before a decision is made on their suitability for a specific environment.

It is also traditional to use to the best advantage the old trees that are found in the gardens. Since their founding, some of the Suzhou gardens have had a long history of preserving the tall trees that are several hundred years old and are still alive. Many new owners preserved these age-old plants as priceless relics and made ingenious use of them to harmonize with the hillocks, pools, and buildings when these gardens were rebuilt. The cypress and the Chinese yew standing south of the Kansongduhua Xuan (Looking-at-the-Pine-and-Painting Hall) in Wangshi Yuan (The Retired Fisherman's Garden), the tall poplars in the central part of Zhuozheng Yuan (The Humble Administrator's Garden), the ginkgo and the Chinese hackberry in the central part of Liu Yuan (Lingering-Here Garden) (Fig. VI-40), and the ginkgo in front of Wenmei Ge (Asking-for-Plum-Tree Two-Storied Pavilion) in Shizilin (The Forest of Lions Garden) are all good examples of how old trees were turned to good account.

The Choice of Plants

The natural conditions in Suzhou are favorable for growing a great variety of flowers and trees, including many that are found in the earth's temperate zones. There are more than a hundred different kinds of flowers and trees in the large gardens in Suzhou, while thirty to seventy species can be found in the medium-size and smaller gardens (Figs. VI-11 through-VI-18).

In choosing flowers and trees to plant, the local practice of selecting the proper plants is followed so as to exploit the climatic conditions of the district to fullest advantage. Therefore the flowers and trees in most Suzhou gardens are primarily deciduous; these are matched with some evergreens, and further supplemented by wisteria, bamboo, banana trees, and herbs. These mark the key principle for growing plants in the gardens.

In the past, the choice of plants for the classical gardens of Suzhou was based on the garden owners' individual desires and whims. For instance, many owners liked to watch and enjoy certain flowers and trees at close range for detailed examination, so they paid more attention to those flowers and trees with luxuriant but well-spaced branches and leaves, light and pliant contours, and refined colors and quiet fragrances. Therefore, antiquity, quaintness, and refinement were the qualities those garden owners had in mind when they chose plants.

The flowers and trees commonly planted in Suzhou gardens according to their usefulness and and botanical types may be roughly grouped into the following categories:

Flowers for Observation

Because of their attractive colors and delectable fragrances, flowers of this category are the chief object for appreciation and pleasure. Among the evergreens are camellia, laurel, magnolia from Guangdong, golden pear, June-fragrance, orchids in vases, tan-chun (a-maying in spring), huang-su-xin, and han-xiao (the names of flowers in south China). Among the deciduous plants are peony, plum, apricot, begonia, wisteria, Chinese redbud, big-leaf hydrangea, jin-dai-hua ("embroidered-sash" flower), winter jasmine, forsythia, false spiraea, kerria, prune, and flowering plum. Of these, the peony is known as "the king of flowers," because the flower is large and beautifully colored; often it is the outstanding flower on the garden terrace. Begonia and wisteria are not only attractive in shape and color, but fit in well everywhere, whether on the hills, beside the pools, or in the courtyards. There are four types of begonias: the "xi-fu" (literally, west mansion), the "chui-si" (literally, drooping silk), the "tie-geng" (literally, glued to the stem), and the "mu-Gua" (literally, Chinese flowering quince). Though the shapes of these four types are different from each other, they are all worthy of observation and appreciation. The "chui-si" type has swirling branches and twigs and is very frequently planted in gardens. The laurels and the camellias are evergreens, and both can flourish in the shade. What is more, the camellias are delightfully colorful and the laurels very fragrant, so they are often planted. The wintersweets are both fragrant and colorful and, as important objects for observation and appreciation, are also frequently planted in courtyards.

Fruits for Observation

Plants that bear fruit are planted to be enjoyed in the summer and autumn seasons, or as decoration in the winter. Among the evergreens are the loquat, tangerine, nandina, holly, and coral. Among the deciduous plants are the pomegranate, Chinese pear-leaved crabapple, persimmon, wuhua guo, Chinese wolfberry (or matrimony vine), and the date tree. Of these, the golden fruit of loquat not only is delightful to look at but also is edible, so it is planted in most gardens. The nandina, also called Tian zhu (literally, heavenly bamboo), bears fruit in the winter; it is frequently found in Suzhou gardens with wintersweets.

Leaves for Observation

These plants are indispensable. The evergreens that belong to this group are: the melon-seed Chinese littleleaf box (or boxwood), pomegranate, pear-leaved coral, hexagon-golden-plate, glossy privet, silken orchid, and palm. The deciduous plants of this group include the maple, Chinese sweet gum, Chinese tallow tree, weeping willow, mountain hemp (or mountain flax), quaint-shaped willow, and red-leaved plant. Of these, the palms have the most variety in color, posture, and the shape of their leaves; they are excellent plants for observation and appreciation, whether planted singly or in groves.

Forest and Shade Trees

These trees are the chief components of forests on the hill or shades of green in the garden; they are also the basis for the choice of plants in gardens. The evergreens in this group are the Chinese yew, the pine, white pine, masson pine, "hui-bai" (a kind of cypress), cryptomeria, and fragrant camphor. The deciduous trees in the group include the kolanut (Chinese plane tree), feng-yang (a kind of poplar), tree of heaven, chinaberry, silk tree or mimos, Chinese catalpa, Chinese golden thread, and Chinese honey locust. Of these, the feng-yang (a kind of poplar) grows relatively quickly; its branches and twigs are tortuous, and its top provides dense shade, so it can easily produce a luxuriantly green environment. It is planted extensively in Suzhou gardens.

Creepers

Creepers are the chief plants that climb along the rocks, hills, walls, and flower shelves in the garden. Because they tend to climb upward, they can fill the blank spaces on walls and give the garden a lively look. Of the creepers, the evergreen group includes the rambler rose, banksia rose, climbing fig, Chinese star jasmine, Chinese ivy, honeysuckle, and crawling cypress. The deciduous plants include the wisteria, Chinese trumpet vine, wall-climbing ivy, and grape vine. Of these, the wisteria not only serves as a creeper, but may be trimmed into all sorts of shapes. The popular banksia rose has numerous twigs and branches and emits a fragrance that reaches far and near.

Bamboos

Bamboos are especially fond of a warm climate and fertile soil. Their posture is straight and handsome, they can withstand the winter weather without withering; they are valued as highly as the pines and cypresses. Because they grow quickly in both sun and shade, at the foot of a wall, and beside a pool, they are frequently planted. Their varieties include:

- Elephant bamboos
- "Ci-xiao-zhu" (a kind of bamboo)
- Indocalamus
- China pink
- Fernleaf hedge bamboo
- "Shou-xin-zhu" (another kind of bamboo)
- Mottled bamboo
- Black bamboo
- Square-shaped bamboo
- Inland-gold-and-green-jade bamboo

The elephant bamboo is long-stemmed and straight. Usually it is planted in large patches, and the greenery is most pleasing. Since it is low in height and is grown in a grove, the wide-leaved indocalamus generally is planted on hills and between rocks, and can add to the feeling of wild life among the hills and rills. The black bamboo and the square-shaped bamboo have slender stems and narrow leaves, and are planted along shady walls and at the corners of buildings. They are also used to fill bank space in order to block a line of vision.

Herbs and Water-Based Plants

There are also herbaceous plants and those that grow in water. The frequently seen specimens of herbaceous plants include the banana tree, Chinese herbaceous peony, chrysanthemum, tawny daylily, shu-dai-cao (otherwise known as mai-dong, a kind of Chinese medicinal herb), broccoli, yuan wei, black calyx, fragrant plantain lily, begonia, mirabilis jalapa (or four o'clock), garden balsam, cockscomb, hollyhock, hibiscus, dayflower, and saxifrage. Of these, the banana tree usually is planted in the courtyard in front of a window, or at the corner of a wall. Its branches and leaves are luxuriant and well-spaced, and the green shade it provides is like a canopy. The commonly seen plants that grow in water are the lotus, the sleeping lily, and the reed.

Ways of Growing Plants

Flowers and trees in the classical gardens of Suzhou are grown according to their characteristics, shapes and contours, and colors and scents.

A single species by itself is commonly planted; its color, scent, and contours then may be displayed to best advantage. Only when a single plant is grown in isolation can it be seen and appreciated at close range and within a small space. An isolated single flower or tree often can serve as the chief attraction in a courtyard. Instances of this may be found in the magnolia and the laurel standing in front of Yulan Tang (Magnolia Hall) in Zhuozheng Yuan (The Humble Administrator's Garden) (Fig. VI-11). The red-leaved plum is grown in front of the Sheya Lang (Corridor for Shooting Ducks) and the Suoyiqi (The Straw-Cape Maple) is planted beside the Xiaoshanconggui Xuan (Little-Hillock-and-Laurel-Grove Hall) in Wangshi Yuan (The Retired Fisherman's Garden) (Fig. VI-20).

Sometimes it is possible to set off to advantage a single tree, with its tortuous branches and treetop full of luxuriant and well-spaced leaves, by planting it in isolation on the cliff of a hill to enhance the impression of the perilous steepness of a precipice. Or growing it beside a pool may achieve a vivid, inverted reflection in the water. The crape myrtle that jut out from the precipice of a rockery in Huanxiu Shanzhuang (Mountain Villa of Encircled Elegance)(Fig. VI-21) and the black pine in front of Zhuwaiyizhi Xuan (A-Branch-from-the-Bamboo Lounge) in Wangshi Yuan (The Retired Fisherman's Garden) (Fig. VI-23) are good examples of these techniques.

Planting a single flower or tree with fine contours beside a building at one end of a bridge or path, or at the bend of a pool, is also a common phenomenon. In this way, the single plant can serve as a foil, or as contrapositional scenery, and add to the charm of the whole garden layout,. Cases of this kind include the feng-yang (a kind of poplar) that towers in front of the Wuzhuyouju Ting (Pavilion amid-Secluded-Wutong-and-Bamboo) (Fig. VII-32) and the lacebark pine that stands at one end of a bridge in Wangshi Yuan (The Retired Fisherman's Garden) (Fig. VI-19). Planting a single tree as embellishment to a grove of nearby trees is also common. Its intent is to break the monotony of massed plants of a single kind by adding variety. This device may be found in the single magnolia from Guangdong that is planted in front of the grove of elephant bamboo at the northeastern part of Liu Yuan (Lingering-Here Garden), and in the single ginkgo growing amid the maple grove in the western part of the same garden.

Planting several of the same kind of trees together or a whole grove of the same plant can call attention to the specific features of a flower or tree, and thereby introduce a striking new quality to the entire garden scene. Numerous examples include the grove of loquat trees in the loquat garden inside

Zhuozheng Yuan (The Humble Administrator's Garden), the laurel grove around Wenmushixiang Xuan (Smelling-the-Fragrance-of-Osmanthus Lounge) in Liu Yuan (Lingering-Here Garden) (Fig. VI-24), the bamboo groves in Liu Yuan (Lingering-Here Garden), Canglang Ting (The Surging-Wave-Pavilion Garden), and Shizilin (The Forest of Lions Garden). Also, there are the magnolias from Guangdong in front of the Yuanxiang Tang (Distant-Fragrance Hall) in Zhuozheng Yuan (The Humble Administrator's Garden) and the plum grove in Yi Yuan (Happy Garden). Planting trees in groups or groves in some cases may give immense pleasure to visitors who can enjoy the beauty of the scene they create. Observers can also delight in the fragrance of the plants. In other cases, a fascinating and satisfying scene results from the combined attractions of enchanting colors, gratifying fragrance, and delectable contours all at once.

Planting many kinds of flowers and trees in groups or groves is like making a drawing or painting a picture, where there is lovely order amid much complexity; yet, the peculiar qualities of any particular plant can still be enjoyed.

In group planting it is essential to properly combine the evergreens and deciduous plants. Pines and cypress, which are evergreens, give an impression of solemnity, while deciduous trees appear more lively but may produce a sense of desolation and bleakness when autumn arrives. Mixed-group plantings of different kinds of trees is therefore often adopted in Zhuozheng Yuan (The Humble Administrator's Garden), Liu Yuan (Lingering-Here Garden), and Canglang Ting (The Surging-Wave-Pavilion Garden). In these gardens, one can see large, lofty trees planted in conjunction with slender, tall ones, while underneath are shrubs or bamboo groves. The effect, a rise and fall in general contour and a feeling of variety and depth.

Whether the group planting is of the same flowers and trees or not, it is essential to try to avoid uniformity and monotony and the repetition of plant shapes and sizes. The goal is to combine plants large and small, left and right, rear and front, so that all the flowers and trees together achieve the harmonious effect of echo and response.

Just as space is arranged in a variety of ways in the classical gardens of Suzhou, the tree and flower plantings must also vary with the specific surroundings and make adjustments for each locality. Tree and flower plantings within small spaces facilitate close-range observation and appreciation in the courtyards among buildings, and in the small courts formed by the corridors and walls that separate them from the rest of the garden. One's vision is limited in these small courtyards or courts, so it is best to plant flowers and trees that are colorful and fragrant, and have fine postures. These plants are sometimes matched with well-shaped, limpid lake stone, or placed against a background of white walls so that a variety of spectacles appear to change with the hours and the succession of seasons. This is especially evident when the sun shines upon the scene, and shadows of different tints are reflected upon the white walls; many lively designs then become visible (Figs. VI-25 through VI-30). In such cases, the flowers and trees most commonly planted are the bamboo, the tianzhu (literally, heavenly bamboo), wintersweet, camellia, begonia, and banana; in slightly larger courtyards, magnolia, laurel, crape myrtle, Chinese parasol, lacebark pine, yew podocapus, Chinese boxwood, and chicken's claw maple are generally planted; in order to keep the growth of trees under control, frequent trimming and pruning are necessary.

It is also a common practice to make creeper plants climb up white walls to break the monotony of the white surface; at the same time the composition offers the viewer a strong sense of green vegetation and an impression of depth and variety inside the limited confines of the garden space. Good examples of such an arrangement include: the wall-creepers in the small court

Huabuxiaozhu in Liu Yuan (Lingering-Here Garden) (Fig. VIII-12) and the Chinese trumpet vines in the back courtyard of Xiexiu Lou (Picking-the-Elegant-View Two-Storied Building). In Wangshi Yuan (The Retired Fisherman's Garden), the banksia rose climbs up the side wall of a studio in an unidentified residence at Wangxima Lane, and the wall creepers and the Chinese star jasmine climb up the walls in Hu Yuan (Kettle Garden) in Miaotang Lane (Temple-Hall Lane). Also commonly seen in Suzhou gardens are the Chinese rose and the rambler rose, both of which are breathtakingly beautiful when in bloom.

In spacious areas, lofty trees are planted because they can play an important role in creating a general contour for the whole garden. The large trees can link the various buildings of the garden into a compact design, and can divide the entire garden space into several separable areas. For instance, the general contour of the area south of the pool in the central part of Zhuozheng Yuan (The Humble Administrator's Garden), with its rise and fall and its irregularity and complexity, is notable for several big towering trees, halls, lounges, winding corridors, and pavilions. The green maple tree south of the pool in the central part of Liu Yuan (Lingering-Here Garden) links up into one entity the lower, open hall and the much taller Mingse Lou (The Bright-Zither Two-Storied Building).

Because Chang Yuan (Carefree Garden) in Miaotang Lane (Temple-Hall Lane) occupies only a rather long and narrow strip of space along the southern bank of the pool, tall trees are planted alternately with dwarfish ones in an effort to extend the perceptual dimension of the garden space and avert the shortcoming of everything being unfolded to view all at once.

Another device to achieve such an effect is using one kind of tree as the main theme of a garden and planting other kinds in between, such as the use of lacebark pines on the hillock in Shizilin (The Forest of Lions Garden). The ginkgos on the hillock in the central part of Liu Yuan (Lingering-Here Garden) and the maple grove on the hillock in the western part of the same park both serve admirably well as the main themes of their respective gardens (Fig. VI-35). Otherwise, by planting different kinds of trees in irregular patterns and varying densities, it is also possible to achieve the effect of perceptual depth in scenery as one stretch of trees after another is unfolded before one's eyes.

Flowers and Trees in Relation to Buildings, Hillocks, and Pools

Arrangement of Flowers and Trees near Buildings

The flowers and trees near buildings not only provide shade and fragrance, and serve as objects to be observed and appreciated, but can also harmonize with the buildings and enhance their beauty. Examples are the feng-yang (a kind of poplar) standing in front of the Quxi Lou (Winding-Creek Two-Storied Building) in Liu Yuan (Lingering-Here Garden) (Fig. V-26), the magnolias from Guangdong planted near Yuanxiang Tang (Distant-Fragrance Hall) in Zhuozheng Yuan (The Humble Administrator's Garden), and the lacebark pines grown on one side of Ouxiang Xie (Lotus-Root-Fragrance Waterside Pavilion) (Fig. VI-37); all of these contribute a great deal to the garden scenery as a whole.

In planting flowers and trees in front of or behind halls and lounges, it is proper to choose those that excel in color, fragrance, and contour. In order for them not to overshadow the outside of a building or obstruct daylight, these plants should not be grown in great numbers; also, it is essential that tall trees be planted at a reasonable distance from a building.

In order that scenic objects inside a pool can be seen and enjoyed from an adjoining building, small groves of trees should not be planted immediately beside the pool. Only a limited number of flowers and trees should be planted in front of the building so as not to obstruct the viewer's line of vision (Figs. VI-41 and VI-42); however, big, towering trees may be planted behind corridors to serve as foils (Fig. V-82).

The pavilions in the garden, whether located on a hillock or beside the water, ought to be flanked by trees instead of being left in isolation. Generally, there are two ways of planting trees near a pavilion: one is to build pavilions amidst big patches of tree groves, as in the cases of Shuxiao Ting (Comfortable-Whistle Pavilion) in the western part of Liu Yuan (Lingering-Here Garden) (Fig. VI-35) and the pavilion on a hillock in Canglang Ting (The Surging-Wave-Pavilion Garden) (Fig., VI-34); the other way is to plant a few tall trees beside a pavilion as foils, and also plant some low trees and flowers to match, as in the cases of Xiuyi Ting (Embroidered-Silk Pavilion) in Zhuozheng Yuan (The Humble Administrator's Garden) (Figs. V-65 and V-66) and Shanmian Ting (Fan-Shaped Pavilion) in Shizilin (The Forest of Lions Garden).

Flowers and trees with luxuriant and well-spaced branches and leaves generally are planted in front of the windows through which one observes the scenery at a distance; outside the rear windows, which are used mainly to let daylight in, bamboo groves or other flowers and trees are planted to conceal the unsightly aspects of the enclosing wall and to create a feeling of freshness and verdure everywhere. Casementless windows and tracery windows along corridors, transit halls, and flower halls are built primarily to link up the indoors with the outdoors and also to create an impression of spaciousness as one travels through these transient spaces. The plantings outside these windows, therefore, should be few and sparse, allowing, for example, one leaf of a banana tree here, and a few stalks of slender bamboo there, sometimes visible and sometimes not. A beautiful painting seems to appear before one's eyes (Figs. VI-30 and VI-31).

Planting Flowers and Trees on Hills

The flowers and trees that are planted should go well with the size and the shape of the rockeries. In Suzhou gardens, on rockeries with more earth and less rock, large deciduous trees are planted with low evergreens to form the main body of the hill and forest. Planted beneath are dwarf bushes of thick growth, with indocalamus or herbaceous flowers planted still further below to conceal the piled stones below the hill and the shores of the pool. Viewed from a great distance, the whole hilly forest appears like an open wilderness. Once inside the forest, one seems to find oneself in the midst of a wild mountain where trees intertwine and the thick shade shuts out the sunlight. On the two islets in the central part of Zhuozheng Yuan (The Humble Administrator's Garden) and the earthen hill in Canglang Ting (The Surging-Wave-Pavilion Garden), one can readily experience this feeling (Fig. VI-38).

The arrangement of trees and shrubs in three layers as described above should not, however, be applied rigidly and uniformly in the design of forest hills, because planning a garden demands variety and flexibility. When planning a hill where such an arrangement is adopted, variations of the theme must be expected because of the variety of available plant species and the laws of nature in which trees are allowed to have their natural growths, and vie among themselves for height and density, and for superiority.

In rockeries with more rocks and less earth, the steepness and precipitousness of the rocks should be emphasized and articulated. This can be accomplished by having a small number of trees sparsely planted around the rockeries with a few bushes or bamboo groves, and flowers or herbs planted under them. Such a scene can be found in many of the Suzhou gardens including Shizilin (The Forest of Lions Garden), Yi Yuan (Happy Garden), Liu Yuan (Lingering-Here Garden), and Huanxiu Shanzhuang (Mountain Villa of Encircled Elegance).

As for the mixed plantings of evergreens and deciduous trees on hills, they are often left to random arrangement, as no specific way can be prescribed. In Yi Yuan (Happy Garden) and Shizilin (The Forest of Lions Garden), for example, evergreens are planted on the front of the hills while deciduous trees are found at the back to serve as foils. By contrast, deciduous trees are planted on the most prominent side of the rockery in the central part of Liu Yuan (Lingering-Here Garden), while the evergreens are concealed on the west side.

On the precipice of a hill, regardless of the presence of a pool, usually a pine or a Chinese hackberry tree, or a wisteria is planted. In each case, it would be chosen for its tortuous habit of growth. These usually grow with their branches and stems reaching outward toward the sunlight. With proper clipping and trimming, they lean aslant beyond the precipice and form delightful and attractive postures. Fitting this description are the lacebark pine north of the pool in Yi Yuan (Happy Garden), the hackberry in the central part of Liu Yuan (Lingering-Here Garden), and the coarse-leafed tree on the yellow stone rockery in front of the Yuanxiang Tang (Distant-Fragrance Hall) in Zhuozheng Yuan (The Humble Administrator's Garden) (Figs. VI-39 and VI-40).

Planting Flowers and Trees beside a Pool

Flowers and trees planted beside a pool add to the beauty of a water scene. A few relatively bulky deciduous trees or evergreens planted around a poolside building can serve as foils for the building, and can help to link buildings of various shapes and sizes. For instance, there are only a few trees around the pool in Wangshi Yuan (The Retired Fisherman's Garden), yet they are excellent foils for the other garden scenery.

Flowers and trees planted on the opposite shores of a pool should be varied as to shape, size, and tone or color if they are to produce delightful rhythmic contrasts. The flower and tree planting north of Xiaofeihong (Little-Flying-Rainbow Corridor-Bridge) in Zhuozheng Yuan (The Humble Administrator's Garden) (Fig. VI-41) is a good example of this.

A fairly large deciduous tree usually can serve as the center of interest among the flowers and trees on the shores of a pool. It can go well with the flowers and the smaller trees; it may have an exquisite shape and the posture of a graceful dancing figure as its top naturally leans outward (Fig. VI-40).

If the shore of the pool is higher than the water, drooping winter jasmines or tan-chun (literally, a-maying in spring) can be planted. Climbing figs and Chinese star jasmines should spread out and stretch over the surface of the rocks, and above them are grown tawny daylilies, fragrant plantain lilies, fringed irises, garden balsams, June snow (Liu-Yue-Xie, white flowers from south China), and begonias. These latter plants contrast with the taller flowers and trees behind them (Fig. VI-44).

When planting flowers and trees at the side of the footpath along the shore of the pool, it is more appropriate to aim for sparsity. One usually grows just a few tall trees at intervals, or plants some bushes to enrich the beauty of the poolside scene but keep the field of vision unobstructed. This device is adopted when planting flowers and trees along the footpath between the two islets in the central part of Zhuozheng Yuan (The Humble Administrator's Garden) and at the path along the pool in Wangshi Yuan (The Retired Fisherman's Garden) (Figs. VI-2 and VI-42).

The inverted images of garden elements in a pool, whether on the hottest day of summer or in the depth of winter, whether seen in the morning mist or on a moonlit night, and whether as smooth and transparent as a mirror or mildly rippled by a breeze, always make beautiful pictures. To preserve this reflective surface, it is a good policy not to plant lotuses at the foot of a hill, under a bridge, or near a waterside pavilion. In the cases where lotuses are planted in those locations, their growth must be carefully controlled. The flowers and leaves of sleeping lilies usually are small and level with the surface of the waters, so they are the kind most suited for small pools (Fig. VI-45). In addition, reeds planted at one corner of a bay, as in Zhuozheng Yuan (The Humble Administrator's Garden), also can add to the ideal of natural delight. Water plants, including algae, rarely are grown in Suzhou gardens; perhaps only a few of these are used to serve as a background for the fish that swim by.

Flower Terraces and Miniature Landscapes

Flower Terraces

Usually, there are flower terraces in the classical gardens of Suzhou. Frequently they are found in front of a hall or behind a lounge, beside a corridor or a veranda, and at the foot of a hill or by the side of a pool. Whether they are made of lake stones or yellow stones, their shapes and patterns are designed to look natural. Very few brick-laid flower terraces are found in regular patterns (Fig. VI-48). The layouts and levels of the terraces made of lake stones or yellow stones generally are irregular. On them are flowers, bushes, and trees, which, complemented by a rocky peak here and some stalagmites there, capture the image of landscapes in nature. The lake stone flower beds south of Chuyue Xuan (Hoeing-on-the-Moon Hall), otherwise known as Ouxiang Xie (Lotus-Root-Fragrance Waterside Pavilion) in Yi Yuan (Happy Garden) are good examples (Figs. VI-46 and VI-47).

The most frequently planted herbaceous flowers on flower terraces are the Chinese peony, banana tree, tawny daylily, garden balsam, cockscomb, and hollyhock. Also popular are hibiscus, chrysanthemum, iris (or fringed iris), purple calyx, sepal, fragrant plantain lily, and saxifrage. Flowers and trees that belong to the category of woody plants include the peony, azalea, pomegranate, clover, plum, begonia, camellia, Tianzhu (literally, heavenly bamboo), wintersweet, bigleaf hydrangea, crape myrtle, winter jasmine, and banksia rose. These flowers and trees generally are arranged in groups according to the season in which they blossom so that scenery for each of the four seasons is represented.

Miniature Landscapes (Potted Landscapes) and Plants Grown in Pots

Miniature landscapes and plants grown in pots are common elements in classical Suzhou gardens. Due to their portability, they may be placed anywhere to serve any given purpose. They not only can serve as objects for indoor display, they also can be used outdoors to fill the gaps between the flowers and trees planted in the garden.

The peculiar characteristic of a miniature landscape is its ability to contain the world of nature in a fairly small bowl to form a living three-dimensional landscape. Classified by their appearance, there are three categories of miniature landscape: dry pots, watery pots and watery-dry pots.

Miniature landscape has had a history of more than a thousand years. It has a rich and varied content and is grown extensively in Suzhou gardens. No garden is usually built on the spacious terrace in front of a hall, but large and small specimens of miniature landscapes are often exhibited there for viewing and appreciation. The large miniature landscape in the courtyard next to the music room in Wangshi Yuan (The Retired Fisherman's Garden) really is a miniature terrace and fits in extremely well with the surroundings) (Fig. VI-50).

In a broad sense plants grown in pots are a special type of miniature landscape. They are the flowers and trees, planted inside the pots or jars, which have undergone some sort of artistic cultivation. Plants in pots are mostly tree stumps, otherwise called tree stumps in pots. These tree stumps are made to undergo long years of artistic cultivation including clipping, trimming, tying up, and twining about in order to give them the appearance of ancient trees. Usually short, grey, and tortuous, these plants work well with one or two pieces of stone or stalagmite inside the pots. Plants in pots are now generally listed as a type of miniature landscape.

In addition, flowers in pots (Fig. VI-51) and other plants in pots also are popularly grown for the enjoyment of their blossoms, fruits, and leaves.

Notes

1. The term "Distant Fragrance" originated from the fragrance coming from the Lotus. (See *Essay on Fondness for the Lotus*, by Zhou Dunyi of the Song Dynasty). Distant-Fragrance Hall was so named because it was located right next to the lotus. The expression, "leaning on the jade" is based on a line of verse in the Humble Administrator's Garden written by Wen Zhengming of the Ming Dynasty: "Leaning on a pillar of the hall to watch ten-thousand jadelike bamboos." The hall was so named because in front of it there were bamboos; "fragrant snow" refers to plums, while "colorful clouds" refers to the dense grove of trees on the hill. "Waiting for the Frost" refers to the fact that with the first coming of frost the tangerines begin to turn red, and the pavilion was so named because there were tangerine trees planted by its side.
2. Pavilion amid-Secluded-Wutong-and-Bamboo was so named because there were Wutong trees and bamboos grown beside it. In front of the Wind-from-the-Pine Pavilion there were pine trees. In front of the Winding-Path-under-Willow-Shade Corridor there were willow trees. "Mantuoluo" is just another name for camellia.

part Two
Chinese Classical Gardens

VII

Zhuozheng Yuan
(The Humble Administrator's Garden)[1]

Zhuozheng Yuan, located at Dongbei Street inside Lou Men (Lou Gate), was first built in the middle of the Ming Dynasty more than four hundred years ago. It is acclaimed as the model for all the classical gardens south of the Changjiang (Yangtse) River.

This garden originally was located on the site of Dahong Temple. During the reign of Emperor Zhengde (1506–1521) in the Ming Dynasty, Wang Xianchen, the censor occupied the temple and converted it into a private garden and villa.[2] Later, the ownership of the garden changed hands several times: it became the private garden of an official-landlord, a part of a government office, and then again the dwelling of commoners; it was rebuilt many times during this process.[3]

The garden was completely repaired and expanded in the 1950s. Now it contains three parts: the central part, "Zhuozheng Yuan" proper, the western part (formerly "Supplementary Garden"), and the eastern part (originally, "Guitianyuanju," "Dwelling upon Return to the Countryside") (Figs. VII-5, VII-6, and VII-9), with a total area of about 4 hectares.[4]

Water is a major element in the layout of Zhuozheng Yuan. The entire garden site originally was a low-lying, water-logged land. When the garden was first built, the water-logged land was utilized; it was dug out and shaped into a pool surrounded by groves of trees. A beautiful garden was thus created, with water as its chief component. According to *Records of the Wang's Zhuozheng Yuan*, and "Painting of Zhuozheng Yuan," as well as the record in inscriptions and verses of Wen Zhengming of the Ming Dynasty, when the garden was first built in the middle of the Ming Dynasty it had just a few sparsely-constructed buildings, and was densely planted with trees. It had a tortuous pool, a bright and spacious water area, and groves of trees that extended into the distance. The whole scene closely resembled the world of nature (Fig. VII-2).[5] Actually, the whole scope of the garden at that time comprised all the three parts of it that it has today.

By the end of the Ming Dynasty, the first Zhuozheng Yuan was practically abandoned; the eastern part was separated from the rest and there the Dwelling upon Return to the Countryside was constructed. The central and western parts of the garden were not restored and reconstructed until the reign of Emperor

Shunhi early in the Qing Dynasty. Prior to that, they were used as the villas of governmental officials. Then, in the years of Emperor Kangxi, construction of the gardens went on rapidly: hillocks were piled, ravines dug, and more buildings erected, so that a big change came about that altered the original appearance of the place.[6] When the Painting of Zhuozheng Yuan was later drawn during the reign of Emperor Yungzheng, there were already one earthen hillock and a two-story building in the garden proper (Fig. VII-3).

At the beginning of Emperor Qianlong's reign, Zhuozheng Yuan was again divided into two parts: the central part, knows as "Fu Yuan" (The Restored Garden), and the western part, called "Shu Yuan" (The Book or Study Garden). After that, only the central part was still called Zhuozheng Yuan. The original single, unified garden now became three gardens separated from one another, each of them an entity in itself.

The central part, which continued to be known as Zhuozheng Yuan, was the principal part of the garden. According to records, in the middle of the Qing Dynasty (during the reigns of Emperors Qianlong and Jiaqing), the central part of the garden twice underwent repairs. Both times, however, the restoration and repairs were made on the original foundations of the garden, and no large-scale modifications were introduced.[7]. In the Painting of Zhuozheng Yuan which was drawn some time later, Yuanxiang Tang (Distant-Fragrance Hall), Pipa Yuan (Loquat Orchard), Liuyinluqu (Winding-Path-under-Willow-Shade Corridor), and Jianshan Lou (Seeing-the-Hill Two-Storied Building) were located at the same spots as they are today; however, there was a different two-story hall, constructed on the site where Xuexiangyunwei Ting (The Pavilion of Fragrant-Snow-and-Colorful Clouds) now stands. Also there was a waterside corridor there extending southward in front of the Hefengsimian Ting (Breeze-from-the-Lotus-in-Four-Directions Pavilion) (Fig. VII-4) of today.[8]

The buildings in the garden now essentially preserve the appearance they had in the later period of the Qing Dynasty (Fig. VII-4).[9] The arrangement of the hillock and the ravine inside the pool can be traced back to the early years of the Qing Dynasty. The unique characteristics of the garden ever since its founding, with water as the major phenomenon, the spacious surface of the pool, and the naturalness of the scenery, have remained unchanged to this day (Figs. VII-22, VII-25, and VII-37).

The present appearance of the western part of the garden gradually took shape during the reign of Emperor Guangxu in the last years of the Qing Dynasty. During that time, the layout went through several significant changes (Fig. VII-38). In the eastern part, the original Dwelling upon Return to the Countryside was abandoned. In fact, it was made a part of Zhuozheng Yuan only after 1949 when it underwent much modification and renovation, which articulated the flat high mound and meadows with the hillock and pool, the pavilions, and the two-story buildings (Figs. VI-16 through VII-18).

Zhuozheng Yuan is located to the north of the owner's residence. The main gate of the garden, newly constructed in 1962, is located south of the former Dwelling upon Return to the Countryside that occupied the eastern part of the garden (Figs. VII-6 and VII-16). The original gate of the garden had been an entrance that opened onto the residential lane. One had to pass through a small winding lane in order to reach the former inner gate. Inside the main gate, there is a yellow stone rockery that had obstructed from view all of the scenic objects in the garden. Behind the rockery there is a small pool. Then, as one walks on along the corridor by the pool, one comes upon the garden's major scenic area (Fig. VII-19), which is especially spacious and bright. This is the frequently employed technique of using contrast in Chinese classical gardens: one emerges from a small, narrow space and finds oneself suddenly in broad, spacious surroundings.

The central part is the creme de la creme of the garden, occupying an area of a little over 1 hectare, of which one-third is water surface. The focal point of the general layout is a pool. "All the pavilions, balustrades, terraces and waterside pavilions turn to face the water."[10] Beside the pool, buildings of all shapes and sizes are scattered about in apparent confusion, thus revealing a characteristic picture of the water country south of the Changjiang (Yangtse) River (Fig. VII-25). Buildings that formerly served as living quarters and places for pleasure-taking for the garden owners, such as Yuanxiang Tang (Distant-Fragrance Hall), Yulan Tang (Magnolia Hall), Xiangzhou (Fragrant-Isle Landboat), Xiaocanglang (Little-Surging-Wave Watercourt), and Haitangchunwu (Spring-Begonia-Cove House), are clustered together in the southern part of the garden and located adjacent to the residence (Figs. VII-23, VII-26, and VII-28). They are practically extensions of the residence. In the northern part of the garden there is a balanced stress on hillock and pool, and flowers and trees, with the buildings secondary in importance (Figs. VII-22, VII-24, and VII-37).

Yuanxiang Tang (Distant-Fragrance Hall) on the southern shore of the pool is the center of all activities for the central part of the garden. Surrounded by a hillock, a pool, and a grove of trees, it is the principal scenic area in the garden. Several other groups of buildings are placed in the environs. They are described in the paragraphs that follow.

A flower lounge called Yulan Tang (Magnolia Hall) (Fig. VII-21) is located right next to the residence in the southwestern corner of the garden, and it forms an independent and isolated courtyard area. Inside the courtyard magnolias of flower terraces where bamboos and Tianzhu (literally, heavenly bamboo) are planted, along with a few lake stones. The building and the courtyard are linked together very naturally and closely.

A waterside two-story pavilion named Xiaocanglang (Little-Surging-Wave) is also located in the southwest corner of the garden. This quiet waterside courtyard is linked to the rest of the garden by a corridor-bridge called Xiaofeihong (Little-Flying-Rainbow Corridor-Bridge) (Fig. VII-27). To the east of the courtyard are the inner gate and Yuanxiang Tang (Distant-Fragrance Hall), while on the south the courtyard opens onto the residence.

Pipa Yuan (The Loquat Orchard) and Haitangchunwu (Spring-Begonia-Cove House) are located in the southeastern corner of the garden, with the former being screened off by a wavy wall and the latter by a flowery wall, so that each is a small court; they are named, respectively, after the loquat and the begonia planted there (Figs. VII-35 and V-8).

Inside the pool, which is located on the northwestern side of the earthen hillock in the northern part to the garden, is Jianshan Lou (Seeing-the-Hill Two-Storied Building). West of the building, a winding corridor named Liuyinluqu (Winding-Path-under-Willow-Shade Corridor) screens the area off and forms a corridor-court with rocks, flowers, and trees as its center of attraction. In this way the space inside the court is cut off from the outside and at the same time is intertwined with the space beyond. Some old poplars are planted here to serve as a background for the design, and the result is a pleasant feeling of depth and layered scenery.

The main building, Yuanxiang Tang (Distant-Fragrance Hall), is bordered by the hillock and the pool, and has a broad space around it. The hall is built to face all four directions, with long, transparent windows on all sides, so that one can take in the scenic objects all around as if viewing a continuous scroll painting (Figs. VII-22 and VII-24). The yellow stone rockery south of the hall, standing between the building and the inner garden-gate, serves merely as a screen that obstructs a direct view of the hall; the rockery is not a bulky one, but the pile of rocks appears quite natural, making it one of the best yellow stone hillocks in Suzhou. The trees on the hillock are scattered but orderly, and they harmonize with the luxuriant and well-spaced magnolias in front of Yuanxiang Tang; the deep, clear water in the pool serves as a background and foil. All of these add to the variety and richness of the scenery in the front court of the hall (Fig. VII-19).

To the north of Yuanxiang Tang, the water surface of the pool is clear and spacious, and there a broad terrace faces the pool (Fig. VII-23). Within the expanse of the pool, stones and earth are piled up to form two small hills, the western and the eastern hills, which are separated by a little creek. But the hills and the creek actually constitute one entity to divide the surface of the pool in two and to separate the two spaces into the south and the north.

On the western hill, Xuexiangyunwei Ting (The Pavilion of Fragrant-Snow-and-Colorful Clouds) is oblong in shape while on the eastern hill Daishuang Ting (Waiting-for-the-Frost Pavilion) is hexagonal (Fig. VII-36). These different shaped pavilions add variety to the two hills, both of which are built mainly of earth, supplemented with stones.

On the sunny side, the shore of the pool is paved with yellow stones; it rises and falls in an irregular fashion. To the rear of the hills, the earthen slope and patches of weeds produce a natural scene. Trees are planted everywhere on the hills, predominantly with deciduous plants, with evergreens in between; together, they provide desirable scenery year-round.

On both sides of the winding paths and amid the hills, bamboo groves and tall trees conceal one another, and their dense shade obstructs the sunlight. This leads to a forest-on-a-hill kind of atmosphere, which is typical south of the Changjiang River (Fig. VII-38). Along the shore of the pool are crape myrtles and other creepers and bushes, whose low twigs touch the water and add to the sense of a full-to-overflowing water country (Fig. VII-22).

Over the ravine and the creek that separate the two hills are small bridges, including a winding bridge on the east that leads to Wuzhuyouju Ting (Pavilion amid-Secluded-Wutong-and-Bamboo), on all sides of which are round, leafless gates. As one looks at the pool through these round gates, the scene seems to be circular and enters into one's vision through the circle (Figs. VII-32 and VII-33).

At the southwestern corner of the western hill and within the pool is a pavilion named Hefengsimian Ting (Breeze-from-the-Lotus-in-Four-Directions Pavilion) on the west, south of which are two bridges; the bridge on the west leads to Liuyinluqu (Winding-Path-under-Willow-Shade Corridor); after crossing it, one can turn north towards Jianshan Lou (Seeing-the-Hill Two-Storied Building). The bridge on the south is linked with Yiyu Xuan (Leaning-on-Jade Hall). Although these two bridges divide the pool into three parts, they look transparent because of their low railings, which are full of apertures; because of these, the pool seems divided into three sections and yet actually is one entity. Thus, it gives the impression of a broad and vast body of water (Figs. VII-24 and VII-37).

Zhuozheng Yuan is linked with Yiyu Xuan on the west. The water in the pool branches off from Yiyu Xuan, and one stream of it flows south all the way to the wall. The stream here is known for its seclusion and tortuosity. The corridor-bridge Xiaofeihong (Little-Flying-Rainbow Corridor-Bridge) and the two-story waterside pavilion Xiaocanglang (Little-Surging-Wave) both stretch across the water from east to west, while on both sides of the stream there is a chessboardlike arrangement of pavilions and corridors that form a calm and quiet waterside court (Figs. VII-27 and VII-28).

Further north are the landboat Xiangzhou (Fragrant-Isle) and a laurel grove. Leaning on the balustrade at Xiaocanglang (Little-Surging-Wave Water Court) and looking northwards, one can see beyond Xiaofeihong (Little-Flying-Rainbow Corridor-Bridge) and Hefengsimian Ting (Breeze-from-the-Lotus-in-Four-Directions Pavilion), with Jianshan Lou (Seeing-the-Hill Two-Storied Building) in the distance. Seeing the scenic objects, tier upon tier stretching out in the distance, one gets a sense of special depth (Figs. VII-25 and VII-28).

Xiangzhou (Fragrant-Isle Landboat) and Yiyu Xuan (Leaning-on-Jade Hall) (Fig. VII-1) face each other directly. The former is horizontal and the latter vertical, and the pool between the two is rather narrow. There is a big mirror inside the landboat Xiangzhou to reflect the scenic objects in and around Yiyu Xuan beyond the pool. This is another device to create a sense of depth in the garden scenery.

To the east of Yuanxiang Tang (Distant-Fragrance Hall) there is another earthen hill piled with yellow stones, and on it is Xiuyi Ting (Embroidered-Silk Pavilion) (Fig. VII-20). To the south of it is Pipa Yuan (Loquat Orchard) (Fig. VII-35). The hill and the rockery south of Yuanxiang Tang are in harmony with each other because both of them have stone precipices and stone slopes; the wavy wall of Pipa Yuan weaves the two hillocks together in an organic whole.

South of the hill, there are few buildings in the area around Pipa Yuan, and the arrangement inside the various courtyards is simple and unadorned. In the courtyard of Haitangchunwu (Spring-Begonia-Cove House) for example, there are just a few begonias, one elm tree, and a grove of bamboos. Yet, as major scenic objects they are outstanding, and the whole place is well-organized around them (Fig. V-8). The buildings in this area are linked by winding corridors, and several separate compounds are formed in a none-too-large space. But they are interwoven by many tracery windows and leafless gates.

At the wavy wall north of Pipa Yuan (Loquat Orchard) there is a round leafless gate named Wancui (Evening Green). Looking southward through this gate, there is a beautiful scene around Jiashi Ting (Fine-Fruit Pavilion). Then, looking northward through this gate from inside the Pipa Yuan, there is another beautiful scene with Xuexiangyunwei Ting (The Pavilion of Fragrant-Snow-and-Colorful Clouds) as the major attraction. The pavilion is partly revealed and partly concealed amid a grove of trees (Fig. II-31). Here is an excellent example of a contrapositional scene in garden design.

At the southern end of the Liuyinluqu (Winding-Path-under-Willow-Shade Corridor), there is a half-pavilion called Bieyoutongtian (Unique-Beauty) (Fig. VII-29). West of this half-pavilion is the western part of the garden, known in the last decades of the Qing Dynasty as Bu Yuan (Supplementary Garden). Here again, the pool is used as the focal point, and to locate the main building on the pool's south shore adjacent to the residential area (Fig. VII-39). The pool is shaped like a crooked ruler, and on its southwestern corner one branch extends southward (Fig. VII-41). At the northern end of the pool is a rockery, and on top of it and beside the pool are a pavilion and a two-story pavilion (Fig. VII-38).

The 36-Mandarin-Duck Hall to the south (Fig. V-19) is the main building; it may be reached from the residential quarters by way of a winding corridor. The hall is square-shaped, and is divided into two parts, the north and the south, by a wooden partition and an ornamental, netlike wooden panel hanging from the beam. It became a sort of twin hall, with the northern half called the 36-Yuanyang Guan (36-Mandarin-Duck Hall) and the southern half called the 18-Datura Hall. In the four corners of the hall there are four small annexes which in by-gone days were used as backstage for acting troupes hired to entertain the garden owners and their guests (Figs. V-19 through V-28).

In the southern part of the hall there is a small court in which camellias are planted. The court faces the winding pool on the north and stands directly opposite the major garden scenery (Fig. VI-38). But the hall is very large and the strip of land on which it is built is small and narrow. The building is obliged to jut out northward to beetle over the water, seeming to bear down on the surface of the pool; thus, the entire space appears crowded and cramped. The peculiar style of the building cannot be fully viewed, and the pool itself loses its feature of spaciousness. Because of this, the pool to the west of the hall does not seem to have the quality of tortuousness alternating with openness of view.

The eastern part of the hall has stones piled into a hill, on top of which is a pavilion (Fig. II-36). From the pavilion one not only can look downward at the different scenic objects inside the garden, but also observe the distant scenery in the central part of the garden (Fig. II-35). It is therefore called Yilian Ting (Fit-to-Observe-Scenery-in-Two-Directions Pavilion).

Going north from the pavilion and along the eastern shore of the pool, there is a long corridor that links the pavilion with Daoyin Lou (Inverted-Image Two-Storied Building) at the northeast corner of the garden. Built over the water, this corridor winds about rising and falling, and vaulting the water surface in a wavy structure that is unique in form and shape. Daoyin Lou (Inverted-Image Two-Storied Building) and Yilian Ting (Fit-to-Observe-Scenery-in-Two-Directions Pavilion) stand opposite each other across the pool, thus serving as a contrapositional garden scene (Fig. VI-40). With their inverted images reflected in the crystal clear water, they constitute the most delightful scenery in the western part of the garden.

The water in the pool in this area originally was directly connected with that in the central part of the garden. At the time the garden was divided up into the western and central parts, a wall was constructed to obstruct the flow of the water; the surface of the pool was thus cut in two. In the 1950s, the western part was again united with the central part, and a water cave was dug to link up the pool on both sides of the wall. On the wall of the wavelike corridor, tracery windows were also constructed, thus producing an excellent effect upon the enriched garden scenery.

The newly rebuilt eastern part of the garden was constructed on the old site of Guitianyuanju (Dwelling upon Return to the Countryside), occupying an area of about two hectares. Big patches of meadows and buildings, including teahouses and pavilions and waterside pavilions were set up for rest and recreation (Fig. VII-18).

To the west of the meadows across the water is an earthen hill, on top of which are thickly overgrown trees; around it are winding streams coiling about and flowing east to form a clear pool. The surface of the water is broad and open, and on the shores of the pool are rows of green willows and many kinds of flowers. A pavilion named Fangyan (Taking-a-Broad-View), stands on the summit of the hill, while in the midst of the water is a waterside pavilion named Furong Xie (Lotus Waterside Pavilion) (Fig. VII-8). Both pavilions are focal points of the garden design and stand opposite each other for observers to enjoy. For the most part the trees are planted in large groups and groves of pines, magnolias from Guangdong, laurels, maples, camphor trees, and so forth.

Notes

1. According to *Records of the Wang's Zhouzheng Yuan*, by Wen Zhengming, in the twelfth year of the reign of Emperor Jiajing of the Ming Dynasty. (As quoted in an album of painting entitled, *A painting of Zhuozheng Yuan of Wen the junior secretary at court*, published by Chung Hwa Book Co., Ltd.,

and in *Postscript to Verses on the Painting of Zhuozheng Yuan*, by Wang Xianchen, in the eighteenth year of the reign of Emperor Jiajing of the Ming Dynasty. Wang Xianchen was not so successful in his political career and so compared himself to Pan Yue of the Western Jin Dynasty. He quoted what Pan Yue wrote in his *Verse on Idly-Staying at Home*, as follows:

It is my wish for fleeting happiness (i.e., floating clouds) to build a house and plant trees and to lead a free and happy existence of idleness; let there be a pond to fish from, and let me tax the lands instead ploughing, let me water the garden and sell the vegetables in order to provide for my daily meals, let me tend the sheep and sell the milk in order to pay the expenses in hot summer and cold winter, let me pay my respects to my parents and show my affection to my brothers; that is how a humble person administers his domain.

> —(quoted from *Complete Essays in the Dynasties of Qin, Han, Sanguo (The Three Kingdoms), Wei, and Jin)*

This passage was quoted to explain the title of this garden. Wang Xianchen also said:

I have engaged in a political career for over forty years. While some of my contemporaries attained high officialdom, I myself retired after having become a county official. Since my official position was inferior to that of Pan Yue, I called my garden by this name.

> —(See Wang Xianchen, *Postscript to Verses on the Painting of Zhuozheng Yuan*).

Here the meaning of the name for the garden is clearly explained. The so-called "free and happy existence," as described by Pan Yue in his *Verse on Idly-Staying at Home*, was a picture of an official who was dismissed from his post, and now led a life of exploitation as a landlord, while his words, "It is my wish for fleeting happiness," are purely bombastic speech to muddle other people.

2. According to what Wen Zhengming said in *Records of Zhuozheng Yuan owned by the Wang's Family*:

You just started to rise in your political career in the prime of your life, but soon you gave up your officialdom and came home to stay. You spoke of building a house and planting trees, of watering your garden and selling the vegetables you raised, of leading a happy and free existence of enjoying your idle life at home; you actually have already done all this for no less than twenty years.

If we count back twenty years from the time Wen Zhengming wrote this passage, it would mean that the garden was first built in the eighth year of the reign of Emperor Zhengde of the Ming Dynasty. Again, according to what Wang Xianchen wrote in *Postscript to Verses on the Painting of Zhuozheng Yuan*:

Upon my retirement from political life, after I came back I daily trained my pages and my servants, cleaned up my house and planted trees, fed the cows and sold the milk, carried a shovel and filled the earthen jars, engaged in farming in order to provide for my daily needs, passed many summers and winters, worked for a long time before the garden was completed, though therein the house and hall, the terrace and the waterside pavilions were actually only roughly finished. I consulted old sayings and applied them to personal events of recent years, and the name of the garden evolved. Xianchen did not go to the lakes and the mountains, did not attend feasts and funerals; although there were summer heat and winter cold, wind and rain, I was never away for one day, but lived here quietly and humbly for almost thirty years.

If we count back thirty years from the time Wang Xiancheng wrote this passage, the garden would have been built around the fourth year of the reign of Emperor Zhende.

3. The son of Wang Xiancheng gambled and lost the garden to a man named Xu, in the eighth year of the reign of Emperor Chongzhen. The eastern part of the garden, known as "Dwelling upon Return to the Countryside," was owned by Wang Xinyi, but remained abandoned till before liberation. In the early years of the reign of Emperor Shunzhi of the Qing Dynasty, the central and western parts of the garden were the residence of a battalion commander, but soon they were converted into the Office of the General of Garrison Troops and Defense Troops Transit Hostel. Then the garden was owned by Wang Yungning, the son-in-law of Wu Sangui (in *Comments on Verses on the Painting of Zhuozheng Yuan*), but Qing Yung of the Qing Dynasty mistook him for Wang Yungkang.

   When Wu Sangui came to grief, the garden became public property. In the eighteenth year of the reign of Emperor Kangxi, the placed was turned into the New Office of the Shire of Suzhou, Songjiang, and Changshu. When this new office was dissolved, the garden again was used as residences for the common folk.

   By the early years of the reign of Emperor Qianlong, the central part of the garden belonged to Jiang Qifu, and the western part became Ye Shikuan's study. Still later, the central part belonged, successively, to Pan Shiyi, Cha Shitan, and Wu Jing (when it was called "Wu Garden"), while the western part belonged to Shen Yuanzhen. At the time of Taiping, both parts belonged to Zhongwang Fu of Li Xiuchen. After the fall of the Taiping Uprising, the central part again became public property, and was used by the District Guild of Eight Bannermen from Fengtian and Chili Provinces. The western part belonged to a certain Wang's family, and then, by the third year of the reign of Emperor Guangxu, it became "Supplementary Garden," owned by Zhang Luqian.

4. The area of each of the gardens mentioned in this book is calculated according to the plan survey used herein. The figures given, except for Wangshi Yuan (The Retired Fisherman's Garden), do not include the residential part of each of the gardens.

5. According to what is recorded in *Records of Zhuozheng Yuan Owned by the Wang Family*, in "Painting of Zhuozheng Yuan," and in inscriptions and verses, the Yuanxiang Tang (Distant-Fragrance Hall) of today was originally Ruoshu Tang, while the Yiyu Xuan (Leaning-on-Jade Hall) of today was already built near its present site during the Ming Dynasty. At that time the latter hall faced Mengyin Lou (Indistinct-Dream Two-Storied Building) across the water; between the two buildings there was a Xiaofeihong Qiao (Little-Flying-Rainbow Corridor-Bridge) that linked them together. The two earthen hillocks within the pool today, as well as the present Jianshan Lou (Seeing-the-Hill Two-Storied Building) and the western part of the garden, in those days were no more than a wild nature area, with bamboo trees stretching into the gloomy depth and water spread all over the space. The area north of Mengyin Lou then had only the grove of pines, while east of it stood an orchard, a flower nursery, and a bamboo grove. The buildings in the garden at the time consisted of just one two-story hall, another hall, and a few pavilions and verandas, a total of eight.

6. During the reign of Emperor Kangxi in the Qing Dynasty, Xu Qianxue, in his *A Record of the New Office of the Shire of Suzhou, Songjiang, and Changshu*, which was vol. 26 of *Zhan Yuan*, wrote:

I have not yet had the time to introduce any changes, and so I have to turn to Yungning [referring to Wang Yungning], for the earlier occupants here all followed the old ways of the original Zhuozheng Yuan; but after Yungning began to build hillocks and ravines and then improved on the carvings and engravings, the garden no longer looked the same as before.

Also, in an entry on Zhuozheng Yuan, in vol.17 about mansions, residences, gardens, and pavilions in *Annuals of Changzhou County*, published in the twenty-third year of the reign of Emperor Kangxi, it was recorded thus:

In the last twenty years, the garden [referring to Zhuozheng Yuan] had a succession of owners, although new buildings had been put up, and they looked majestic and elegant; yet the quiet refinement of the hills and rills that was to be found in the past is gone.

7. In the twelfth year of the reign of Emperor Qianlong of the Qing Dynasty, Shen Deqian in this *Fu Yuan Ji (Records on The Restored Garden)*, wrote:

Between the two city gates of Lou Men and Qi Men in Suzhou there is a famous garden. An official named Jiang restored the old garden and gave it the name Fu Yuan. For a hundred years this garden had fallen into ruins, as luxuriant weeds grew all over the place and foxes and hares made their homes there. Then the owner bought the place.... He built a hillock out of an earthen mound and created a pool in the low-lying ground.... The halls and lounges are not changed but the open halls and verandas are higher and brighter and seem to be of greater depth than before; the surroundings are the same, but the buildings and paths are tortuous and criss-cross and appear new to the eye....

In the thirteenth year of the reign of Emperor Daoguang, Qian Yuan in his *Comments on Verses on the Painting of Zhuozheng Yuan*, wrote:

...It again belongs to the native of the county Prefect Jiang Qi who named it Fu Yuan.... But after that, for fifty years the pool and the buildings were deserted; reeds and mosses spread over the paths, and there were no longer the looks of the old days. Then, during the reign of Emperor Jiaqing, Scholar of Second Degree Cha Shanyu bought the place, and cut down the weeds and dredged the pool, watered the flowers and planted trees for over a year, and the garden was restored to its old appearance. Recently, however, it has become a pawnshop for the family of prime minister Wu Songfu.

From the above records, it is obvious that both times repairs were made on the old garden to turn it into a new one, but its general appearance did not change much.

8. The "Painting of Zhuozheng Yuan," by Wang Jun, was probably painted during the reign of Emperor Xiangeng. On it we see rows of wooden stakes in the pool west of Yiyu Xuan (Leaning-on-Jade Hall), which probably were the ruins of waterside corridors.

9. The appearance of the garden as shown in the "Painting of Zhuozheng Yuan" by Wu Juan in the reign of Emperor Tongzhi of the Qing Dynasty, and in the "Map of the District Guild of Eight Bannermen from Fengtian and Chili Provinces," drawn during the twenty-seventh year of the reign of Emperor Guanxu, closely resemble the present condition of the buildings that are still preserved.

10. This is a quotation from *Records of Zhuozheng Yuan owned by the Wang Family*, by Wen Zhengming of the Ming Dynasty.

VIII

Liu Yuan
(Lingering-Here Garden)[1]

Liu Yuan (Lingering-Here Garden), located outside the city gate of Changmen and occupying an area of about two hectares, is one of the spacious classical gardens in Suzhou. During the reign of Emperor Jiajing of the Ming Dynasty, Xu Taishi of Taipu Temple built two gardens: Dong Yuan (East Garden) and Xi Yuan (West Garden). He collected all kinds of odd-shaped rocks for Dong Yuan, and asked Zhou Bingzhong, otherwise known as Shichen, to construct a rockery there.[2] Xi Yuan later became a Buddhist temple named Jiezhuanglisi (Set of Monastic Regulations Temple).

During the reign of Emperor Jiaqing of the Qing Dynasty, the former east garden was rebuilt and named Hanbizhuang (Cold-Emerald Villa), and twelve peaks made of Taihu stones were collected and placed in the garden. It became one of the famous gardens of the time, stretching from Yifeng Xuan (Salute-to-the-Peak Hall) on the east to the region of Hanbi Shanfang (Cold-Emerald Mountain-House) on the west (Fig. VII-2).

Later, the place was deserted until the early years of the reign of Emperor Guangxu, when the garden was rebuilt and expanded. More buildings were erected, and it was renamed Liu Yuan (Lingering-Here Garden) (Fig. VII-11). In 1961 the State Council listed the garden as one of the major national cultural relics for preservation.[3]

The garden may be divided roughly into four areas (Figs. VIII-3 through VIII-10). The central part, based on the original Hanbizhuang (Cold-Emerald Villa), has been under intermittent care and management for the longest time of all parts of the garden. It is still the best part of the garden today (Figs. VII-13 and VII-14). The eastern, northern, and western parts all were added to the original garden during the reign of Emperor Guangxu.

The central part again may be divided into two sections, the eastern section and the western section. The hillock and the pool are the major features of the western section, while the buildings and the courtyards dominate the eastern section (Figs. VIII-17 and VIII-18). The whole garden originally was located at the back of the residence, and the entrance to the garden from the residence was placed near Hesuo (Crane Hall) east of Wufeng Xianguan (Five-Peak Celestial House). But at that time, the private gardens frequently were open to the public in the spring season, so another gate to the garden was constructed.

The entrance to Liu Yuan today still follows the original path. After entering the gate, one passes through a long winding corridor and two courtyards before reaching Gumujiaoke (Old-Trees-Intertwining-One-Another). From there, through the tracery windows one can already have a partial view of the hillock and the pool, as well as the main garden's pavilions and two-story pavilions. One can then look through the casementless windows on the west of Gumujiaoke and view Loying Xuan (Green-Shade Lounge) and Mingse Lou (Bright-Zither Two-Storied Building), where the scenery unfolds, tier after tier, in great depth.

The area of the hillock and the pool roughly consists of a hillock on the northwest, a pool in the center, and buildings on the southeast. This kind of arrangement places the major scenic objects, the hillock and the pool, in positions facing the sunlight; this exposure is commonly adopted in the large-size classical gardens in Suzhou. There are more than ten tall trees of ginkgo, poplar, cypress, and elm in the garden, quite a few of which are over one hundred years old. They bring to the garden the atmosphere of a dark and luxuriant forest and hill.

The poplars in front of Quxi Lou (Winding-Creek Two-Storied Building) and the maples beside Loying Xuan (Green-Shade Lounge) are graceful in appearance and carriage, and add to the beauty of garden scenery (Fig. VIII-14). However, the poplars that were originally grown in front of Quxi Lou (Winding-Creek Two-Storied Building) are no longer there. The hillock is piled with earth, and stones are piled only to serve as stone steps on the hill path.

When one views the scene as a whole, the rocks on the hill look craggy and jagged, and the general impression is pretty good. Chiefly yellow stones are employed here, and they appear simple, vigorous, and especially fine in the southwestern section. But the lake stone peaks placed above the yellow stones give it a feeling of triviality and lack of harmony.

Between the western and northern hills is a water gully which creates the impression that there is a source for the water in the pool. At the entrance to the gully, a rock projects into the water; on the rock is a rocky beam; unfortunately, the rock is too big and appears to have concealed the water gully; thus the effect is bad.

On the rockery north of the pool, Ke Ting (Just-Right Pavilion) serves as the focal point of the garden design. On the western hill, there is a grove of laurel trees, and a hill-climbing corridor that goes all the way up to Wenmuxixiang Xuan (Smelling-the-Fragrance-of-Osmanthus Lounge) at the hill's summit. When one gets there and looks down, one can see all the scenery in the garden (Fig. VIII-14) at a glance.

The water forms a bay southeast of the pool, but its shore in this area is regular and straight, so it seems a bit dull and monotonous. In addition, the Loying Xuan (Green-Shade Lounge) is a little too high above the water, and therefore, in terms of location it is not as appropriate as, for example, Zhuoying Shuige (Washing-Tassel Waterside Pavilion) in Wangshi Yuan (The Retired Fisherman's Garden).

To the east of the pool, a little islet called Xiaopenglai (Small-Fabled-Immortal-Abode) and a level bridge cut off a small part of the water surface and they form a small scenic area with Haopu Ting (River-Moat Pavilion) and Qingfengchi Guan (The Fresh-Breeze-Pool House), the featured architectural elements. Formerly, there was an ancient tree projecting out and facing the pool, and the surroundings here were gloomy and secluded in contrast to the area beyond. But Xiaopenglai (Small-Fabled-Immortal-Abode) is located too close to the center of the pool, so it lacks a feeling of an overflowing and extensive water country. In addition, the shape of the frame on which the crape myrtle creeps on the islet fails to harmonize sufficiently with the environs, another defect.

In the area containing the Quxi Lou (Winding-Creek Two-Storied Building) east of the pool, there are several outstanding buildings in a row (Figs. VIII-14 and VIII-15). South of the pool are several other buildings including Hanbi Shanfang (Encompassing-Jade Mountain House), Mingse Lou (Bright-Zither Two-Storied Building), and Loying Xuan (Green-Shade Lounge), which are scattered about and are in various sizes, volumes, and structures. The whitewashed wall and grey tiles are matched with chestnut-colored doors, windows, and other decorations, and their mild colors harmonize with each other and with the surroundings. These are considered excellent examples of the architectural art in the Suzhou classical gardens. Although the buildings south of the pool are placed along the garden walls, among them are small courts of differing shapes and sizes where bamboos and rocks, and parterres are used for decoration. The whole is a beautiful arrangement for a garden border.

North of the hillock and the pool, along the garden walls, originally there were two buildings: Zizai Chu (Place of Comfort) (located where now Yuancui Ge or Distant-Green Two-Storied Pavilion is) and Banye Caotang (Half-Field Cottage); a winding corridor links them up and marks the borders of the garden on the north. Banye Caotang no longer exists, and only a long corridor is left there, along with a bamboo grove and a few trees (Fig. V-84). On the earthen hill in the western part of the garden, there is the rise and fall of wavy walls, outside of which are a high mound and a maple grove that serve as the scenery in the distance. They give the viewer a rich feeling of depth in garden scenery.

To the east of Quxi Lou (Winding-Creek Two-Storied Building) are several courtyards which were the places for the official-owners of the past to indulge their pleasure-seeking activities. The main hall, large and luxurious Wufeng Xianguan (Five-Peak Celestial House), is the focal point of Liu Yuan. It is surrounded by Huanwodushu Chu (The Restored-to-Me Study), Yifeng Xuan (Salute-to-the-Peak Hall) Jigudegeng Chu (The Place of Drawing-Water-from-Ancient-to-Find Rope), Xi Lou (West Two-Storied Building), Hesuo (Crane Hall), and other accessory buildings (Figs. VIII-16 through VIII-18). Nanmu is used for the cross-beams and pillars in Wufeng Xianguan (The Five-Peak Celestial House), which is therefore also called Nanmu Hall.

In the front court of the hall is a lake-stone rockery which is the largest of its kind in all Suzhou gardens (Fig. VIII-16). In the middle of the courtyard and in front of Yifeng Xuan (Salute-to-the-Peak Hall) stands a lake-stone peak, around which is a corridor that winds about on all four sides. The walls and the corridor form small courts in which lake stones, some stalagmite, and green bamboos and banana trees are planted (Fig. VIII-18). Facing the window of Yifeng Xuan (Salute-to-the-Peak Hall) is another picturesque composition of bamboos and stones.

East of Yifeng Xuan is a group of buildings constructed primarily to highlight Guanyun Feng (Cloud-Topping Peak). The whole layout in this area is intended to give distinction to this stone peak. Guanyun Feng (Cloud-Topping Peak) is the highest lake-stone peak in all the Suzhou gardens, and is said to have been an old structure in the days of Dong Yuan (East Garden) in the Ming Dynasty. There are other peaks, Ruiyun Feng (Auspicious-Cloud Peak) and Xiuyun Feng (Hill-Cloud Peak), standing at either side of it. The chief observation spot from which to fully appreciate this group of stone peaks is at the Mandarin-Duck Hall south of the pool. It is also appropriately called Linquanjishuozhi Guan (House for the Aged Giants of Groves and Springs).

To the north of Guanyun Feng (Cloud-Topping Peak) is Guanyun Lou

(Cloud-Topping Two-Storied Building), which serves as the screen for the famed peak (Figs. VIII-19 and VIII-20) . From the second story of Guanyun Lou one can view Huqiu (Tiger Hill) in the distance, and there we find an example of borrowed scenery. To the east and west of Guanyun Feng are winding corridors, along with buildings such as Zhuyunan (Lingering-Cloud House) and Guanyun Tai (Cloud-Topping Terrace). But the whole area lacks tall trees, so there is no feeling of depth in space.

North of the western part of the garden is an earthen mound which is the highest spot in the whole garden. Originally, it was possible to enjoy the borrowed scenery from the mountains such as Huqiu (Tiger Hill), Tianping Mountain, Shangfang Mountain, and Shizi Mountain, and also from Xi Yuan (West Garden). There is a grove of maple trees on the mound whose red leaves in the fall match those of the ginkgo, producing rich variegated colors that harmonize with each other (Fig. VIII-22). To the south of the western part of the garden is level ground, and to the north is a winding creek that flows slowly around the foot of the hill.

The spatial arrangement of the buildings in this garden is superb. There is variety and contrast everywhere in the arrangement of garden spaces, whether one enters the garden from Hesuo (Crane Hall), passes through the areas of Wufeng Xianguan (Five-Peak Celestial House), Qingfengchi Guan (The Fresh-Breeze-Pool House), and Quxi Lou (Winding-Creek Two-Storied Building), and finally reaches the hillock and the pool in the central part of the garden, or enters at the garden, passes through Quxi Lou (Winding-Creek Two-Storied Building) and Wufeng Xianguan (Five-Peak Celestial House), and goes into Dong Yuan (East Garden). There are contrasts between large and small, bright and dim, open and closed, and high and low spots. And the total garden forms a rhythmic interlacing of numerous spaces. It sets off to best advantage the peculiar characteristics of the courtyards, so that there is rich variety and depth in the garden scenery.

If one enters from the garden gate and first goes through a stretch of narrow, winding corridors and small courts, one's line of vision is very restricted. Then, when one gets to the area of Gumujiaoke (Old-Trees-Intertwining-One-Another), the space becomes a little broader. From the south of Gumujiaoke the light comes from the small courts where two or three minor scenic objects are placed. Toward the north and through the tracery windows, one may vaguely see the hill and the pool, and the pavilions and two-story pavilions in the garden. After passing through the above-mentioned "prelude" of a series of smaller spaces and going round to LÖyin Xuan (Green-Shade Lounge), one suddenly comes into the bright and open space, and can see the spacious and luminous scenic objects, the hillock and the pool.

From thence eastward, after passing through the winding and close-knit indoor spaces of Quxi Lou (Winding-Creek Two-Storied Building), one reaches Wufeng Xianguan (Five-Peak Celestial House), the main building of Liu Yuan. At this point of the garden tour, one instantly feels that the indoor space is particularly broad and open. All the aforementioned experiences result from the use of contrast in garden design.

The smaller buildings around the main hall, such as Hesuo (Crane Hall) and Jigudegeng Chu (The Place of Drawing-Water-from-Ancient-Well-to-Find-Rope), are smaller and low-ceilinged because they originally were used as accessory buildings. The area of Yifeng Xuan (Salute-to-the-Peak Hall) to the east of the main hall is composed of six or seven small courtyards. They overlap each other and merge into one another. The viewer is confronted with a many-tiered scene, so there is no feeling of being cramped or crowded in. If one goes further east to Linquanjishuozhi Guan (House for the Aged Giants of Groves and

Springs), one again finds the hall tall and wide, and the front court spacious and open, with stone peaks towering above. This is the major scenic area in the eastern part of the hall. Between these groups of buildings, there are short corridors or small rooms to serve as links and transitions and to add more contrast.

Liu Yuan is large and contains numerous buildings, and its halls and lounges are spacious, tall, and magnificent. Its variety and contrast, and the ingeniously designed buildings demonstrate the high degree of artistic talent and the inventive ingenuity of the architects and craftsmen of ancient times.

Notes

1. During the reign of Emperor Qianlong of the Qing Dynasty this garden belonged to a high official named Liu Shu (also known as Rong Feng) (Fig. VIII-2). After repairs, the garden was completed in the third year of the reign of Emperor Jiaqing. "The bamboos look fresh and cool, the pool appears clear and green; they give distinction to the garden, and so we call it the Cold-Emerald Villa" (quoted from "Preface to the poem written at a Feast in Cold-Emerald Villa," by Qian Daxin, in the sixth year of the reign of Emperor Jiaqing). Later it was also called Hanbi Shanzhuang (Cold-Emerald Mountain-Villa), and popularly known as "Liu Yuan." After the days of the Taiping uprising, only this one garden remained outside the city gate of Changmen. In the second year of the reign of Emperor Guangxu, high official Sheng Kang, also named Xu Ren, owned this garden. He used a different Chinese character with the same sound as Liu Yuan, for the garden of the Liu family, and called it "Liu Yuan" (meaning Lingering-Here Garden). This event may be verified by *Hanbizhuang Ji* (*Records of Cold-Emerald Villa*), by Fan Laizhong; by the characters written by Wu Yung on the inscribed horizontal board for Liu Yuan; and by Records of Liu Yuan, by Yu Yue.

2. In vol. 14 of Mr. Yuan Zhonglang's Complete Works by Yuan Hongdao of the Ming Dynasty, it is written:

   The garden of Xu Jiongqing (i.e., Xu Taishi) is located in Xiatang outside the city gate of Changmen. It is magnificent and spacious. There is a two-story building at the front and there is a lounge in the rear, and in both places banquets can be held for the guests. The stone screen (i.e., rockery) is piled by scholar Zhou Shichen, 30 chi* high and about 20 chi wide, delicate and precipitous, resembling a picture of hills and rills on a horizontal hanging-scroll, with no traces of breaks or continuations. It is truly done with ingenuity and skill.

   In the central part of Liu Yuan, the lower parts of the rockery north and west of the pool are now piled with yellow stones, seemingly built in those days of the past. The upper parts or the rockery have been repaired several times with lake stones that are broken and strewn about.

3. On March 4, 1961, the State Council published A *List of the First Batch of Major National Cultural Relics for Preservation*. This garden is No. 124 on the list.

---

*1 chi = 1/2 meter

IX

Shizilin
(The Forest of Lions Garden)[1]

Shizilin (The Forest of Lions Garden) is located on Yuanlin Road (literally, Forest of Gardens Road) in northeastern Suzhou. In the second year of the imperial rule of Zhizheng, toward the end of the Yuan Dynasty, the followers of the Buddhist Monk Weize (otherwise known as Chan master Tianru) built a hermitage here for him. At first it was named Shilinsi (Lions' Forest Temple), and later was renamed Pudizhengzong Si (Orthodox Bodhi Temple). It was also called Shizilin (Forest of Lions).

The garden is north of the temple. Originally it was the site of a deserted garden in the Song Dynasty where bamboo groves and odd-looking rocks were abundant. In the first years of the imperial reign of Hongwu in the Ming Dynasty, a painter named Ni Zan (also named Yunlin) painted a picture called Shizilin Tu (Fig. IX-2).

Following the layout of the garden, the pool is situated north of the central part; south and east of the pool, rocks are piled into hillocks. The buildings are mainly placed to the east and the north of the pool, with a long corridor stretching forth in four directions (Figs. IX-4 through IX-7). The total area of the garden is about 1 hectare, including the part where the ancestral hall is situated.

Now the garden gate is in the east where the ancestral hall used to be. After entering the garden gate, one goes through a passageway west of the ancestral hall to reach Yanyu Tang (Famed-for-Swallow Hall), which was built in the fashion of the Mandarin-Duck Hall or Twin Hall. Parterres and stalagmites are found in the courtyard in front of Yanyu Tang, with a magnolia tree on each side. This is considered an effective courtyard design (Fig. IX-3). North of the hall there is a small, square lounge named "Yuanshechenqu" ("A visit to the garden is interesting").

The stone peaks in this court, as well as in Five-Old-Pine Park, are very varied in shape and size. Sometimes they seem to be looking upward and sometimes gazing downward. In the bodies of the peaks there are many cavities and holes, through which stone tablets are suspended by means of iron hooks, and which are filled with cement. All these peaks were piled between 1918 and 1926, and they represent the prevailing practice of piling rockeries at that time.

West of the small, square lounge is Zhibai Xuan (Pointing-at-Cypress Hall)

(Fig. IX-11), the main hall of the garden. It is two-storied and rather large. To the south of the hall is a rockery, on top of which are several stone peaks and stalagmites, with dim caves winding about. In the cavities between rocks on the rockery, the roots of ancient trees twist around. In the middle of the rockery is a patch of level ground where a two-story building named Woyun Shi (Lying-in-Cloud Chamber) is built (Fig. IX-10). Yanyu Tang (Famed-for-Swallow Hall) and Small Square Lounge are within easy reach of Woyun Shi. To the west of the rockery is a narrow ravine, and further west of it is a group of rockeries amidst the pool (Fig. IV-8). At the northern end of the ravine, two rockeries are linked together over a ravine, and they appear to be a unified body. Over the ravine is Xiuzhu Ge (Tall-Bamboo Pavilion).

Westward from Zhibai Xuan (Pointing-at-Cypress Hall), Guwusun Yuan (Five-Old-Pines Park) can be found. At the front court, stone peaks and ancient trees stand separately, resulting in a secluded and quiet environment. To the south and facing the pool are Hehua Ting (Lotus Hall) and Zhengqu Ting (True-Interest Pavilion), the main spots from which to observe and admire the garden (Fig. IX-8). Further to the west is Anxiangshuying Lou (Hidden-Fragrance and Sparse-Shadow Two-Storied Building). The group of buildings from Hehua Ting (Lotus Hall) to this point are all placed horizontally to facilitate east-west orientation. Here the contours are stiff and straight, and lacking depth.

In the western part of the garden there is an earthen hill (Fig. IX-1)which was piled with the earth dug from an adjacent pool when the garden was expanded in recent times. On top of the hill are Feipu Ting (Flying-Waterfall Pavilion), Wenmei Ge (Asking-for-Plum-Tree Two-Storied Pavilion), Shuangxiang Xianguan (Double-Fragrance Celestial Hall), and other buildings. Wenwei Ge is the focal point in the western part of the garden (Fig. IX-5), but it is too bulky. Between Wenmei Ge and Feipu Ting is a ravine, which is stone-piled all the way up. On top of the two-story pavilion is a big cabinet that can hold and store a great amount of water. The water can be made to flow along the ravine down to the pool, like an artificial waterfall.

As one travels from Wenmei Ge along the wall, follows the corridor south-ward, and turns eastward, Shanzi Ting (Fan Pavilion) can be found at the southwestern corner of the garden. Behind Shanzi Ting is a small courtyard with bamboos and rocks that resemble a miniature artistic sketch. Along the south wall, a long corridor rises and falls; there are two half-pavilions along the way to break up the monotonous stretch of corridor. In front of the corridors and along the shore of the pool embankment are stone arrangements. The stony path along the pool is tortuous and circuitous to compensate for the straight, high walls on the south. All along the pool's stone embankment, with the only exception being Xiaochibi (Little Red Cliff), yellow stones are used to build an arched bridge in imitation of a natural solvent stone cliff cave, closely resembling one in the world of nature. Especially noteworthy is the use of a narrow bridge that vaults over a long, narrow, belt-shaped strip of water surface. This is a case where rocks in a garden were piled successfully (Fig. III-12).

The corridor along the south wall becomes a double corridor at the east end, through which one can approach the building and courtyards in the eastern part of the garden and finally reach Lixue Tang (Standing-in-the-Snow Hall).

Note

1. For the naming of Shizilin, it is necessary to quote from Records of Shizilin Pudizhengzong Si (*Records of Orthodox Bodhi Temple in the Forest of Lions*), by Ouyang Xuan, in the fourteenth year of the imperial reign of Zhizheng in the Yuan Dynasty:

Inside the city of Gusu [i.e., Suzhou] there is a forest named Shizi.... In the forest there are ten thousand bamboos, and under the bamboos there are many bizarre rocks, some of which are shaped like lions or wild animals; therefore it is called the Forest of Lions. Besides, the lions learned the religion from the national Buddhist master Puying, Zhongfeng Ben, who preached at Shiziyan in Tianmu Mountain, so the name was also used to indicated where the lions learned the religion.

In addition, Weisu of the Yuan Dynasty in his *Records of Shizilin* (*Records of the Forest of Lions*) wrote:

The Forest of Lions is the hermitage of Chan master Tianru, who had learned the religion from Chan master Zhongfeng Ben of Tianmu Mountain.... In the forest the slopes are steep and high, and the mountain peaks stand separately, of which the one that looks bizarre and stands in the middle is the highest and has the appearance of a line.... In other parts of the forest rocks are in disorder and piles of them are in mixtures of high and low and look like lions and wild horses, so the forest is named Forest of Lions. Besides, there is a rock cliff names Shizi in Tianmu Mountain, and so this name is used to demonstrate the source.

All these are quoted from *An Anthology of Records of the Scenery in Shizilin*, as edited by Xunzhon, a Buddhist monk, in the Ming Dynasty.

X

Canglang Ting
(The Surging-Wave-Pavilion Garden)

Canglang Ting (The Surging-Wave-Pavilion Garden), located near Sanyuan Fang in the southern part of the city, has the longest history of all the classical gardens in Suzhou. Near the end of the Five Dynasties, the site of the present garden was occupied by the villa of General Sun Chengyou of Wu in the state of Wuyue. Later, the villa was deserted.

In the middle of the Song Dynasty, Su Shunqing, also named Zimei, built a waterfront pavilion named Canglang Ting (The Surging-Wave-Pavilion), and he expanded it into a garden. At that time, there were "high mounds and broad waters" and "many different flowers and tall and slender bamboos" in the garden.[1] In other words, the scene was filled with beauty.

At the beginning of the Southern Song Dynasty Han Shizhong used to live there and he expanded it and made it a very large garden. Still later, the place became a part of a Buddhist temple and gradually was abandoned. In the Ming Dynasty, it was already "a deep grove of bamboo and trees, and very much like a village."[2] In the thirty-fifth year of the reign of Emperor Kangxi of the Qing Dynasty, the garden was rebuilt, and Canglang Ting was moved onto the mound.[3] Open halls, corridors, and other buildings were erected to face the pool, while a stone bridge was constructed as the entrance gate. By that time, foundations had already been laid for the plan of Canglang Ting of today[4] (Fig. X-5).

In the seventh year of the reign of Emperor Daoguang, the garden was again repaired when the memorial hall for five hundred famous persons of virtue was built. During the reigns of Emperor Xianfeng and Tongzhi, the garden was destroyed; it was rebuilt in the twelfth year of Emperor Tongzhi's reign when, except for the location of the pavilion Canglang Ting, all the other features of the garden underwent radical changes.[5]

The total garden area is about 1 hectare. Its layout centers around a mound. While the water, which is located outside the garden, provides an external scene, buildings have been constructed around the mound (Figs. X-1, X-3, X-4, and X-6). The garden gate is at the northwestern corner, facing the clear pool outside. Almost immediately in front of the gate is a bridge. As one crosses it into the garden, one immediately meets an outstandingly high hill, which stretches along the path from west to the east. There is an earthen mound at the pool, on which are piled stones to protect the slopes on all four sides. Along the slopes of the mound are paths with steps. On the eastern section of the hill, the path is paved with yellow stones that were piled at an earlier date. On the hill's western section, the path was built partly with lake stones, and was somewhat weedy. There are stone paths winding about in circles on the hill, and there is a dim and gloomy forest of trees, with indocalamus covering the soil beside the paths. The scenery seems very natural (Fig. X-6)in this section of the garden. This is, in fact, one of the best rockery scenes in all the gardens of Suzhou.

Encircling the hill is a winding corridor that rises and dips with the topography, and there are pavilions and waterside pavilions at key locations. At the highest point of the earthen mound is Canglang Ting Pavilion, the garden's namesake (Fig. X-6). To the south, however, Mingdao Tang (Comprehending-the-Doctrine Hall) and the Memorial Hall for Five-Hundred-Famous-Persons-of-Virtue crowd together in front of Canglang Ting and obstruct the view.

Although the place is higher than the elevation at which it is built, it is not possible to look far into the distance. Another building, Kanshan Lou (Looking-at-the-Hill Two-Storied Building) had to be built in front of the memorial hall to enhance the viewpoint.

In the front court of Mingdao Tang (Comprehending-the-Doctrine Hall) and the Memorial Hall for Five-Hundred-Famous-Persons-of-Virtue, the arrangement is dreary and scattered. It lacks the spirit and atmosphere of a good garden. To the south of the memorial hall, in Cuilinglong (The Delicate Emerald Hall) and its environs, there are tiny buildings winding about amidst the bamboo grove. Here, in an obvious interpretation of a line of a verse by Su Zimei, "Sunlight penetrating through the bamboos like an emerald delicately wrought," a refreshing and secluded environment is thus created.

From this point on, one walks along a corridor around the southwestern corner of the small pool and then turns north and passes by Yubei Ting (The Imperial-Tablet Pavilion). Then one returns to the garden gate. To the west of the gate there are several buildings, include Ouxiang Shuixie (Lotus-Root-Fragrance Waterside Pavilion), Wenmiaoxiangshi (Smelling-the-Wonderful-Fragrance Chamber), and Yaohua Jingjie (Land of Glistening Jade). They form a courtyard by themselves.

The northern part of the hill faces the pool. To the west is a waterside pavilion called Mianshui Xuan (Facing-the-Water Pavilion) (Fig. X-9), while to the east is a square-shaped pavilion named Guanyu Chu (Place for Watching the Fish) (Fig. X-7). The two pavilions are joined by a double corridor (Fig. X-10); on its walls are tracery windows, to link up the scenery inside and outside the garden.

Most of the private gardens in Suzhou are surrounded by high walls, within which are piled hillocks and dry pools. Garden owners usually are concerned about their gardens' isolation from the outside world. But this garden was originally a Buddhist temple turned an ancestral hall. It has preserved the custom of being open to the public. Its layout includes, in part, "borrowed scenery" from the outside and a double corridor linking the water outside the walls with the hillock inside them. This is an excellent example of rills. Its topographical advantages, such as the green and fragrant groves of trees and the winding corridor facing the pool, contribute to some of the best scenery in the garden.

Notes

1. See the *Records of Canglang Ting* (The Surging-Wave-Pavilion Garden), by Su Shunqin, of the Song Dynasty. Quoted in vol. 14 of *Annals of Wu County*, by Fan Chenda, of the Song Dynasty.

2. See *Poems to Record a Visit to Caoan, with an Introduction*, by Shen Zhou of the Ming Dynasty. Quoted in vol. 1 of *Brief Record of Canglang Ting*, by Song Luo of the Qing Dynasty.

3. See *A Record of the Rebuilding of Canglang Ting*, by Song Luo, in the reign of Emperor Kangxi of the Qing Dynasty.

4. See the map attached to *Brief Record of Canglang*, by Song Luo, and the map attached to *Grand Ceremony of Imperial Tour to the South*, during the reign of Emperor Qianlong.

5. See *A Record of the Rebuilding of Canglang Ting*, by Zhang Susheng, in the twelfth year of the reign of Emperor Tongzhi of the Qing Dynasty (quoted in *A New Record of Canglang Ting*, 1928).

XI

Wangshi Yuan
(The Retired Fisherman's Garden)

Wangshi Yuan, at Kuojietou Lane, south of Daicheng Bridge originally was the site of Wanjuan Tang (Ten-Thousand-Volume Hall). Owned by a high official, at that time it was called "Yuyin" (Fisherman's Hermitage). This old garden was later abandoned. Then in the middle years of the reign of Emperor Qianlong of the Qing Dynasty it was rebuilt and renamed "Wandshi Yuan".[1] Toward the end of the reign of Emperor Qianlong, the garden once again became dilapidated, but was again repaired and renovated, and the foundation for the layout was built at the present scale.[2]

After that time, the garden underwent several cycles of prosperity and decline as some new buildings were built. For instance, Xiexiu Lou (Picking-Elegant-View Two-Storied Building) was built during the reign of Emperor Guangxu. After 1949, some buildings were added, such as the courtyard in the vicinity of Tiyun Shi (Ladder-Cloud Chamber), as well as Lengquan Ting (Cold-Springs Pavilion) and Hanbi Quan (Enclosing-Emerald Springs). This famous garden, long the dwelling of civilians, was renovated and once again became new and elegant.

The garden is west of the residential quarters, with a total area of more than 4 hectares (including a nursery, halls, and lounges). (Figs. XI-1 through XI-5).

Inside the main gate of the residence at Kuojietou Lane, there is what used to be called the sedan chair hall. To the west of it is a small door. On the lintel over it are engravings on a stone slab: "Wangshi Xiaozhu," meaning Small House for the Fisherman. This used to be the entrance to the garden. Then, at the back of the residence there is a side door leading to the garden. The official garden gate now is the rear gate at Shiquan Street, and one has to pass Tiyun Shi (Ladder-Cloud Chamber) to enter the garden.

There are numerous buildings in the garden which, when grouped together, may be viewed as two large sets of courtyards. On the south, Xiaoshanconggui Xuan (Little-Hillock-and-Laurel-Grove Hall) (also called Daogu Xuan, or Discussing-Ancient-Event Hall), plus the area of Daohuo Guan (Pursuance-of-Harmony House) and Qin Shi (Music Room), constitute a small courtyard to serve as living quarters and places for banqueting and assemblage. On the north, Wufeng Shuwu (Five-Peak Study), Jixuzhai (The Gathering-the-Void Study), Kansongduhua Xuan (Looking-at-the-Pine-and-Painting Hall), and Dianchuanyi

(Late-Spring Chamber), form another set of larger courtyards, with the study a major attraction (Fig. XI-2 and XI-10). At the central part of the garden, flowers and trees, hills and rocks, and buildings, make up the major scenic area, with the pool at its center (Fig. XI-6).

Xiaoshanconggui Xuan (Little-Hillock-and-Laurel-Grove Hall) is the principal building in the garden, but it is small compared to the flower halls of other gardens in Suzhou. In front of the hall and at its back are piled stones. On the south, laurel trees are planted in a low, dwarfish parterre made of lake stones. But on the north, the yellow stone rockery called "Yungang" (Cloudy Heights) is rather lofty and steep. On top of the rockery are several maples, laurels, and magnolias, producing a variety of colors. From the hall one can go along the corridor to reach Daohuo Guan (Pursuance-of-Harmony House) and Qing Shi (Music Room). In this area the garden space is narrow and is enclosed by winding corridors—a gloomy, deep, and tortuous environment.

From Xiaoshanconggui Xuan (Little-Hillock-and-Laurel-Grove Hall), where hilly rocks are scattered about in apparent disorder, one passes through a section of small, low, and dim corridor to reach the central part of the garden. The garden pool there drifts about, and the surroundings suddenly become bright and spacious. This illustrates the device of using dimness contrasted with brightness, and a hillock and rocks contrasted with water in the pool.

The pool in this part of the garden occupies an area of about 330 square meters. The shape of the surface is somewhat square and is seen as one continuous whole instead of being divided up; there are only two branches extending out into bays at the southeastern and northwestern corners. The pavilions and corridors, the two-story waterside pavilion, and the stone bridges built on the shores of the pool are all low, and seem to bend down over the surface of the water. The expanse of the pool is bright and spacious and its shores are low. On its yellow stone embankments, stones are piled to form the shape of caves, so the surface of the pool seems to consist of broad and extensive waves coming from a remote, undiscernible source. No water-lilies are plated in the pool so the light from the sky, colors of the hills, corridors and halls, and shadows of trees, may all be reflected in the water to make the whole scene rich and full of variety.

The main buildings, including Kansongduhua Xuan (Looking-at-the-Pine-and-Painting Hall) and Jixuzhai (The Gathering-the-Void Study), seem to recede into the background. They are separated from the pool either by rockery and parterre or by courtyards and trees, so that the taller halls do not appear to press down onto the surface of the water, but nevertheless add to the feeling of tiers and depth in the garden scenery. As one looks northward from south of the pool, the comparatively low building Kansongduhua Xuan (Looking-at-the-Pine-and-Painting Hall) seems concealed among the groves of trees. On the northeast, two-story buildings stand apart in an irregular arrangement, with one in the front and another at the back. There are also lofty ancient cypresses, winding bridges, and rock seats that almost touch the water, and Zhuwaiyizhi Xuan (A-Branch-from-Bamboo Lounge) faces the water and appears transparent and delicate (Fig. II-20). All of these combined form an irregular and complexly-patterned picture (Fig. XI-6)

South of the pool there is the light and delicate Zhuoying Shuige (Washing-Tassel Waterside Pavilion). The simple and vigorous hill precipice called Yungang (Cloudy Heights) stands in strong contrast to the pavilion (Fig. XI-7). To the east of the pool and immediately next to the residence there is a stretch of high walls. There, open pavilion, open corridors, horizontal architraves, and fake tracery windows are used. Also, a rockery is piled there and creeperlike wisteria and climbing figs are planted to avert the feeling of stiffness and relieve the monotony of the wall surfaces.

In the northern part of the garden, two-story halls for reading and chambers for painting, such as Kansongduhua Xuan (Looking-at-the-Pine-and-Painting Hall), Jixuzhai (The Gathering-the-Void Study), and Dianchunyi (Late-Spring Chamber), form courtyards by themselves. In the courtyards are parterres with piled stones, groves of bamboo, flowers and trees, and stone peaks for scenery (Fig. XI-10). At the back of the building is a small court for light and ventilation. In it are some lake stones, sparsely planted bamboo, plum trees, and banana trees, all for viewing through the window. The studies and courtyards are in the northwest corner of the garden, known for the many Chinese herbaceous peonies planted there. Peaked rocks stand in prominence in these courtyards, trees appear sparse and bright, and everything is arranged simply. With the addition of the newly constructed Lengquan Ting (Cold-Springs Pavilion) and Hanbi Quan (Enclosing-Emerald Springs), the courtyard scene has become more elaborate.

The buildings in this garden are distinguished by their attractive and charming structures, and their delicacy and exquisiteness. The pavilions and two-story pavilions around the pool especially are known for their characteristics of petiteness, low height, and transparency; the furniture and interior decoration are also exquisite.

The stones employed in this garden are used in different surroundings according to their qualities. For instance, yellow stones are used for rockeries, the parterre around the pool, and the embankments of the pool. Lake stones are employed in the courtyards. The two kinds of stones are not mixed, for a good reason. Vertical-shaped stones are used underneath the horizontal stones on the pool embankments. The horizontal pieces are placed to form all sorts of cavities, holes, and convex spots. The stone paths and stone shores are tortuous and irregular, and an effort is made to put together big pieces of stones, so that the observers don't find the stone assemblage either dull and monotonous or confusing and disorderly, common defects often found on the shores of pools. As for flowers and trees, just a few kinds are used, but they are of good quality. The total number of trees planted in the garden is relatively small, and the species include sweetgum, maple, laurel, lacebark pine, pine, Chinese wisteria, and magnolia. As they are kept properly trimmed, they achieve the designed effect when closely observed.

Notes

1. In the middle of the reign of Emperor Qianlong in the Qing Dynasty, the garden owner Song Zongyuan, who was junior minister of Guanlushi (Bureau of Imperial Refection Service) used the original meaning of "Yuyin" (Fisherman's Hermitage) and considered himself a fisherman; so he renamed the garden "Wangshi," which means fisherman.

2. In the sixteenth year of the reign of Emperor Qianlong of the Qing Dynasty, Qian Daxin wrote in his *Records of Wangshi Yuan*:

   South of Daicheng Bridge, it was the site of Wanjuan Tang (Ten-Thousand-Volume Hall) owned by a man named Shi in the Song Dynasty.... About thirty years ago, Song Guanlu bought the place, built a villa for his old age, therefore called himself a fisherman and gave it as the name of the garden, pretending to be a fisherman and hermit.... After he died, the garden grew dilapidated, the tall trees and ancient rocks were mostly lost, and only the deep and clear water of the pool remained pure and bright. Then Mr. Qu Yuancuan bought and owned the place. On its original foundations he built new buildings, piled stones and planted trees, arranged everything properly, added new pavilions and halls, replaced old buildings with new ones.

   This record is engraved in a stone inscription, and is now preserved in the garden.

XII
Yi Yuan
(Happy Garden)

Yi Yuan (Happy Garden)[1] was founded during the reign of Emperors Tongzhi and Guangxu toward the end of the Qing Dynasty. It was a high official's private garden. On the west side it was linked with the adjacent ancestral halls, while on the south side it faced the owner's residence, which was across from an alley. The hillocks, the pool, and the halls in the garden now are essentially the same as they appeared in the original layout (Figs. XII-1 and XII-2).[2]

The plan of this garden is long and narrow, stretching from east to west. The total area is about one-half hectare, and is divided into two parts (Figs. XII-3 through XII-8). The eastern part of the garden originally was the site of an official's residence in the Ming Dynasty, while the western part was built as an extension when the garden was founded in the last period of the Qing Dynasty. The two parts are separated by a double corridor: To the east are chiefly buildings and courtyards, while to the west is the main garden proper, with a pool in the middle, surrounded by a rockery, flowers and trees, and buildings. Now the garden gate is located at the garden's northeastern corner on Renmin Lu (People's Road).

From the gate one enters a small court in the eastern part of the garden (Fig. XII-9), passes through a winding corridor and a pavilion called Yuyan Ting (Jade-Extending Pavilion), and reaches Sishixiaosa Ting (Spirited-and-Unrestrained-through-the-Four-Seasons Pavilion). From here, two different routes may be taken. One route follows the corridor and goes west, passes by Yuhong Ting (Jade-Rainbow Pavilion) and Shifang (Stone Landboat), reaches Suolo Xuan (Locking-up-Greenery Hall) at the north end of the double corridor; then one may enter the western part of the garden (Fig. XII-14).

The other route follows the corridor south, passes through the main building in the eastern part to Poxian Qinguan (Hill-Slope-Fairies Music House), also named Shiting Qinshi (Stone-Listening-to-Music Chamber), and then to Baishi Xuan (Bowing-to-the-Stone Hall), also known as Suihan Caolu (Cold-Season Cottage). One then turns west to reach Nanxui Ting (Southern-Snow Pavilion) at the southern end of the double corridor, and finally arrives at the southeastern corner of the western part of the garden.

There are courtyards in front of Poxian Qinguan (Hill-Slope-Fairies Music

House) and Baishi Xuan (Bowing-to-the-Stone Hall); in the middle of each courtyard stands a stone peak and a parterre made of lake stones and planted with ginkgos, wintersweets, maples, cypresses, camellias, silver roses, and bamboos. The double corridor meanders and winds about, and the tracery windows on the walls between the two lanes of the corridor link up the scenes on both sides and intensify the feeling of the depth of the scenery.

In the middle of the western part of the garden is a pool, long and narrow, stretching from east to west. North of the pool is a hill with lake stones, while to its south are buildings. The main hall was Ouxiang Xie (Lotus-Root-Fragrance Waterside Pavilion), which, with its once-exquisite interior decorations, was destroyed during World War II. The interior of this hall assumes a mandarin-duck or twin-hall pattern: the north half-hall, called Ouxiang Xie (Lotus-Root-Fragrance Waterside Pavilion) (Fig. XII-12) or Hehue Ting (Lotus Hall), has a terrace facing the pool (Fig. V-12), where one can observe the lotus flowers in the summer; the south half-hall called Chuyue Xuan (Hoeing-on-the-Moon Hall), faces southward to an irregular lake stone parterre, uneven in height and irregular in arrangement; it is planted with peonies, Chinese herbaceous peonies, China firs, laurels, and lacebark pines (Fig. VI-46). To the east of the parterre are scores of plum trees, so south half-hall is also called Meihua Ting (Plum-Blossom Hall).

To the east of the hall is a corridor linking it with Nanxue Ting (Southern-Snow Pavilion). Walking northeast from the hall, one passes over a winding bridge to reach the environs of Jinsu Ting (Golden-Millet Pavilion) and Suolo Xuan (Locking-up-Greenery Hall). Going west from the hall, one comes to Biwuqifeng Guan (Green-Wutong-Sheltering-Phoenix House) and Mianbi Ting (Facing-the-Cliff Pavilion). The rockery to the north of the pool is piled with lake stones. The stone cliffs and the hill cave on the rockery appear quite natural, with big, whole pieces of rock on the surface that reveal the technical skill of the craftsmen (Fig. XII-1 and XII-11). The shore of the pool, however, is a bit too straight and stiff. Also, the stone peak at the east end of the hill is a bit too broken up, and the height of the stone wall is too low to be in good proportion to the dimensions of the hall and the pool.

In the western section of the pool there is a water gate through which the water in the pool flows north and bends around toward the northwest to form a small pond. There is a landboat at the end of the pond, Huafang Zhai (Painting Landboat Study), where the decorations are the most exquisite and beautiful of all the landboats in the locality. To the extreme west, there is Zhanlu Tang (Crystal-Clear-Dew Hall), an independent, closed court, where a parterre is built for peonies, lacebark pines, laurels, wisterias, and other flowers and trees. From north of Huafang Zhai (Painting Landboat Study), one turns east to reach the stone cave of the rockery. After one passes through the cave and walks up the steps that wind around up the rockery, one comes to Luoji Ting (Snail-Shaped Coiled-Hair Pavilion) (Fig. XII-13), and there one can look down and view the whole garden beneath. One then passes through Xiaocanglang Ting (Little-Surging-Wave Pavilion) on the hill and reaches Jinsu Ting (Golden-Millet Pavilion) and Suolo Xuan (Locking-up-Greenery Hall) at the northeastern part of the garden. All around Jinsu Ting (Golden-Millet Pavilion) are laurel trees and numerous stone peaks, which stand there to form a forest, all of which add up to a sparse but graceful aspect. There, one can see the hillock and the pools to the west and the groves of trees in the garden, some tall and some low, some concealed and some visible, giving great depth to the garden scenery.

Notes

1. Yu Yue of the Qing Dynasty wrote in his *Records of Yi Yuan*:

   Provincial High Commissioner Gu Zishan, after founding his Spring Shades Country house for charity, built a garden east of it, in order to keep himself fit to lead a long life, and he called the place Yi Yuan (Happy Garden).

   See Records of County Wu, vol. 39, part 1 of the Minguo period. Gu Wenbin, known also as Zishan, was a follower of Guan Wen, Hu Linyi, Li Hongzhang, etc., who were the executioners of the Qing Dynasty, to suppress the revolutionaries of Taipingtianguo. Later he was a high official in the eastern part of Zhejian, Dao-Yin (or chief magistrate) of the Dao of Ningbo, Shaoxing, and Taizhou. He exploited the people very cruelly. Then, in Suzhou he built an ancestral hall, a garden, and a residence. On the construction of one garden alone, he spent about 200,000 ounces of silver.

2. What was described in Yu Yue's *Records of Yi Yuan* on the whole is the same as the conditions that presently exist.

XIII
Ou Yuan
(Twin Garden)

Inside the residence at No. 6 Xiaoxinqiao Bridge Lane, there are two gardens, namely the East Garden and the West Garden. Therefore, they were named Ou Yuan or the Twin Garden. The East Garden, also called She Yuan (Involved Garden), was founded at the beginning of the Qing Dynasty, and was later abandoned. Toward the end of the Qing Dynasty, the garden was expanded and it began to assume its present shape.[1] (Fig. XIII-2).

The West Garden was west of the central axis of the residential quarters. A study in the middle called Zhilian Laowu (Curtain-Weaving Old-Lodge) divided it into two small courts. In front of the study, to the south, is a spacious terrace and an irregular-shaped courtyard. There is a rockery on the southwest corner of the courtyard. Elsewhere, there are varieties of flowers, trees, and lake stones everywhere. At the back of the study is another courtyard in which there is a two-story studio and a hillock, rocks, and trees. This is a good example of a studio hall beside a courtyard.

East of the main hall on the central axis are a parlor, two small courts, and a smaller parlor. Further east is the East Garden (Fig. XIII-3), which occupies an area of about one-third hectare; its layout centers around a hillock and a pool, its focal points.

The main building, a double-eaved two-story hall, is a rare specimen in the gardens of Suzhou. The southeastern corner of the East Garden projects out somewhat, and there are three small courts where several halls and intricate pathways lead to the residence on the west. The whole area is called Chengqu Caotang (City-Corner Cottage) (Fig. XIII-4). In the middle is a three-room main hall where the garden owners used to give parties and feasts. In front of it there is a wide stretch of meadows on a gentle hill-slope, and on the other side of it is a simple and majestic rockery piled with yellow stones.

To the east of the rockery is a long, narrow pool that stretches toward the north. There is a corridor to the east of the pool which leads to the eastern part of the main hall in the north and a small pavilion beside the pool in the south, just where the latter extends south from the rockery and a winding bridge vaults over it. At the southern end of the pool is a two-story pavilion called Sanshuijian (Waterside Pavilion amid-the-Hillock-and-Pool) straddling the water (Fig. XIII-6). Sanshuijian, the waterside pavilion, faces northward toward

Chengqu Caotang (City-Corner Cottage). There is a yellow-stone rockery between, and they make up a major scenic area, with the rockery as the principal element (Fig. II-23).

South of Sanshuijian there is another hall, which is linked to another two-story building by a pathway along the precipice. The small two-story building is called Tinglu Lou (Listening-to-the-Scull Two-Storied Building) (Fig. XIII-7). It stands alone at the extreme southeastern end of the garden. North of the hall is a stone path on a hilly slope, and flowers and trees are planted along the path, creating a small scenic area of gloom and isolation.

The yellow-stone rockery in front of Chengqu Caotang (City-Corner Cottage) has two sections: The eastern half is larger, and one can go along the stone path in front of the hall to reach the terrace, which lies between a rockery to the east and a stone lodge to the west. Further east from the terrace, the hillock rises and leads to a precipice that beetles over the pool below. At the southeastern corner of the precipice is a stone-step path leading down the slope to the shore of the pool. Here the piled stones appear majestic and steep, and constitute the most attractive part of the whole hillock. The western half of the rockery is smaller, and it gets lower by gradations from east to west as the slope becomes gentler. The rockery ends at the right wall of the small parlor.

Between the western and the eastern halves of the rockery is a ravine a little over one meter wide. On the both sides of the ravine the rocks become hanging cliffs, and the whole area looks like a sort of gorge and therefore is called "Suigu" (Deep Gorge) (Fig. VI-12). The cliff on its east faces the pool, and there the surface of the water is broad and the dimensions of the rockery are in good proportion to the width of the pool.

From Sanshuijian (Waterside Pavilion amid-the-Hillock-and-Pool) or from the small pavilion in the east, one can see the steep, simple, but majestic hill in the distance across the pool. No two-story pavilions are found on top of the hill, but at its summit and back are flowers such as camellias, big-leaf hydrangeas, crape myrtles, wintersweets, Tianzhu (heavenly bamboos, a kind of Chinese bamboo), and trees like glossy privets, Chinese little box-trees, flat-leafed cypresses, and Chinese scholar trees, sparsely planted. A few trees jut out from the precipice to match the hanging kudzu vine and Chinese wisteria.

All these echo the striking features of the natural world of hills and rills (Fig. XIII-1). For here on this hill, the precipices, stone steps, ravines, and piled rocks, all appear real and natural. The big and small stones alternate with one another. Some of them are convex and others concave, some vertical and others horizontal, and they appear to be thrown at random and in disorder. They are mainly horizontal stones, and the whole arrangement resembles the naturally split veins of yellow stones. They look almost the same as the yellow-stone rockery in Yu Yuan (Comfort Garden) of Shanghai, which was piled by Zhang Nanyuan during the reign of Jiajing in the Ming Dynasty.

It can be speculated that they might possibly be the relics of the She Yuan (Involved Garden), dating back to the beginning of the Qing Dynasty.

East of Sanshuijian and south of Tinglo Lou, the parterre on the earthen slope serves as contrapositional scenery. Together, these scenic objects make up a separate area of attractions. Yellow stones serve as boundaries for the earthen slope. Covered with earth, these stones serve as terraces, between which there is a winding stone path. There is a bamboo grove on the slope and sparsely planted apricot trees, plum trees, magnolias from Guangdong, crape myrtles, and other flowers and trees. With the whitewashed walls as a background and the bamboo grove as a foil, the whole region seems fresh and lively, and harmonizes with the yellow-stone rockery far beyond the pool. This is effective use of striking contrast.

The hillock is the major attraction of the East Garden, and the pool serves as its foil. These are the two principal objects that stand out prominently. The yellow-stone rockery in particular in this garden is recognized as a successful example of the rockeries in all the Suzhou gardens. Not only are the stones piled naturally, but the rockery itself is well-located. With the main building relegated to the rear of the garden, it is appropriate for the rockery to be built a bit away from the axis so that the scene may be viewed and appreciated from several angles.

Note

1. Two Chinese characters, "Ou" (meaning a team of two, a match, an equal) and "Ou" (meaning mate, spouse) are pronounced exactly alike: She Yuan (Involved Garden) was originally the private garden of a man named Lu Jin, magistrate of Baoning District, in the early Qing Dynasty. It was also known as Xiaoyulin (Small Fragrant Forest). After that, several owners of the garden succeeded each other, with the family names of Zhu, Shen, and Gu, in that order. In the last years of the Qing Dynasty, the garden was owned by a reactionary official named Shen Bingcheng who extended the west part of the garden, and it became Twin Garden. This was recorded in vol. v of *Hermit's life in the City of Wu*, by Gu Zhenghai, during the reign of Daoguang of the Qing Dynasty; and in the "She Yuan" (Involved Garden) in vol. 396 of *Annals of Wu District*, in the age of Minguo.

XIV
Yi Pu
(Art Orchard)

Yi Pu (Art Orchard) is located at No. 5 Wenya Lane and was first founded in the Ming Dynasty. Its first owner was a high official named Wen Zhenmeng, who was a great-grandson of the literary giant Wen Zhengming. At that time, it was called Yao Yuan or Medicine Garden. At the beginning of the Qing Dynasty, it was renamed Yi Pu (Art Orchard) and also was known as Jingting Shanfang (Respect-to-Pavilion Hill-Lodge).[1]

The layout of the garden's hillock and the pool is much the same as those built at the end of the Ming and the beginning of the Qing Dynasties. The total garden area is about one-third hectare. According to the "Map of Yi Pu" drawn by Wang Hui, there was no waterside hall to the north of the pool. There was, however, a terrace next to the pool in the original layout. Also, west of the terrace there was a hall (i.e., Jingting Shanfang or Respect-to-Pavilion Hill-Lodge), which no longer exists today, and the former Lotus-Pool-and-Winding-Bridge was very different in appearance from the present bridge.

Upon entering the garden of the residential quarter, the visitor goes through a long winding lane to reach the front hall Shilun Tang (Ethics-of-the-Age Hall). Then one proceeds west to enter the garden proper. South of the main building named Boya Tang (Rich-in-Learning Hall), there is a small court, and beside the pool, there is a waterside hall of five rooms (running in the width) that projects over the pool. Two of the hall's wing rooms face the pool and are linked with two additional wing rooms, one east and one west of the pool. The pool is the focal point of the garden layout (Fig. XIV-1). While buildings are the major features on the north shore, south of the pool a hillock is piled with earth and stones. There is an abundance of trees on the hillock, and southwest of it is a small court surrounded by walls with a round moon gate that leads to the hillock and pool in the central part of the garden. There is a sparse arrangement of pavilions, corridors, trees, and stones on the pool's western and eastern shores. They serve as a transitional stage between the northern and southern parts of the garden and also as foils (Fig. XIV-4).

One turns south from the east-wing room of the waterside hall, walks on a small path along the eastern shore of the pool, and reaches Ruyu Ting (Breeding-the-Fish Pavilion), a wooden structure of Ming origin. Southeast of this pavilion, the pool water gathers into a pond on which a slightly arched bridge of stone slabs was built. This bridge appears like a miniature of the stone bridges frequently seen in and around Suzhou, most of which were constructed in the early days after this garden was founded. One crosses over the bridge to the foot of the hill, and the path branches out in two directions. In one direction it leads into a cave on the hill and winds up at the rockery near a hexagonal pavilion.

In the other direction it proceeds westward along the cliffs south of the pool and reaches a winding bridge at the southwest corner of the pool. The bridge is low and it practically touches the surface of the water. It leads toward the west to a winding corridor and a small court beyond a round moon gate. In this small court, a smaller pool is dug to link up with the larger one, and lake stones, flowers, and trees are scattered about in the small court. This is the quietest and the most secluded spot in the garden (Fig. XIV-2). The original library (called Jiancao Lou), however, is no longer there.

The pool occupies about 660 square meters of this garden. It is concentrated primarily in one area, except that in its southeastern and southwestern corners it extends out to form two bays. At each of the two entrances to the pool there is a stone-slab bridge. The surface of the water appears broad and spacious, while the two winding bays contrast with the main body of the pool. However, the waterside hall on the north shore is a little too straight and flat, and therefore appears dull and monotonous. On the eastern and western shores of the pool there is also a lack of depth. The rockery south of the pool is piled with earth, and beside the pool are steep precipices and dangerous paths piled with lake stones. When one looks far into the distance from north of the pool, one can see the rocks on the hill, rugged and craggy, and the trees, green and luxuriant. The chief contrapositional scenery in the garden is in this area (Figs. XIV-3 and XIV-4). Stone paths, the pool, and precipices are placed together, and the three serve as foils for each other. This kind of device is also used in Huanxiu Shanzhuang (Mountain Villa of Encircled Elegance), Wangshi Yuan (The Retired Fisherman's Garden), and other gardens, as it was a technique commonly employed when piling rockeries and channeling waters in Suzhou during the Ming and the Qing Dynasties.

Not many stones are used on this hill, but the stone paths are tortuous and the caves and ravines are full of variety. However, the stone cliffs standing against the sunlight lack ever-changing shadows; they appear flat, dull, and lacking in depth. In the eastern part of the garden, two-story buildings and high walls come into view with no obstructions; with nothing to serve as a screen they have to be shut out. This is another defect of this garden.

Note

1. In the last part about the County of Wu, in vol. 3 of *Records of Folk Songs Collected*, by Zhang Songzhai, in the fiftieth year of the reign of Emperor Kangxi of the Qing Dynasty, it was written:

   Yi Pu used to be the Medicine Orchard of Duke Wen Wensu, but it is now the temporary residence of Jiang Jijian from Laiyang, who changed the name of the place to Jingting Shanfang (Respect-to-Pavilion Hill-Lodge).

   Also see Record of Jingting Shanfang, by Wei Xi, and *Records of Jiang's Yi Pu* and *Continued Records of Yi Pu*, by Wang Wan, and *Records of Nianzhuo Tang*, by Huang Zongxi, all of the Qing Dynasty. All these are recorded in the first part of vol. 39 of *Annals of Wu County* in Minguo.

XV

Huanxiu Shanzhuang
(Mountain Villa of Encircled Elegance)

Located at No. 280 Jingde Street, Huanxiu Shanzhuang (Mountain Villa of Encircled Elegance) was first founded during the reign of Emperor Qianlong of the Qing Dynasty. Initially, it was a private garden owned by a high official. Later, it underwent many vicissitudes, when the garden prospered and then declined. In the last years of the reign of Emperor Daoguang, it became part of the ancestral hall of a Wang family and was renamed Huanxiu Shanzhuang.[1] Before 1949, all the buildings in the garden, except for Buqiu Fang (Replenishing-Autumn Landboat) (also called Buqiu Shanzhuang), were destroyed and this garden became dilapidated. The rockery that is preserved to this date, according to records, was designed by Ge Yuliang, a famous rockery artist during the reign of Emperor Qianlong.[2] In artistic excellence, this work should be ranked first among all the lake-stone rockeries in Suzhou (Fig. XV-1).

This garden covers only a little over 660 meters, but its limited space is fully utilized. A hill is made the major scenic object; a pool is second in importance (Figs. XV-2 and XV-3); and winding paths figure largely in the artistic composition, achieving a place of rare beauty. The rockery to the east of the pool is the major part (Figs. XV-1 and XV-5), with the secondary part the hill on the north; the water in the pool winds about between the two parts and serves beautifully as a foil for the rockery. The original flower hall is located south of the pool, and is linked by a corridor in the west with Wenquan Ting (Asking-for-the-Springs Pavilion) and Buqiu Fang (Replenishing-Autumn Landboat) (Fig. XV-8). Along the corridor there is a two-story attic; one can go up there to view the distant scenery.

The secondary part of the rockery leans close to the wall at the northwest corner of the garden, while on the side that faces the pool there are cliffs on which two Chinese characters, "Feixue" (Flying-Snow), are inscribed, indicating the old site of the Feixue Quan (Flying-Snow Springs).

The major part of the rockery may be subdivided into front and rear sections. It rises, with an earthen slope in the northeastern part facing the garden; on the southwest are piles of lake stones. In between there are two ravines, one stretching from south to north, and the other from northwest to southeast. The two meet in the middle of the rockery, dividing it into three areas. The entire front section and all of the outside are piled with rocks that simulate peaks, ridges, and steep precipices; but inside of this rockery there is an empty, hollow cave (Fig. XV-1). At the rear section of the rockery facing the pool, there are stone cliffs made of lake stones and between the two sections there is a ravine 1.5 meters wide and 4 to 6 meters high (Fig. XV-6). Although the two sections of the rockery are detached, they appear to exist as a single entity. Running from west to east, they are much like a mountain range, but they suddenly break up into overhanging cliffs and steep precipices at the shore of the pool, in the words of Zhang Nanyuan, "as if at the foot of a high mountain, severed by creeks and cut off by ravines."[3]

The major peak of the rockery is at the southwestern corner; it is surrounded by the three lower, secondary peaks, as foils, with ravines running on its left and right. Stones are placed over the ravines to serve as beams. In this way there is contrast between solid and void, so that the rockery appears majestic and steep, with a lively shape that is ever shifting (Fig. XV-5 and XV-7).

Starting from Wenquan Ting (Asking-for-the-Springs Pavilion) to the west of the pool, one walks past Qu Qiao (The Winding Bridge) and comes to a small path along the pool. At the side of the path is a stiff cliff four meters high, and underneath is the pool. Inside the hillock are a stone cave and a stone chamber. A small path leads to the stone cave. The diameter of the cave is three meters, and the height is almost 2.7 meters.

Inside the cave are a stone table and several stone seats. There are five or six apertures for lighting and ventilation on the four walls of the cave. Beside the stone table is another stone cave about half a meter in diameter that goes down to the surface of the water. The light form the open sky and the color of the water are both reflected inside this small cave, achieving unique artistic imagery.

Once outside the cave one faces the ravine and the gorges, which are surrounded by overhanging stone cliffs; a secondary rockery in the northwest serves as contrapositional scenery. Here we have come to the most secluded spot in the rockery, and one of great depth (Fig. XV-6) . Outside the ravine one goes up the stone steps that wind around the rear section of the hill; the ground level up there is over four meters above the earth. The hilly path is built along narrow, perilous areas and there one looks down at the winding bridge and the pool as if from an overhanging cliff.

For detailed treatment of rockeries, reference is made to the conditions of natural lime rocks that have been beaten and corroded by rainwater and are piled to assume different shapes: some, like the hill peaks, resemble balls; some, like the vertical objects on the stone cliffs, look like long, narrow strips; some others, like the stone cliffs close to the walls in the southeastern corner, seem somewhat like thin flakes; and still others are in irregular shapes. The main bodies and surfaces of the entire hillock are properly arranged without the defect of containing broken pieces scattered in disorder. The stones are piled like lake-stone veins. Viewed from the southeastern corner of the major section of the rockery or from the yet-unrenovated portions of the summit, the mortar originally used to fill in the crevices of rocks now closely resembles the creviced rocks in the natural world.

The stone caves are built with an arched or vaulted roof, resembling karst-corroded caves. Like real caves, yet very solid and strong, after two hundred years they show no trace of fissures or slight shifts in location. As Ge Yuliang once said:

If only the big and small pieces of stone are hooked and girdled together in the way a ring-shaped bridge is built, the structure can last for a thousand years. Only when it is exactly the same as a real hill or cave can one say a good job has been done.[4]

This can be deemed a true and well-founded statement when we consider the central phenomena as evidence. The overhanging rocks that jut out from the stone cliffs should also be hooked and girdled with lake stones; only then can they last long and appear natural. By adopting the above-mentioned superior approach, the whole hill is brought together as a unified entity. No kudzu vines or wisterias are needed to cover up the ugly spots; the rockery appears to be naturally solid and of one piece.

The use of stone for special needs is observed everywhere on the hill. On peaks, cliffs, caves, gorges, banks along the creeks, and other places that attract attention, stones of fine shapes and in large sizes are used. Careful selection of stones is especially essential for constructing peaks and cliffs. In the rear section of the rockery, located close to a wall encircling the garden and other less-prominent places, the stones used may be of a relatively low quality, and ordinary yellow stones would be good enough for the stones that are perpetually under water in a pool, or used for ravines. In that way the lake stones are used economically, but the result are good.

Notes

1. See the entry of Shen Shixing Zhai in the first part of vol. 39 of *Annals of the County of Wu* in Minguo, and *Records of Feixue Quan* (*Flying-Snow Springs*), by Jiang Gongfei during the reign of Emperor Qianlong in the Qing Dynasty. Also see *Records of Gengyin Yizhuang as Owned by the Wang Family*, in Book 4 of *Manuscripts of Xianzhi Tang* by Feng Guifen in the second year of the reign of Emperor Guanxu of the Qing Dynasty:

   ...The locality for the founding of the garden today used to be known as Yue Pu (Music Orchard), which later became Jingde Shi (Jingde Temple)... then became the residence of Duke Shen Wending. Since the reign of Emperor Qianglong, the following people lived there: Minister of Criminal Law Jiang Ji, Minister Bi Yuan, and Duke San Wenjing, alias Shiyi, in that order. On the east there is a small garden.... It was one of the famous gardens in Suzhou.

2. See entry on "Piling Rockeries," in vol. 12 of *Lu Yuan Conghua* (*Miscellaneous Remarks on Lü Garden*, by Qian Yun of the Qing Dynasty:

   Lately, there is a man named Ge Yuliang, a native of Changzhou, whose way of piling a rockery is even better than the others. ...and the rockery in front of the study-hall in the home of Sun Guyun is also piled under his direction.

   Sun Guyun is Sun Jun, grandson of Sun Shiyi (see note 1), according to vol. 10 of *Molin Jinhua*, by Jiang Baoling of the Qing Dynasty.

3. See Biography of Zhang Nanyuan, included in *Zhangzhang Ji*, by Huang Zongxi of the Qing Dynasty, as quoted in *Zhejiang Lu* (*Records of Clever Handicraftsmen*) in the combined edition of vol. iii and iv of *Collected Publications of Zhongguo Yingzhao Xueshe*.

4. See the entry, "Rockery-Piling," in vol. 12 of *Lo Yuan Conghua* (*Miscellaneous Remarks on Lü Garden*.)

XVI

Yongcui Shanzhuang
(Mountain Villa of Embracing Emerald)

Yongcui Shanzhuang (Mountain Villa of Embracing Emerald) is located to the west of the original site of the ancient Hanhan Quan (Hanhan Springs), inside the second gate of Huqiu (Tiger Hill). It was founded in the tenth year of the reign of Emperor Guangxu of the Qing Dynasty, or in 1884 A.D.[1] After repairs were made in the 1950s, it became a part of the Huqiu Park (Tiger-Hill Park).

The special feature of this garden's layout is the way it utilizes the natural hilly slope of Huqiu (Tiger Hill) (Fig. XVI-7). The general plan of the garden consists of its almost oblong shape, with a total area of more than one-half hectare, and its ladderlike form. It contains four layers, each rising higher than the last as the level of the hill rises, so that the whole assumes the pattern of a platform garden (Figs. XVI-1 through XVI-4).

The garden gate is at the south, while the main building, Linglan Jingshe (The Scholar's-Retreat-amid-the-Fairies'-Billows), is on the north. The plans for the northern and the southern ends are symmetrical, while the central area, which includes Yuejia Xuan (Harnessing-the-Moon Lounge) (Fig. XVI-6) and Wenquan Ting (Asking-for-the-Springs Pavilion), is arranged asymmetrically.

Inside the garden gate is a hall three rooms wide named Baoweng Xuan (Holding-the-Jar Hall), with Hanhan Springs just outside the courtyard wall. Not far north of the hall, a terrace rises above ground level; on it, Wenquan Ting (Asking-for-the-Springs Pavilion) was built. This pavilion is somewhat out of proportion because it is too large for its setting.

North and west of Wenquan Ting is a lake-stone rockery on which sweet-scented oleanders, pomegranates, crape myrtles, boxwoods, lacebark pines, and parasols are planted, and several stone peaks are built. The arrangement is simple and compact. The garden walls are barely visible amid the groves of trees, so that the trees inside and outside the walls merge together as one entity. This part of the garden thus appears particularly lively.

If one walks up the rockery's winding stone steps and reaches the terrace in front of Linglan Jingshe (The Scholar's-Retreat-amid-the-Fairies'-Billows) (Figs. XVI-5), the main building of the garden, one can look down and view the scenery of the whole garden. There are luxuriant green trees and winding stone paths that meander about, and one can delight in the sight of the hills and the groves.

To the east of Linglan Jingshe (The Scholar's-Retreat-amid-the-Fairies'-Billows) and jutting out beyond the garden walls is another spacious terrace where, looking down from a great height, one can enjoy the beautiful scenery all along the foot of Huqui (Tiger Hill). Behind Linglan Jingshe (The Scholar's-Retreat-amid-the-Fairies'-Billows), along the same axis, and beyond a small courtyard is a rear hall, Songchun Yi (Sending-off-Spring Chamber). There the courtyard is encircled by walls; again, the arrangement is simple and shipshape.

Because this garden's topography was used to full advantage, a platform garden was created, and it does not seem to matter whether there is a pool or not. On the one hand, ingenuity was used in making full use of the natural attributes within and nearby, while on the other hand, scenic objects were borrowed from beyond the garden. For example: the view upward at the pagoda on Huqiu (Tiger Hill) (Fig. XVI-7); the distant view of Shizi Shan (Lion Hill); and the view downward at the scenery all along the foot of Hiqiu (Tiger Hill). In each case, a little effort on the part of the observer brings great pleasure. In the central part of the garden, the layout is lively, the field of vision is broad, and one feels in close contact with the natural surroundings. This is a small but truly well-planned scenic area in the Tiger Hill region.

Note

1. See "Records of Yongcui Shanzhuang," by Yang Xian, as given in *Investigations into the Territories*, vol. 19 of *Annals of the County of Wu*, in Minguo.

XVII
He Yuan
(Crane Garden)[1]

He Yuan (Crane Garden), at No. 4 Hanjia Lane, was founded toward the end of the Qing Dynasty. The garden is situated west of the owner's private residence. A pool is at the center of the layout, around which are a hill and rocks, flowers, trees, and buildings (Figs. XVII-2). The total area is nearly 1300 square meters.

The garden gate faces south, and the lounge immediately inside the gate contains five rooms built in the width; it is screened from sight by whitewashed walls and tracery windows so that visitors at the gate cannot look directly into the garden. Emerging from the lounge at the gate in the northeastern corner, one comes to a long corridor that runs all the way through the garden from the south to the north. West of the corridor, there are Simian Ting (Facing-Four-Side Hall), and a big hall toward the north (Fig. XVII-3). Simian Ting is right in the middle, dividing the whole garden into two parts, the northern and the southern parts. Simian Ting faces onto the lounge at the gate, and along the whitewashed walls there are parterres where flowers and trees are planted. The place is further dotted with several vertically erected stones. All this provides contrapositional scenery to the south of Simian Ting.

Simian Ting also faces a big hall on the north, and between the two buildings is a pool, around which are piled lake stones and fair-sized plants such as jasmines, a south China plant named Hanxiao, clover, cherry-apple trees, laurel, sweet-scented oleander, crape myrtle, wintersweet, and some evergreens. This is the garden's major scenic area (Fig. XVII-4).

To the west of the pool is a double-eaved staircase-shaped house, which is linked to the big hall by a winding corridor. The house and the long corridor on its east serve to break the monotony and void of the wall surface and to enrich the garden scenery. The long corridor is tortuous and interesting and, together with the courtyard walls, it forms several small courts where various flowers and tall bamboos are planted. This part is the creme de la creme of the whole garden (Fig. XVII-1).

South of the house is an earthen mound on which there is a small, hexagonal pavilion. Scattered about the pavilion are flowers and trees such as magnolias from Guangdong, parasols, Chinese Yews, lacebark pines, palm trees, hibiscus, and pear trees. Against the wall on the west, are bushes and creepers such as wisterias, banksia roses, monthly-blooming roses, and climbing figs. The high garden walls are barely visible amidst all the greenery (Fig. XVII-5). One branch of the pool water passes through the breach and extends toward the earthen mound to form a bay, over which a bridge is constructed to indicate the distant source of the water.

This garden is rather small, and the layout is closely linked to the residential quarters. The arrangement of the hillock and the pool and the treatment of the scenic details are simple and plain; the outstanding feature of the garden scenery as a whole is its openness and brightness. The corridors and halls on the two flanks are admirably laid out, and their dimensions are visually agreeable. The earthen mound and the water bay in the southwestern section do not follow the hackneyed pattern of being enclosed by the buildings around them. However, the centrality of the pool and the sameness of its three main halls and their orientation indicate a lack of variety and thus are a shortcoming of this garden.

Note

1. See *Records of He Yuan*, by Jin Tianyu of Minguo. On a stone inscription in the garden is written:

   During the reigns of the two Emperors, Guangxu and Xuantong, in the Qing Dynasty, a man named Hong Luting, a district superintendent of Huayang, fixed his residence at Hanjia Lane and built a garden to the west of it ... and called it He Yuan (Crane Garden).

XVIII
Chang Yuan
(Carefree Garden)

Located at No. 22 Miaotang Lane, Chang Yuan (Carefree Garden) lies to the east of its owner's living quarters. At the center of the garden is a pool, surrounded by halls and lounges, landboats, pavilions, and corridors; the layout is a closed-in arrangement with a circular route around it. The garden is small, with an area of a little over one mu; yet there is an abundance of garden scenery and very deep views. It is the most representative of the small gardens in Suzhou (Figs. XVIII-2 and XVIII-4).

The garden gate is placed at the southeast corner, and one passes through the lounge inside the gate and the small courtyard to reach Tonghua Shuwu (Parasol-Flower Studio). Beyond this studio, as one's field of vision is suddenly broadened, one may view the whole garden, including a pool, pavilions, and corridors. The pool is at the center of the garden, stretching long and narrow from south to north. Lake stones pave the pool's shores, where flowers and trees are planted sparsely.

Near the southern end of the pool, a winding bridge divides the water surface in two. To the east of the pool and along the shore, a long corridor winds and meanders, with several rises and falls (Fig. XVIII-1). There are two small pavilions situated along the corridor, both of which face the pool on one side. The southern hexagonal pavilion (Fig. XVIII-6) is named Yanhuichengqu (Extending-Splendor-to-Induce-Delight), while the northern one is called Qijian (Rest Pavilion). Between the winding corridor and the garden wall is a small courtyard inside which lake stones, a grove of bamboos, and banana trees are planted. Along the wall on one side of the corridor, there are cave doors and tracery windows, which seem to resemble painted pictures.

Further north there is a larger, square-shaped pavilion. When turning west, one comes to Liuyun Shanfang (Lingering-Cloud Hill House), the main building of the garden. South of Liuyun Shanfang, facing the pool, is a spacious terrace on level ground (Fig. XVIII-5).

From the winding corridor west of the pool one proceeds on to a boat hall named Diwochenjin (Washing-My-Dusty-Clothing), which stretches long and narrow from south to north and faces the pool on the east. Unfortunately, the boat hall's foundations are stiff and straight and lie too high above the water, a case of poor design judgment.

Going south from here, one passes through the square pavilion and follows the corridor upward to Daiyue Ting (Waiting-for-the-Moon Pavilion) on the southwest. This pavilion is built on the rockery and is the highest point in the garden. As one looks down from here, the whole garden is in view (Fig. XVIII-3). One may go down the stone steps of this pavilion to reach the stone cave below, or follow the slanting corridor toward Tonghua Shuwu (Parasol-Flower Studio), thus completing a circuit of the whole garden.

There are, relatively speaking, many buildings in the garden, and scenic details are treated with particular care. The dimensions of the buildings generally are in good proportion to the surroundings, and the arrangements of hills and rocks and flowers and trees attain the effect of being few but exquisite. The whole garden gives the impression of light delicacy and refined elegance.

XIX

Hu Yuan

(Kettle Garden)[1]

Hu Yuan (Kettle Garden), now dismantled, was located to the west of the owner's residential quarters at No. 7 Miaoting Lane (Fig. XIX-3). The garden gate is shaped like a round cave; inside the gate is a corridor that leads to a hall in the north, a lounge in the south, and a hexagonal half-pavilion in the middle. At the center of the garden is a pool (Fig. XIX-2 and XIX-4). The hall and corridor on the north and east face the water, with the shores of the pool lying low and flat. The terrace in front of the hall on the north projects out above the water, and the hexagonal pavilion hovers right next to the pool, so it enhances the sense of the pool's spaciousness.

There is no rockery in the garden except for a few stone peaks here and there around the pool, but there are mixed plantings of cherry-apple trees, lacebark pines, wintersweets, Tianzhu (literally, heavenly bamboo) and bamboo groves, which have the effect of sometimes concealing and sometimes revealing the pool, the rocks, the pavilions, and the corridors from view.

Two bridges that link up the opposite shores of the pool vault over the pool. These small bridges are low, simple, and plain, and harmonize with the pool; their only shortcoming is that their iron railings fail to match the tone of the rest of the garden. The garden walls on the west are tall and dull-looking, so some tracery windows are set on the upper parts of the walls along with creeper plants such as climbing figs. Also, a parterre, some stone peaks, a bamboo grove, and other trees are placed along the walls to make a more lively picture (Fig. XIX-5). The lake stone parterre in front of the hall at the northwestern corner of the garden matches the pool and the small bridges, and so is unique in style.

The total area of this garden is only about 300 square meters. However, the pool, with its many twists, is picturesque, and the small bridges over it and the trees and lake stones on the pool's shores are placed irregularly; the lacebark pines slant over the pool's surface, adding sufficient variety and a strong feeling of depth to the garden space. Whether one looks from the south to the north or vice versa, one can view an attractive scene formed by a deep grove of dark bamboo trees (Fig. XIX-1). This is a good example of a small garden with a pool as the major scenic object.

Note

1. Because of the need for industrial development, this garden has been dismantled.

XX
Canli Yuan
(Remnant-Grain Garden)

Founded toward the end of the Qing Dynasty, Canli Yuan (Remnant-Grain Garden) was located at No. 34 Zhuangjiaqiao Lane. Originally, it was part of the residence of a salt merchant from Yangzhou.

The residence is made up of three sections, the middle, the eastern, and the western, and the garden is located to the east of the flower hall in the residence's eastern section (Figs. XX-2 and XX-3). The garden is very small, containing about 140 square meters, equivalent only to the area of one of the halls in the larger Suzhou gardens. But the architect made good use of the limited space, so the pavilion, rockery, pool, and flowers and trees in the garden are well arranged in an attractive design that has sufficient rise and fall, tortuousness and depth.

From the rear section of the residence, one passes through a round cave door named Jinke (Brocaded Nest) to enter the garden, a device the Chinese invented to conceal the rest of the garden. The pool is at the center of the layout, and around it are parterres and groves of trees. The pool's shores are paved with lake stones, and rocks project out over its surface. In the southwestern corner of the garden wall and along the shore of the pool are rock peaks which harmonize with the stone peak at the entrance of the garden.

Scattered about are different flowers and trees including laurel, Tianzhu (literally, heavenly bamboo), and wintersweet. All add to the feeling of depth in the scenery. On the walls, in addition to several tracery windows, there are climbing figs, ivy, and other creeper plants sprawling all over, thus giving plenty of variety to the otherwise dull and monotonous wall surfaces (Fig. XX-5).

West of the pool and immediately next to the garden wall is a rockery, inside of which is a stone cave. One enters the cave and goes up the steps to a half-pavilion, Guacang Ting (Green-Juniper Pavilion) (Fig. XX-4) before entering the adjacent flower hall. This half-pavilion is built at the highest point of the garden, and is the chief point from which to enjoy the scenery; it also is one of the focal points of the garden design (Fig. XX-1).

The traditional treatment of small garden space is very successfully employed in this garden. The relative positions of the half-pavilion, stone cave, pool, and parterre fit in well with the rest of the garden design. However, the shores of the pool are a little too high above the water, there are too few rises and falls, and the surfaces of the encircling walls obviously lack variety.

XXI

The Courtyard and Studio at Wangxima Lane

The residence at Wangxima Lane was built during the reign of Emperor Guanxu of the Qing Dynasty. At the southeastern corner and in a secluded and quiet section of the residence are a studio and a courtyard (Fig. XXI-2). There are transparent lattice doors and windows-above-balustrades on all four sides of the studio, so one does not feel cramped in the small room (Fig. XXI-3). On the east, the studio faces the courtyard, while its south and north lead to pavilions and corridors (Fig. XXI-1). There is a small court on the west where lake stones are piled and orange osmanthus trees planted, and there is scenery on all four sides of the studio (Fig. XXI-4).

Inside the courtyard, the pavilion and the corridor are relatively small, and around them are laurels, crape myrtles, cherry-apple trees, and banksia roses. In every season there are some flowers and trees to enjoy. Against the wall on the east is an earthen mound, and lake stones are used to build stone caves, parterres, and tree-pits. Also there is a winding path leading past a pavilion to the mound and then descending through a cave. This courtyard occupies very little space (about 300 square meters), but it is tortuous and full of depth, and there is a proper arrangement of buildings, flowers and trees, and lake stones, where dimensions are in keeping with the rest. This is a good model of a courtyard and studio in an old Suzhou residence.

Fig. I-1 A scene southeast of the central part of Lingering-Here Garden.

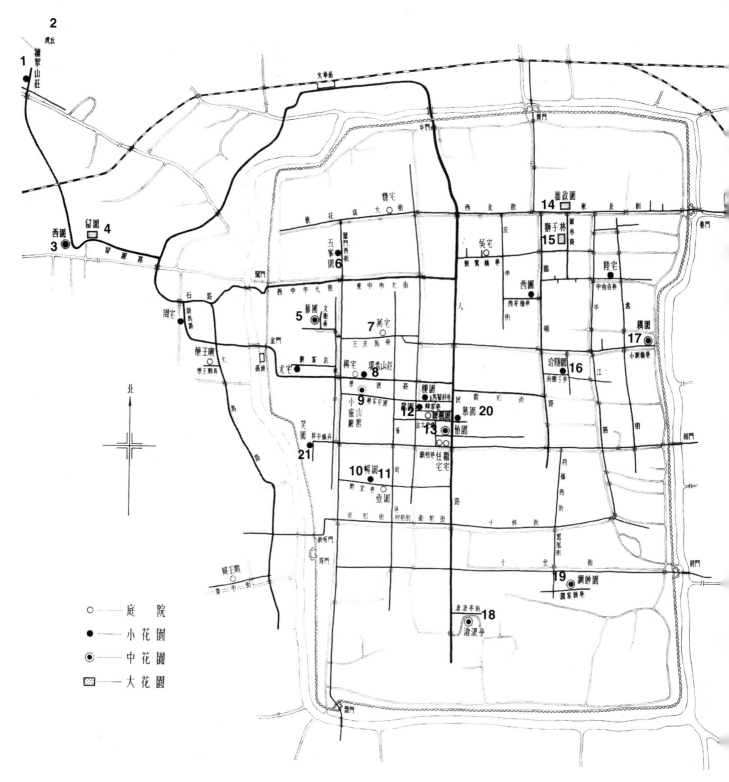

Fig. I-2 Locations of the major classical gardens in Suzhou.

○—residence and courtyard
●—small garden
◉—medium-sized garden
▨—big garden

1. Yongcui Shanzhuang (Mountain Villa of Embracing Emerald)
2. Huqiu (Tiger Hill)
3. Xi Yuan (West Garden)
4. Liu Yuan (Lingering-Here Garden)
5. Yi Pu (Art Orchard)
6. Wufeng Yuan (Five-Peak Garden)
7. The Residence of Wan, Wangxima Lane
8. Huanxiu Shanzhuang (Mountain Villa of Encircled Elegance)
9. Xiaolinyanshan Guan (Little-Linyan Hill-Lodge)
10. Chang Yuan (Carefree Garden)

11. Hu Yuan (Kettle Garden)
12. He Yuan (Crane Garden)
13. Yi Yuan (Happy Garden)
14. Zhuozheng Yuan (Humble Administrator's Garden)
15. Shizilin (Forest of Lions Garden)
16. Qiayin Yuan (Harmony-Hermitage Garden)
17. Ou Yuan (Twin Garden)
18. Canglang Ting (Surging-Wave-Pavilion Garden)
19. Wangshi Yuan (Retired Fisherman's Garden)
20. Mu Yuan (Adoration Garden)
21. Xiao Yuan (Smiling Garden)

144

Fig. II-1 Central part of The Humble Administrator's Garden.

Fig. II-2 Courtyard scene at the residence at No. 12 Iron-Bottle Lane.

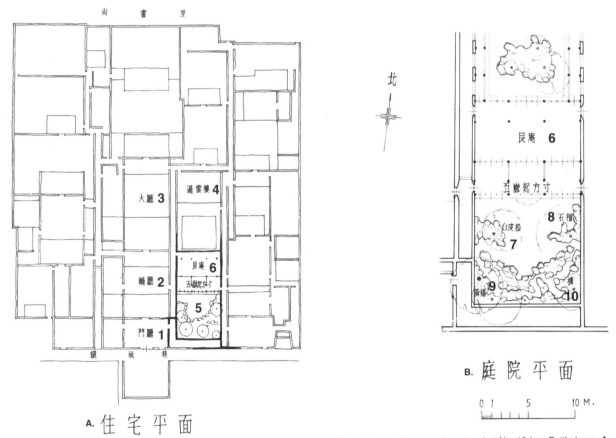

齒書里

大廳 3　　過雲樓 4

喬廳 2

艮庵 6
五嶽起方寸

5

門廳 1

鐵瓶巷

A. 住宅平面

北

艮庵 6

五嶽起方寸

白皮松
7

石榴 8

前場
9

櫸
10

B. 庭院平面

0 1　　5　　10 M.

Fig. II-3 Plan of the residence and courtyard at No. 12 Iron-Bottle Lane. **A.** Plan of the residence: **(1)** Entrance, lobby; **(2)** Lounge; **(3)** Hall; **(4)** Passing-Cloud Two-Storied Building; **(5)** Courtyard.
B. Plan of the Courtyard: **(6)** Building; **(7)** Lacebark; **(8)** Pomegranate; **(9)** Boxwood; **(10)** Chinese hackberry.

Fig. II-4 Courtyard scene at the residence at No. 22 Iron-Bottle Lane.

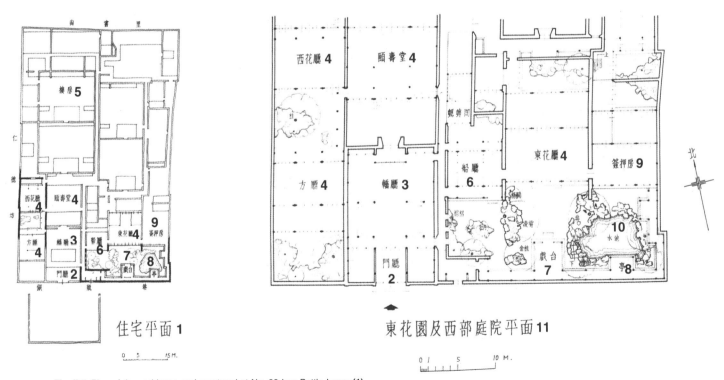

西花廳 4 　頤壽堂 4

樓房 5

西花廳 4
頤壽堂 4

方廳 4
轎廳 3

門廳 2

住宅平面 1

0 5 15 M.

蠡鰤同

西花廳 4　　頤壽堂 4

方廳 4　　轎廳 3　　船廳 6　　東花廳 4　　簽押房 9

門廳 2　　戲台 7　　水池 10　　亭 8

北

東花園及西部庭院平面 11

0 1 5 10 M.

Fig. II-5 Plan of the residence and courtyard at No. 22 Iron-Bottle Lane: (1) Plan of the residence; (2) Entrance, (3) Lounge; (4) Hall; (5) Two-story building; (6) Boat Hall; (7) Stage for Performers; (8) Pavilion; (9) Clerk's room; (10) Pool; (11) Plan of the garden and a part of the residence.

Fig. II-6 Courtyard scene at an unidentified residence.

Fig. II-7 Courtyard of an unidentified residence at Liujiabang.

148

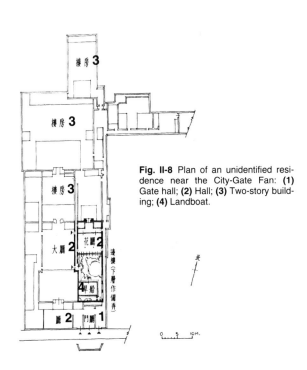

Fig. II-8 Plan of an unidentified residence near the City-Gate Fan: **(1)** Gate hall; **(2)** Hall; **(3)** Two-story building; **(4)** Landboat.

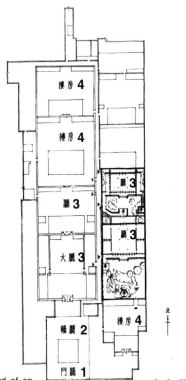

Fig. II-9 Plan of the courtyard of an unidentified residence on Jingde Street: **(1)** Gate hall; **(2)** Lounge; **(3)** Hall; **(4)** Two-story building.

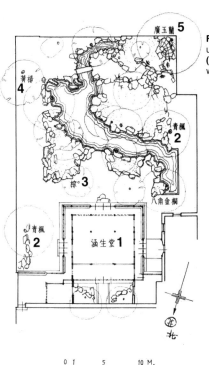

Fig. II-10 Plan of the courtyard of an unidentified residence at Liujiabang: **(1)** Hall; **(2)** Maple; **(3)** Palm; **(4)** Boxwood; **(5)** Magnolia.

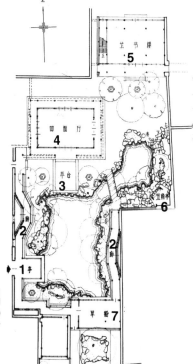

Fig. II-11 Plan of the Half Garden in Middle Yuji Lane: **(1)** Entrance and pavilion; **(2)** Corridor; **(3)** Terrace; **(4)** Hall; **(5)** Library; **(6)** Pentagon pavilion; **(7)** Landboat.

149

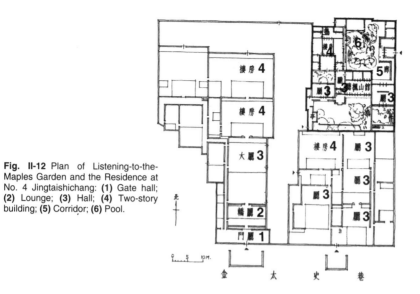

Fig. II-12 Plan of Listening-to-the-Maples Garden and the Residence at No. 4 Jingtaishichang: **(1)** Gate hall; **(2)** Lounge; **(3)** Hall; **(4)** Two-story building; **(5)** Corridor; **(6)** Pool.

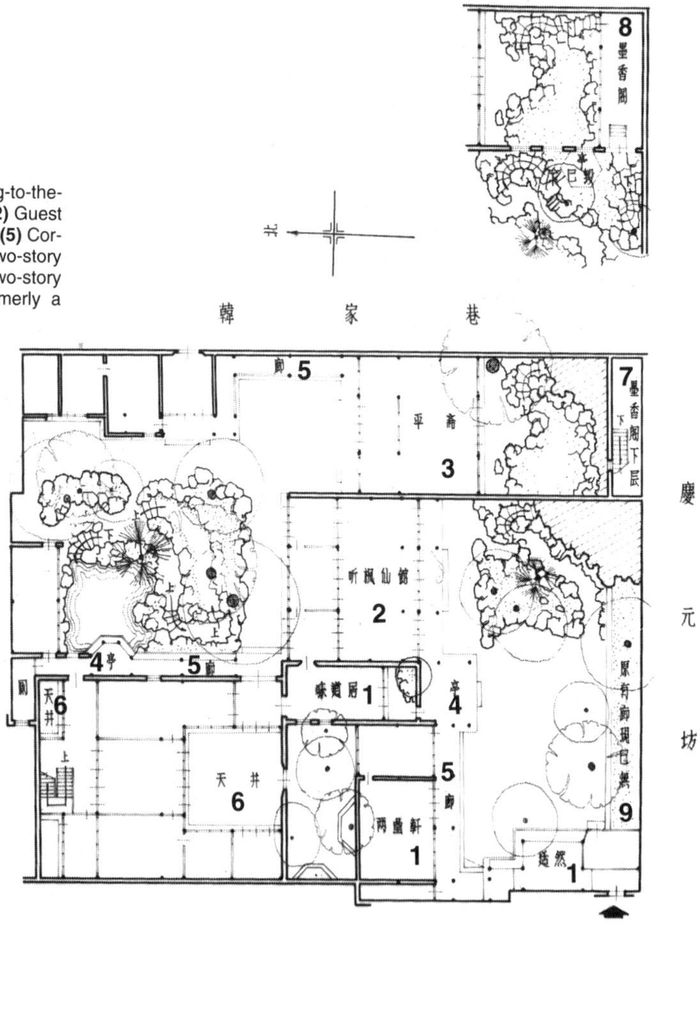

Fig. II-13 Plan of Listening-to-the-Maples Garden: **(1)** Lounge; **(2)** Guest House; **(3)** Study; **(4)** Pavilion; **(5)** Corridor; **(6)** Small yard; **(7)** Two-story pavilion, ground floor; **(8)** Two-story pavilion, upper floor; **(9)** Formerly a corridor, now destroyed.

Fig. II-14 Hillock and pool seen through the tracery windows at the Old-Trees-Intertwining-One-Another of the Lingering-Here Garden.

Fig. II-15 View of the courtyard scene through the casementless windows at Crane Hall in Lingering-Here Garden.

Fig. II-16 Central part of The Humble Administrator's Garden divided up into separable areas, showing the wave-like walls, rockeries, and trees.

Fig. 11-17 Courtyards separated by flower walls in the central part of Lingering-Here Garden.

Fig. 11-18 Watery area divided by Little-Flying-Rainbow Corridor Bridge in The Humble Administrator's Garden.

Fig. II-19 View of the courtyard from inside The House for the Aged Giants of Groves and Springs in Lingering-Here Garden.

Fig. II-20 A Branch-from-Bamboo Lounge in The Retired Fisherman's Garden.

Fig., II-21 Garden scenery in front of Distant-Fragrance Hall in The Humble Administrator's Garden.

Fig. II-22 Garden scenery north of Distant-Fragrance Hall in The Humble
Administrator's Garden.

Fig. II-23 Garden scenery north of Waterside-Pavilion-amid the-Hillock-and-
Pool in the Twin Garden.

Fig. II-24 Garden scenery west of
Waterside-Pavilion-amid-the-Hillock-
and-Pool in the Twin Garden.

Fig. II-25 View of the northeast garden scenery from the Bright-Zither Two-Storied Building in Lingering-Here Garden.

Fig. II-26 Garden scenery viewed from a window of A-Branch-from-Bamboo Lounge in The Retired Fisherman's Garden.

Fig. II-27 A winding corridor in The Retired Fisherman's Garden.

Fig. II-28 Garden scenery at the northeastern corner of the pool in The Retired Fisherman's Garden.

Fig. II-29 Garden scenery viewed from Little Square Hall in Forest of Lions Garden.

Fig. II-30 Just-Right Pavilion in the central part of Lingering-Here Garden.

Fig. II-31 View of Pavilion of Fragrant-Snow-and-Colorful Clouds from north of Loquat Garden in the The Humble Administrator's Garden.

Fig. II-32 View of Fit-to-Observe-Scenery-in-Two-Direction Pavilion, from the Inverted-Image Two-Storied Building in The Humble Administrator's Garden.

164

Fig. II-33 "Borrowed" scenery of the North-Temple Pagoda in the distance, from inside The Humble Administrator's Garden.

Fig. II-34 "Borrowed" scenery of the West-Garden Temple in the distance, from Comfortable-Whistle Pavilion in Lingering-Here Garden.

Fig. II-35 "Borrowed" scenery of adjacent areas in the central part of The Humble Administrator's Garden, from Fit-to-Observe-Scenery-in-Two-Direction Pavilion in the western part of the same garden.

Fig. II-36 View of Fit-to-Observe-Scenery-in-Two-Direction Pavilion in the western part of The Humble Administrator's Garden, from the central part of the same garden.

Fig. II-37 Bird's-eye view of Little-Surging-Wave Watercourt in the central part of The Humble Administrator's Garden.

Fig. II-38 Garden scenery in the central part of The Humble Administrator's Garden.

Fig. III-1 Pool in the western part of The Humble Administrator's Garden.

Fig. III-2 Surface of the pool in the central part of The Humble Administrator's Garden.

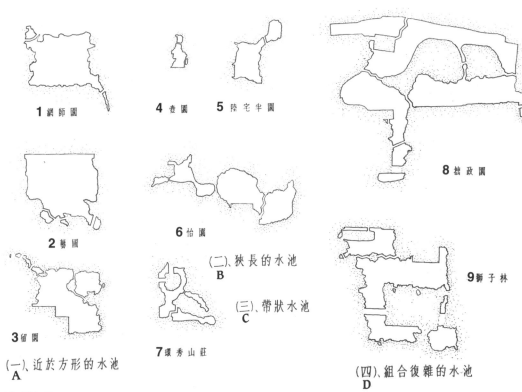

1 網師園　**4** 壺園　**5** 陸宅半園

8 拙政園

2 藝園　**6** 怡園

（二）、狹長的水池
B

3 留園

（三）、帶狀水池
C

7 環秀山莊

9 獅子林

（一）、近於方形的水池
A

（四）、組合復雜的水池
D

Fig. III-3 Plans of various pools.

A. Near-square-shaped
　1. Retired Fisherman's Garden
　2. Art Orchard
　3. Lingering-Here Garden
B. Long and narrow
　4. Kettle Garden
　5. Half Garden in the Residence of Lu
　6. Happy Garden
C. Belt-Shaped
　7. Mountain Villa of Encircled Elegance
D. Assorted
　8. Humble Administrator's Garden
　9. Forest of Lions Garden

Fig. III-4 Garden scenery along the shores of the pool in the central part of The Humble Administrator's Garden.

Fig. III-5 Pool in the central part of The Humble Administrator's Garden.

Fig. III-6 Water gate in Happy Garden.

Fig. III-7 Water gully in Lingering-Here Garden.

172

Fig. III-8 Pool and bridge south of Distant-Fragrance Hall in The Humble
Administrator's Garden.

Fig. III-9 Stone barriers for a lake stone bridge in Adoration Garden.

Fig. III-10 Little-Flying-Rainbow Corridor-Bridge in The Humble Administrator's Garden.

Fig. III-11 Stone bridge in The Humble Administrator's Garden.

Fig. III-12 Little-Red-Cliff Rockery in Forest of Lions Garden.

Fig. III-13 Water gully in The Retired Fisherman's Garden.

Fig. III-14 Yellow stone shore of a pool and reed marshes in the central part of The Humble Administrator's Garden.

Fig. III-15 Shore of a pool in the garden inside a residence at Wenjia'an.

177

Fig. III-16 Yellow stone shore of a pool in the northwestern corner of The Retired Fisherman's Garden.

Fig. III-17 Source of water for the pool built with lake stones in Mountain Villa of Encircled Elegance.

Fig. III-18 Rocky landing beside Breeze-from-the-Lotus-in-Four-Directions
Pavilion in The Humble Administrator's Garden.

Fig. III-19 Earthen shore and grove of trees west of the pool in the eastern part of The Humble Administrator's Garden.

Fig. III-20 Water gully in back of Tall-Bamboo Pavilion in Forest of Lions Garden.

182

Fig. IV-1 Gully under the rockery in Mountain Villa of Encircled Elegance.

Fig. IV-2 Paved path on the earthen hill in the central part of The Humble
Administrator's Garden.

Fig. IV-4 Rockery in Surging-Wave-Pavilion Garden.

Fig. IV-5 Rockery in the garden inside a residence at West-Hundred-Flowers Lane.

186

Fig. IV-6 Rockery and piled stones in the western part of Lingering-Here Garden.

Fig. IV-7 A corner of the rockery in Forest of Lions Garden.

Fig. IV-8 Rockery in the central part of Lingering-Here Garden.

Fig. IV-9 Lake stone rockery in Happy Garden.

190

Fig. IV-10 Lake stone rockery in Mountain Villa of Encircled Elegance.

Fig. IV-11 Yellow stone rockery and pool in Twin Garden.

Fig. IV-12 Southern entrance to the deep gully in the rockery in Twin Garden.

Fig. IV-13 Stone cliff facing the pool in Twin Garden.

194

Fig. IV-14 Rocky shore south of the pool in Art-Orchard Garden.

Fig. IV-15 Small-Forest-Lodge—a cave in the rockery, in Harmony-Hermitage Garden.

Fig. IV-16 Gate of a cave under the rockery in Surging-Wave-Pavilion Garden.

Fig. IV-17 Rocky cliff and gate of a cave in Mountain Villa of Encircled Elegance.

Fig. IV-18 Stone steps west of Encompassing-Jade Mountain House in the central part of Lingering-Here Garden.

Fig. IV-19 Auspicious-Cloud Peak in the former weaving prefect's Mansion.

Fig. IV-20 Cloud-Topping Peak in Lingering-Here Garden.

Fig. IV-21 Piled rocks beside hilly path in the central part of The Humble Administrator's Garden.

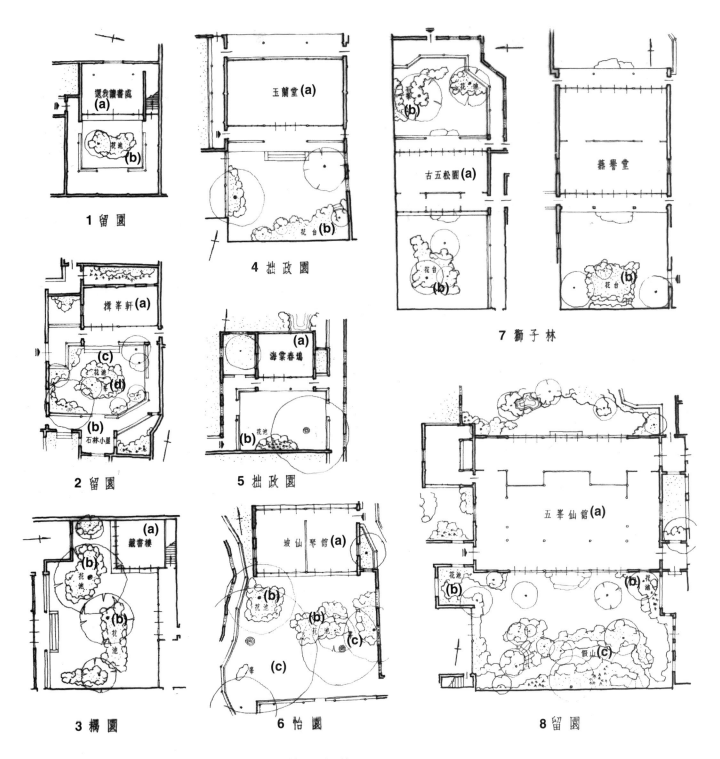

Fig. V-1 Plans of various courtyards in Suzhou gardens: **(1)** Lingering-Here Garden: **(a)** Restored-to-Me Study, **(b)** Flowers; **(2)** Lingering-Here Garden: **(a)** Salute-to-the Peak Hall, **(b)** Small House in the Stone Forest, **(c)** Flowers, **(d)** Rock-Peak; **(3)** Twin Garden: **(a)** Library, **(b)** Flowers; **(4)** Humble Administrator's Garden: **(a)** Magnolia Hall, **(b)** Flowers; **(5)** Humble Administrator's Garden: **(a)** Spring-Begonia-Cove House, **(b)** Flowers; **(6)** Happy Garden: **(a)** Hill-Slope-Fairies Music House, **(b)** Flowers, **(c)** Rock-Peak; **(7)** Forest of Lions Garden: **(a)** Five-Old-Pines Park, **(b)** Flowers; **(8)** Lingering-Here Garden: **(a)** Five-Peak Celestial House, **(b)** Flowers, **(c)** Rockery.

Fig. V-2 Bird's-eye view of the Loquat garden inside The Humble Administrator's Garden.

Fig. V-3 North of Little-Surging-Wave Watercourt in The Humble Administrator's Garden.

Fig. V-3 North of Little-Surging-Wave Watercourt in The Humble Administrator's Garden.

Fig. V-4 Section view in perspective: Little-Surging Wave Watercourt in The Humble Administrator's Garden.

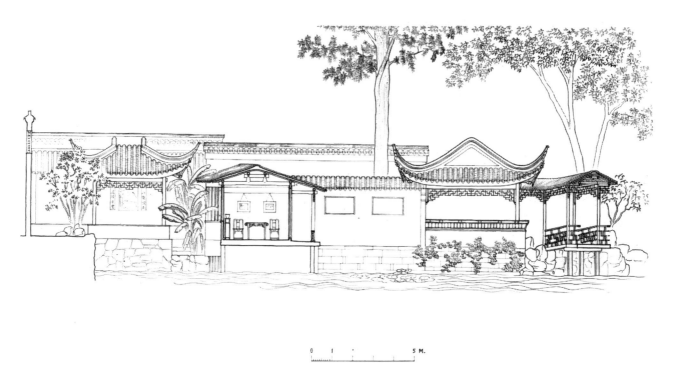

0   1   5 M.

Fig. V-5 West view of Little-Surging-Wave Watercourt of The Humble Administrator's Garden.

204

Fig. V-7 Section view in perspective of Small Courtyard of Stone Forest in Lingering-Here Garden.

Fig. V-8 Full view of Spring-Begonia-Cove House in The Humble Administrator's Garden.

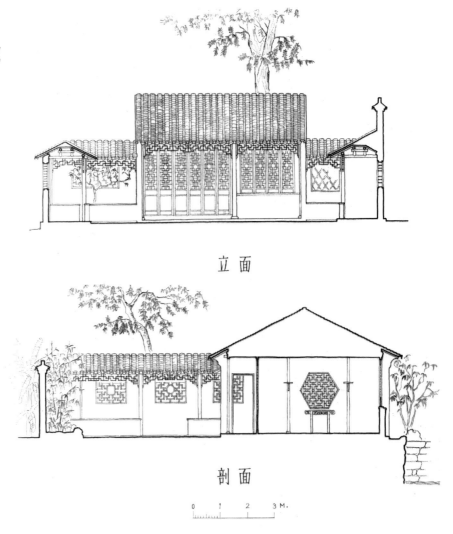

Fig. V-9 Front view and section view of Spring-Begonia-Cove House in The Humble Administrator's Garden.

立 面

剖 面

0   1   2   3 M.

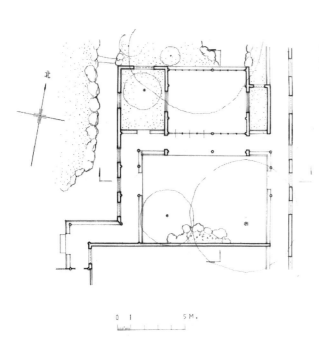

北

0 1   5 M.

Fig. V-10 Plan of Spring-Begonia-Cove House in The Humble Administrator's Garden.

Fig. V-11 Interior of Five-Peak Celestial Hall in Lingering-Here Garden.

208

Fig. V-12 Lotus-Root-Fragrance Waterside Pavilion in Happy Garden.

Fig. V-13 Distant-Fragrance Hall, viewed from outside, in The Humble Administrator's Garden.

210

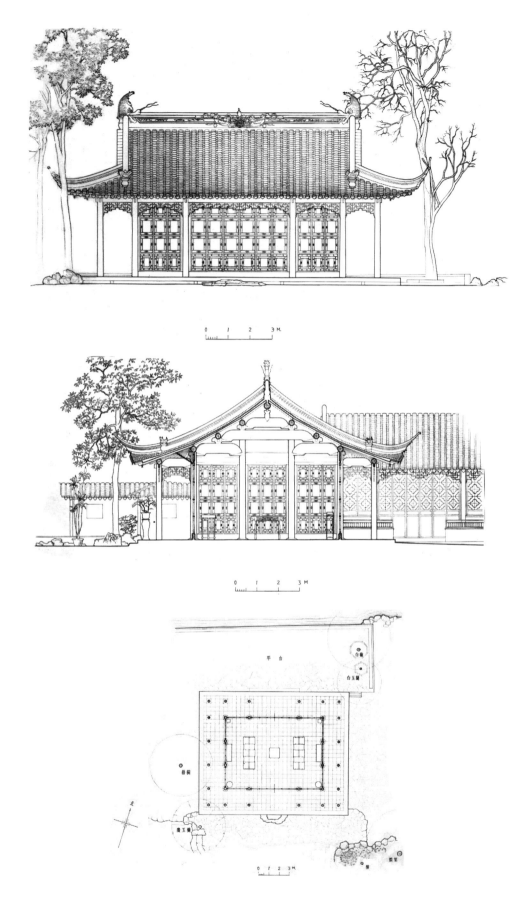

Fig. V-14 Survey drawings of the Distant-Fragrance Hall in The Humble Administrator's Garden.

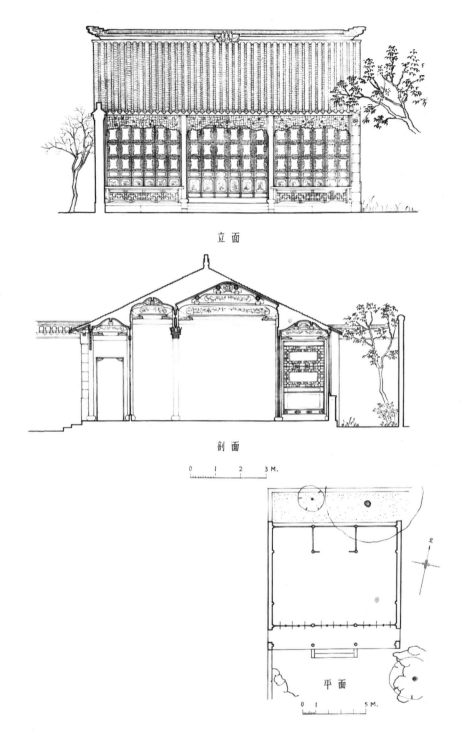

立 面

剖 面

0 1 2 3 M.

平 面

0 1   5 M.

Fig. V-15 Survey drawings of a flower hall in a house at Wangxima Lane.

Fig. V-16 Interior of House for the Aged Giants of Groves and Springs.

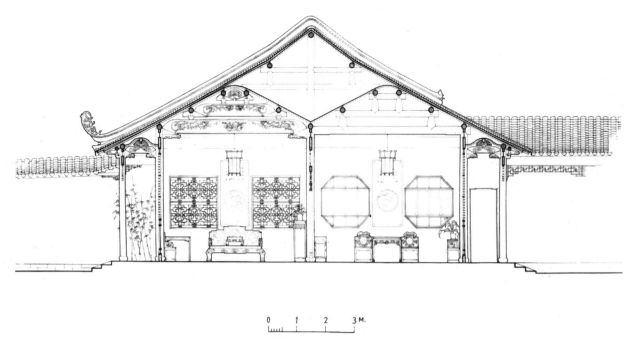

Fig. V-17 Transverse section of House for the Aged Giants of Groves and Springs.

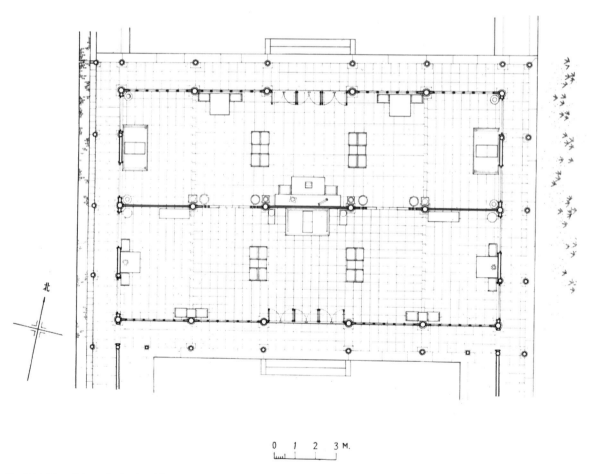

Fig. V-18 Plan of House for the Aged Giants of Groves and Springs.

214

Fig. V-19 Outside view of 36-Mandarin-Duck Hall in Humble Administrator's Garden.

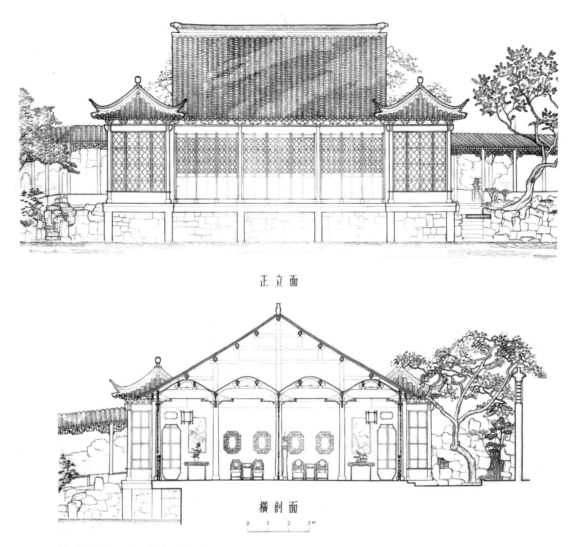

正立面

横剖面

0   1   2   3 M

Fig. V-20 Front view (top) and section view (bottom) of 36-Mandarin-Duck Hall in The Humble Administrator's Garden.

Fig. V-21 Plan of 36-Mandarin-Duck Hall.

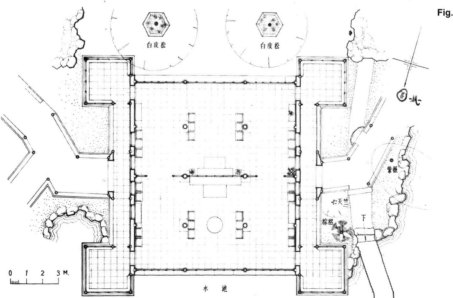

白皮松   白皮松

紫薇

小天竺

棕榈   下

水 池

0   1   2   3 M.

Fig. V-22 Bright-Zither Two-Storied Building and Encompassing-Jade Mountain House.

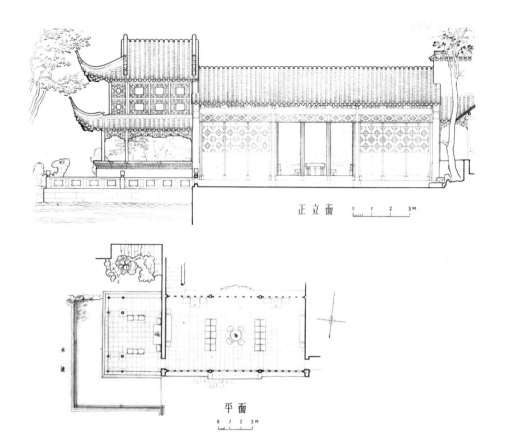

正立面   0 1 2 3M.

平面   0 1 2 3M

Fig. V-23 (1) Survey drawing of Bright-Zither Two-Storied Building.

明瑟樓橫剖面

涵碧山房橫剖面

Fig. V-23 (2) Survey drawing of Encompassing Jade Mountain House.

Fig. V-24 Inverted-Image Two-Storied Building in The Humble Administrator's Garden.

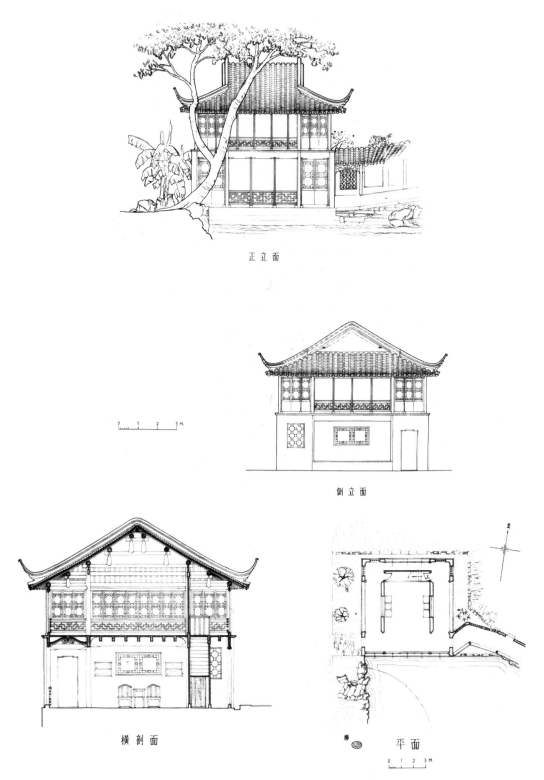

正立面

側立面

橫剖面

平面

0 1 2 3 M.

0 1 2 3 M.

Fig. V-25 Survey drawings of Inverted-Image Two-Storied Building in The Humble Administrator's Garden.

Fig. V-26 Winding-Creek Two-Storied Building in Lingering-Here Garden.

Fig. V-27 Outside view of Looking-at-the-Hill Two-Storied Building in Surging-Wave-Pavilion Garden.

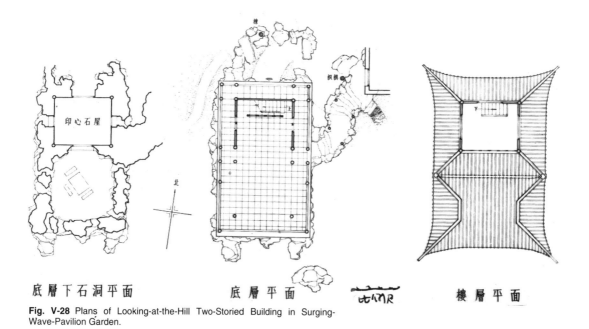

底層下石洞平面　　　　　底層平面　　　　　　樓層平面

Fig. V-28 Plans of Looking-at-the-Hill Two-Storied Building in Surging-Wave-Pavilion Garden.

側 立 面

橫 剖 面

Fig. V-29 Side view (top) and transverse section (bottom) of Looking-at-the-Hill Two-Storied Building in Surging-Wave-Pavilion Garden.

Fig. V-30 Distant-Green Two-Storied Pavilion in Lingering-Here Garden.

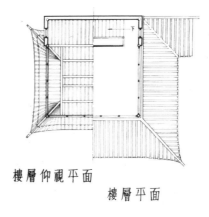

樓層仰視平面

樓層平面

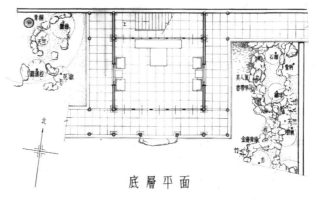

底層平面

Fig. V-31 Plan of Distant-Green Two-Storied Pavilion in Lingering-Here Garden.

Fig. V-32 Front View of Distant-Green Two-Storied Pavilion in Lingering-Here Garden.

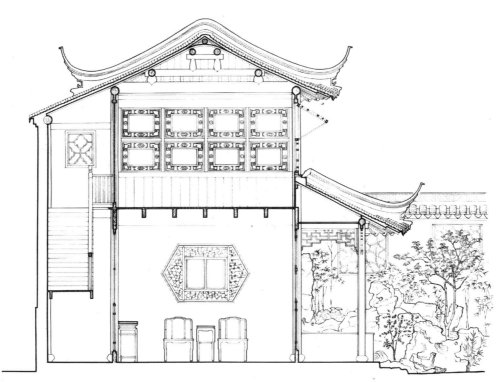

Fig. V-33 Transverse section of Distant-Green Two-Storied Pavilion in Lingering-Here Garden.

225

Fig. V-34 Lying-in-Cloud Chamber in Forest of Lions Garden.

Fig. V-35 Lingering-to-Listen Pavilion in The Humble Administrator's Garden.

Fig. V-36 Lotus Waterside Pavilion in The Humble Administrator's Garden.

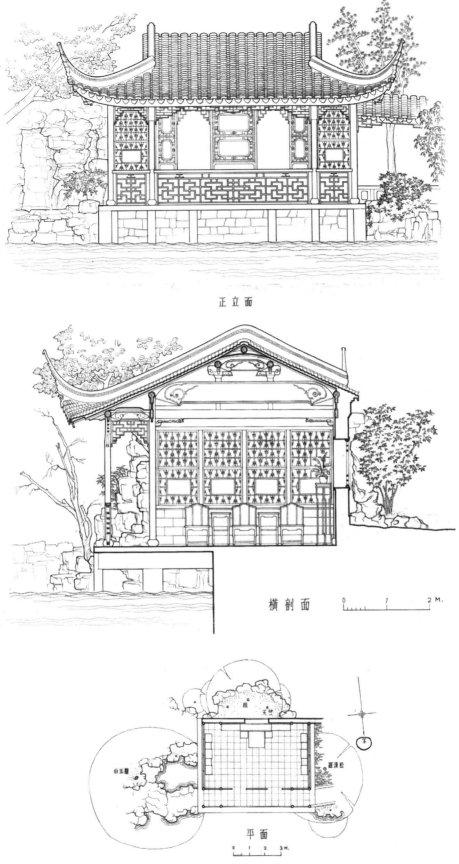

正立面

横剖面　　0　1　2 M.

平面　　0 1 2 3M.

Fig. V-37 Survey drawings of Washing-Tassel Waterside Pavilion in The Retired Fisherman's Garden.

Fig. V-38 Outside view of Washing-Tassel Waterside Pavilion in The Retired Fisherman's Garden.

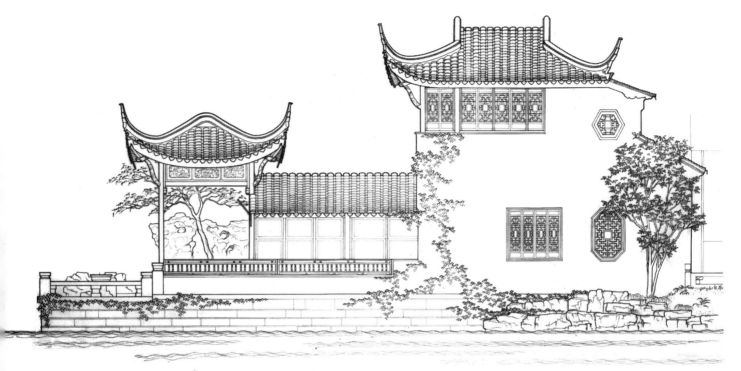

Fig. V-39 Side view of Fragrant-Isle Landboat in The Humble Administrator's Garden.

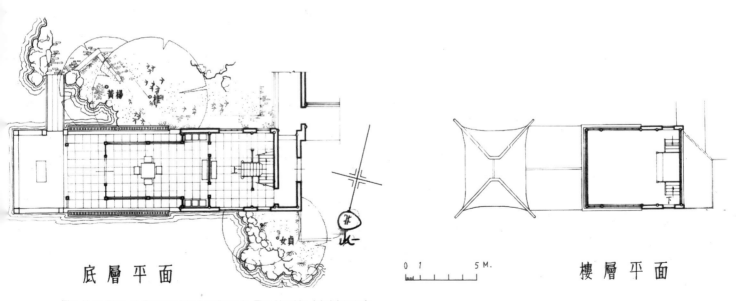

底層平面

0 1　　　　5 M.

樓層平面

黃楊

女貞

Fig. V-40 Plan of Fragrant-Isle Landboat in The Humble Administrator's Garden.

Fig. V-41 Front view of Fragrant-Isle Landboat in The Humble Administrator's Garden.

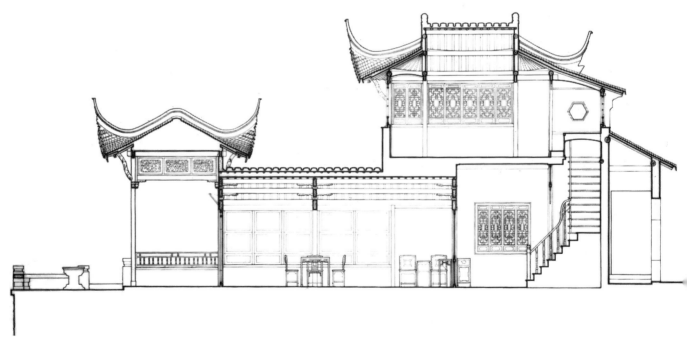

Fig. V-42 Section of Fragrant-Isle Landboat in The Humble Administrator's Garden.

Fig. V-43 Outside view of Fragrant-Isle Landboat in The Humble Administrator's Garden.

Fig. V-44 Outside view of Painting Landboat Study in Happy Garden.

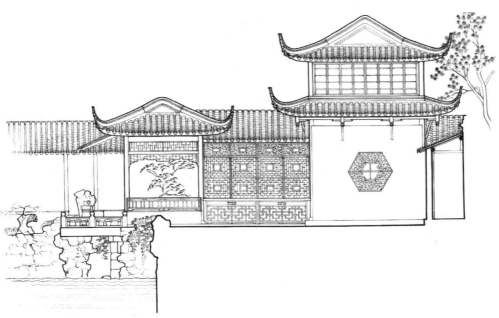

Fig. V-45 Outside view of Painting Landboat Study in Happy Garden.

0   1   2   3 M

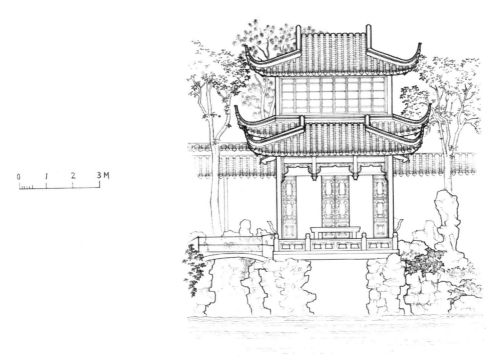

Fig. V-46 Front view of Painting Landboat Study in Happy Garden.

235

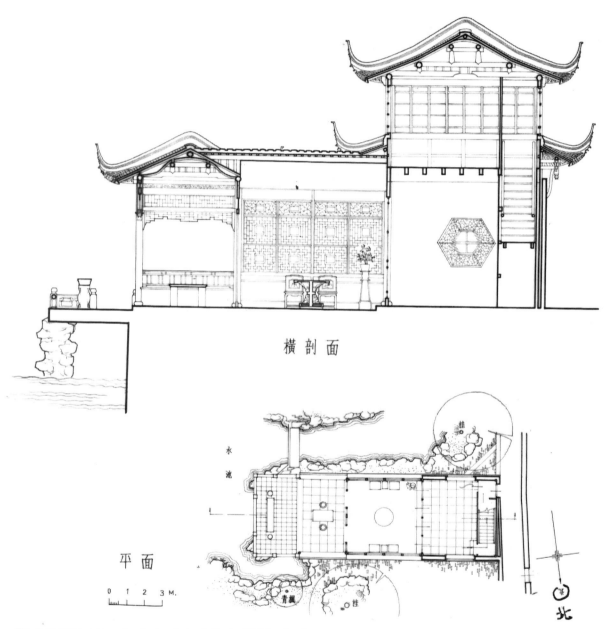

横 剖 面

平 面

0 1 2 3 M.

水池

青枫

桂

桂

北

Fig. V-47 Transverse section (top) and plan (bottom) of Painting Landboat
Study in Happy Garden.

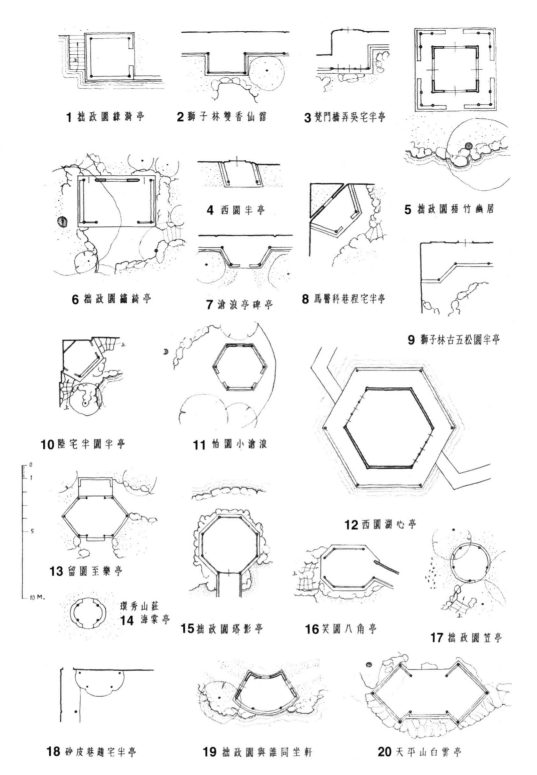

Fig. V-48 Plans of different kinds of pavilions.

1. Green-Ripple Pavilion, Humble Administrator's Garden
2. Double-Fragrance Celestial House, Forest of Lions Garden
3. Half-Pavilion, Residence of Wu, Fanmenqiao Lane
4. Half-Pavilion, West Garden
5. Pavilion amid-Secluded-Wutong-and-Bamboo, Humble Administrator's Garden
6. Embroidered-Silk Pavilion, Humble Administrator's Garden
7. Stone-Tablet Pavilion, Surging-Wave-Pavilion Garden
8. Half-Pavilion, Five-Old-Pines Park, Forest of Lions Garden
9. Half-Pavilion, Five-Old-Pines Park, Forest of Lions Garden
10. Half-Pavilion, Half Garden in the Residence of Lu
11. Little-Surging-Wave Pavilion, Happy Garden
12. Heart-of-the-Lake Pavilion, West Garden
13. Supreme-Happiness Pavilion, Lingering-Here Garden
14. Begonia Pavilion, Mountain Villa of Encircled Elegance
15. Pagoda-Shadow Pavilion, Humble Administrator's Garden
16. Octagonal Pavilion, Smiling Garden
17. Bamboo-Hat Pavilion, Humble Administrator's Garden
18. Half-Pavilion, Residence of Zhao, Shapi Lane
19. With-Whom-to-Sit Lounge, Humble Administrator's Garden
20. White-Cloud Pavilion, Tianping Mountain

Fig. V-49 Outside view of Leaning-on-the-Rainbow Pavilion in The Humble Administrator's Garden.

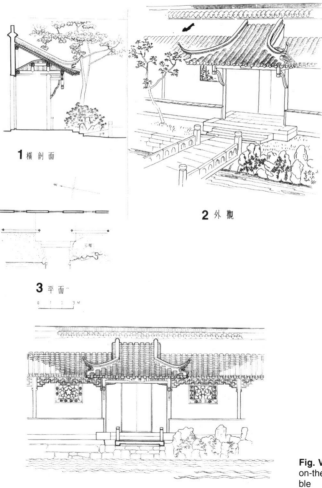

1 横剖面

3 平面

2 外观

4 正立面

Fig. V-50 Survey drawing of Leaning-on-the-Rainbow Pavilion in The Humble Administrator's Garden: **(1)** Outside view; **(2)** Transverse section; **(3)** Plan; **(4)** Front view.

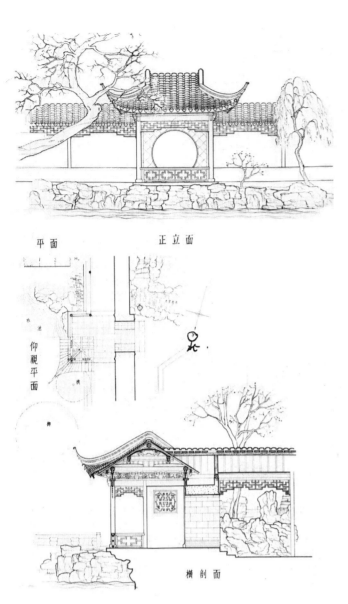

平面　　　　正立面

仰視平面

横剖面

Fig. V-51 Survey drawing of Unique-Beauty Half-Pavilion in The Humble Administrator's Garden.

Fig. V-52 Outside view of Unique-Beauty Half-Pavilion in The Humble Administrator's Garden.

Fig. V-53 True-Interest Pavilion in Forest of Lions Garden.

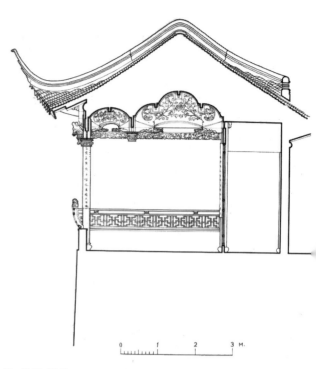

Fig. V-54 (1) Transverse section of True-Interest Pavilion.

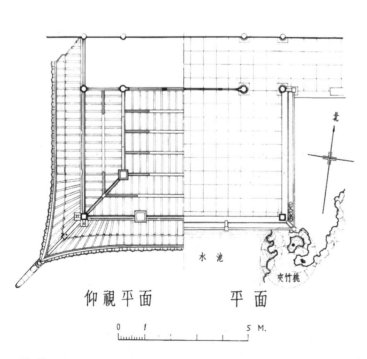

仰視平面　　　平面

水池

夾竹桃

0   1   5 M.

Fig. V-54 (2) Plan and ceiling plan of True-Interest Pavilion.

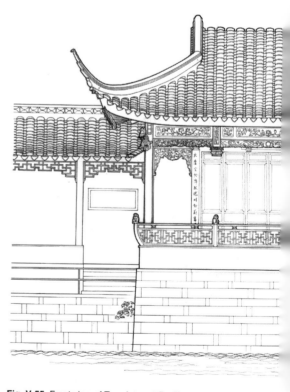

Fig. V-55 Front view of True-Interest Pavilion.

Fig. V-56 Outside view of Green-Ripple Pavilion in The Humble Administrator's Garden.

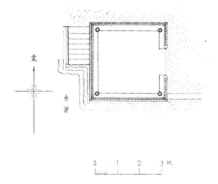

北
水池

0 1 2 3 M.

Fig. V-57 (1) Plan of Green-Ripple Pavilion.

側立面

0 1 2 3 M.

縱剖面

Fig. V-57 (2) Survey drawing of the side view (left) and longitudinal section (right) of Green-Ripple Pavilion.

Fig. V-58 Surging-Wave Pavilion.

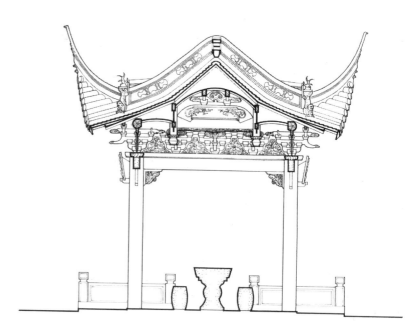

横 剖 面

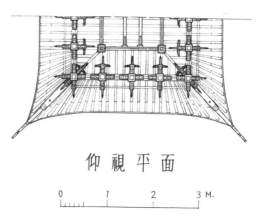

仰 視 平 面

0   1   2   3 M.

Fig. V-59 Transverse section (top) and ceiling plan (bottom) of Surging-Wave Pavilion.

Fig. V-60 Front view of Surging-Wave Pavilion.

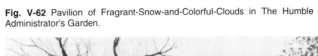
Fig. V-62 Pavilion of Fragrant-Snow-and-Colorful-Clouds in The Humble Administrator's Garden.

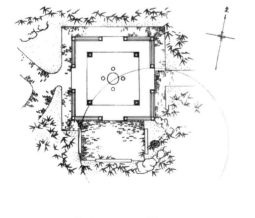

0   1   5 M.

Fig. V-61 Plan of Surging-Wave Pavilion.

Fig. V-63 Embroidered-Silk Pavilion in The Humble Administrator's Garden.

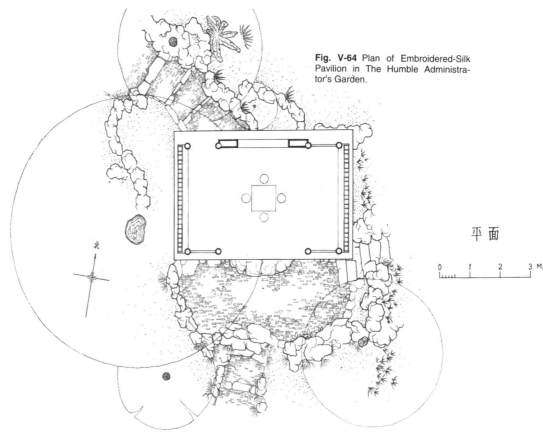

Fig. V-64 Plan of Embroidered-Silk Pavilion in The Humble Administrator's Garden.

平面

0   1   2   3 M.

244

Fig. V-65 Survey drawing of Embroidered-Silk Pavilion, viewed from the front, in The Humble Administrator's Garden.

Fig. V-66 Survey drawing for the transverse section of Embroidered-Silk Pavilion in The Humble Administrator's Garden.

Fig. V-67 Little-Surging-Wave Pavilion in Happy Garden.

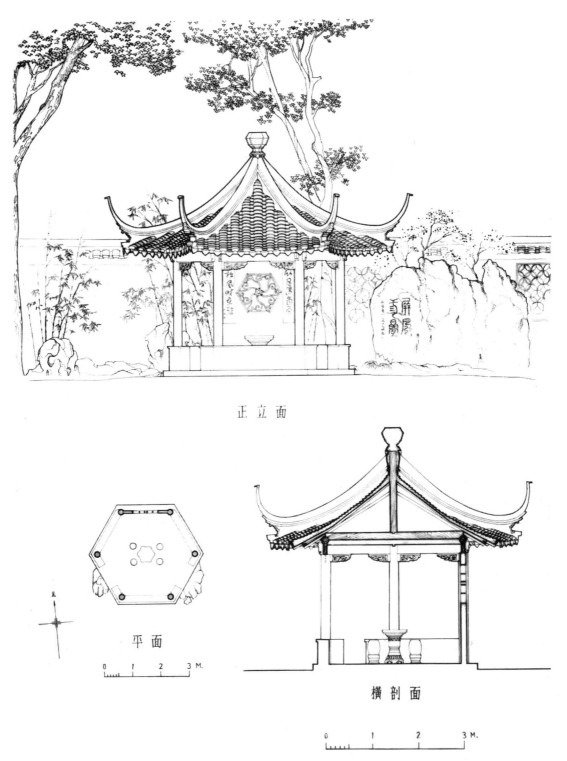

正 立 面

平 面

0   1   2   3 M.

横 剖 面

0   1   2   3 M.

Fig. V-68 Survey drawings of Little-Surging-Wave Pavilion in Happy Garden.

Fig. V-69 Pagoda-Shadow Pavilion in The Humble Administrator's Garden.

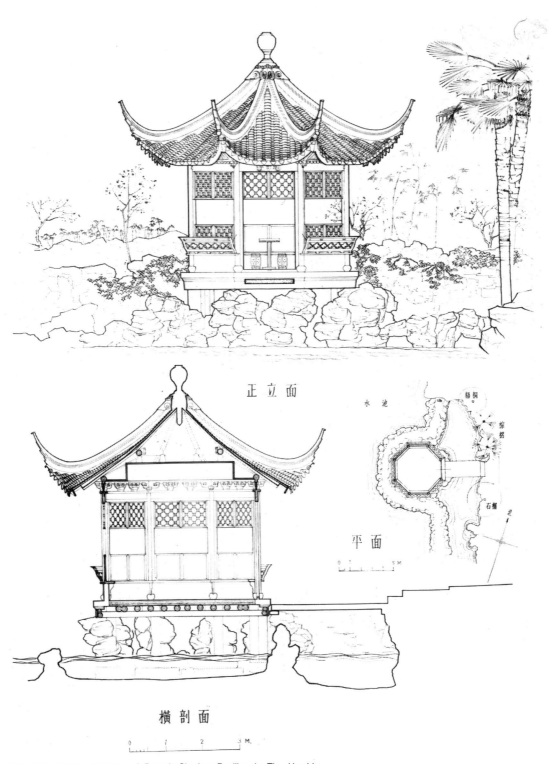

正立面

水池

平面

橫剖面

Fig. V-70 Survey drawings of Pagoda-Shadow Pavilion in The Humble Administrator's Garden.

Fig. V-71 Outside view of Bamboo-Hat Pavilion in The Humble Administrator's Garden.

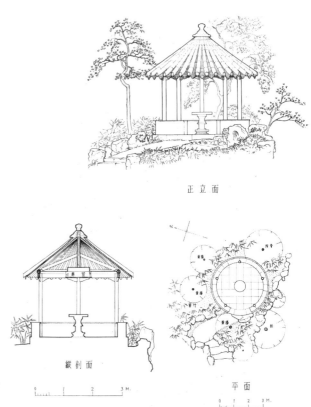

正 立 面

縱 剖 面

平 面

Fig. V-72. Survey drawings of Bamboo-Hat Pavilion in The Humble Administrator's Garden.

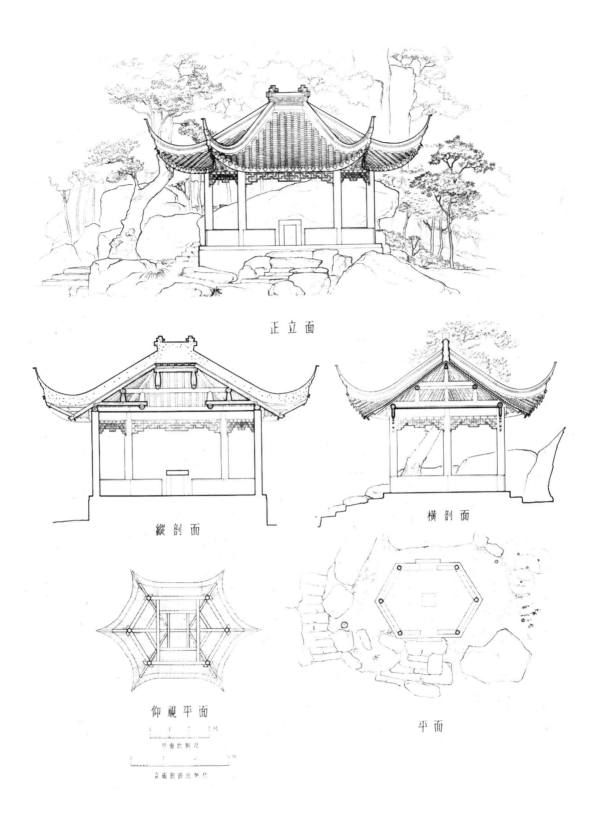

正立面

縱剖面   橫剖面

仰視平面   平面

平面比例尺

立面剖面比例尺

Fig. V-73 Survey Drawings of The Four-Immortals Pavilion in Tianping Mountain.

Fig. V-74 Outside view of Fan-Shaped Pavilion in The Humble Administrator's Garden.

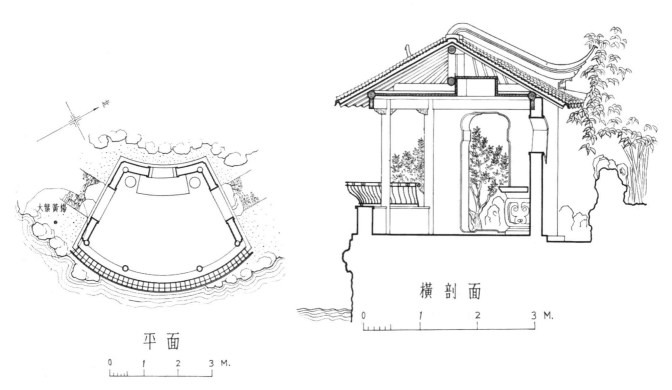

大黃楊

平 面

0   1   2   3 M.

橫 剖 面

0   1   2   3 M.

Fig. V-75 Survey drawing of Fan-Shaped Pavilion in The Humble Administrator's Garden.

Fig. V-76 Fan Pavilion in Forest of Lions Garden.

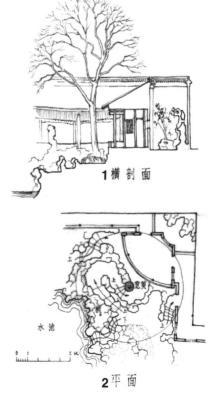

1 横剖面

水池

2 平面

Fig. V-77 Survey drawing of Fan Pavilion in Forest of Lions Garden: **(1)** Transverse section; **(2)** Plan.

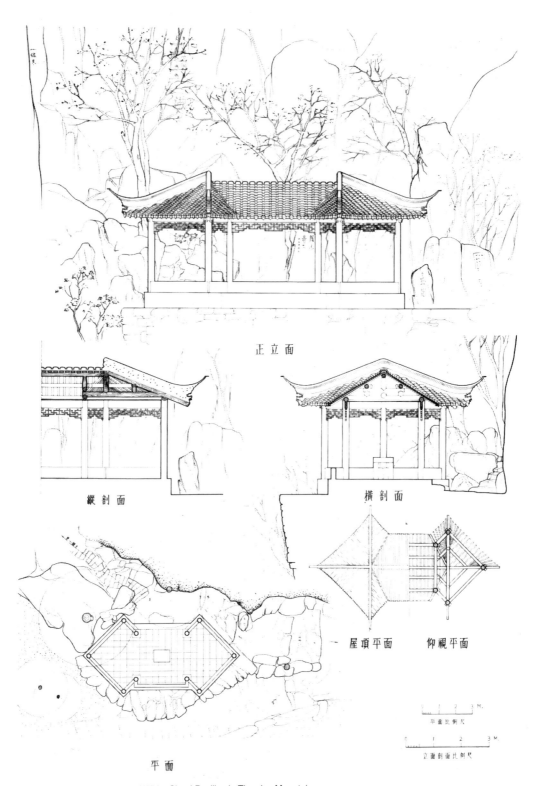

正立面

縱剖面　　　　　　　　　　　　横剖面

屋頂平面　　仰視平面

平面

平面比例尺

立面剖面比例尺

Fig. V-78 Survey drawings of White-Cloud Pavilion in Tianping Mountain.

254

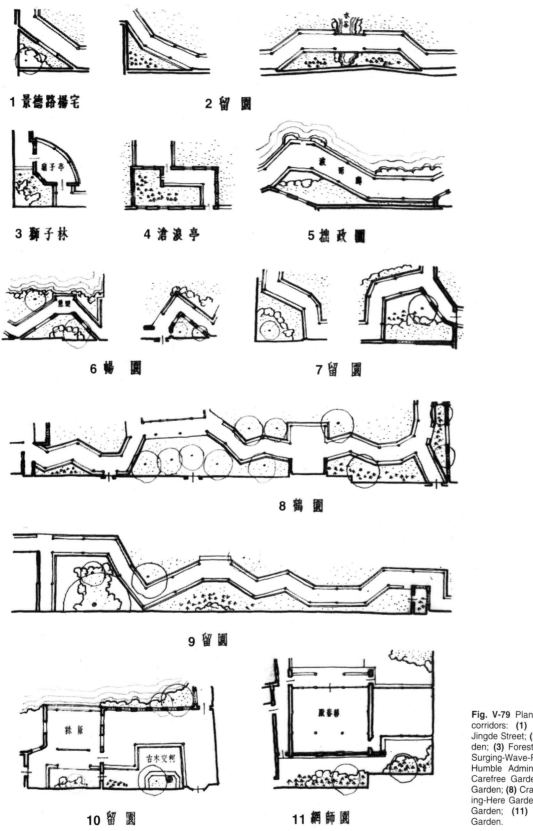

1 景德路楊宅　　　2 留　園

3 獅子林　　　4 滄浪亭　　　5 拙政園

6 暢　園　　　7 留　園

8 鶴　園

9 留　園

10 留　園　　　11 網師園

Fig. V-79 Plans of different kinds of corridors: **(1)** Residence of Yang, Jingde Street; **(2)** Lingering-Here Garden; **(3)** Forest of Lions Garden; **(4)** Surging-Wave-Pavilion Garden; **(5)** Humble Administrator's Garden; **(6)** Carefree Garden; **(7)** Lingering-Here Garden; **(8)** Crane Garden; **(9)** Lingering-Here Garden; **(10)** Lingering-Here Garden; **(11)** Retired Fisherman's Garden.

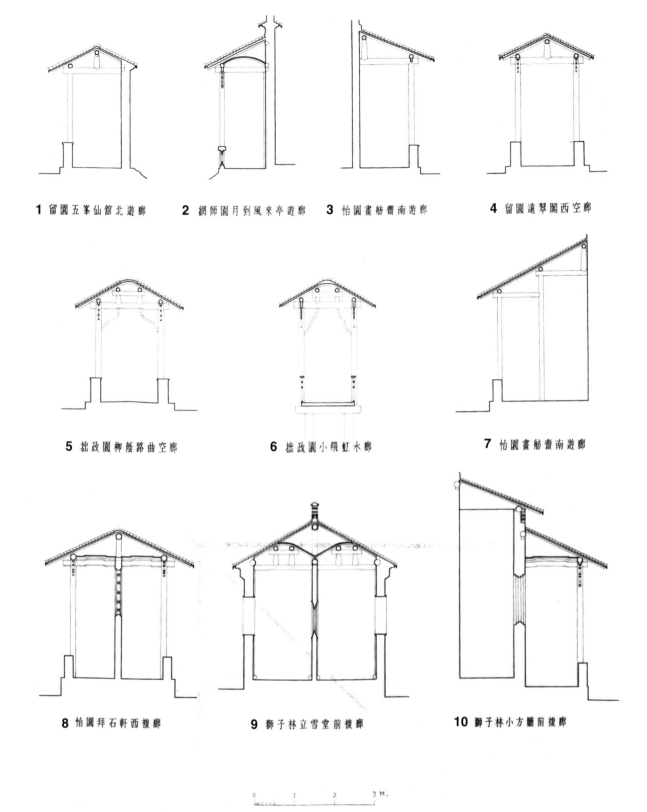

1 留園五峯仙館北遊廊   2 網師園月到風來亭遊廊   3 怡園畫舫齋南遊廊   4 留園遠翠閣西空廊

5 拙政園柳蔭路曲空廊   6 拙政園小飛虹水廊   7 怡園畫舫齋南遊廊

8 怡園拜石軒西複廊   9 獅子林立雪堂前複廊   10 獅子林小方廳前複廊

0   1   2   3 M.

Fig. V-80 Survey drawing of sections of various corridors: **(1)** Corridor north of Five-Peak Celestial House, Lingering-Here Garden; **(2)** Corridor at Moon-Appearing-and-Breeze-Coming Pavilion, Retired Fisherman's Garden; **(3)** Corridor south of Painting Landboat Study, Happy Garden; **(4)** Corridor west of Distant-Green Two-Storied Pavilion, Lingering-Here Garden; **(5)** Corridor at Winding-Path-under-Willow-Shade, Humble Administrator's Garden; **(6)** Little-Flying Rainbow Corridor-Bridge, Humble Administrator's Garden; **(7)** Corridor south of Painting Landboat Study, Happy Garden; **(8)** Double-corridor west of Bowing-to-the-Stone Hall, Happy Garden; **(9)** Double-corridor in front of Standing-in-the-Snow Hall, Forest of Lions Garden; **(10)** Double-corridor in front of Little Square Hall, Forest of Lions Garden.

Fig. V-81 Open corridor at Winding-Path-under-Willow-Shade in The Humble Administrator's Garden.

Fig. V-82 Waterside corridor in the western part of The Humble Administrator's Garden.

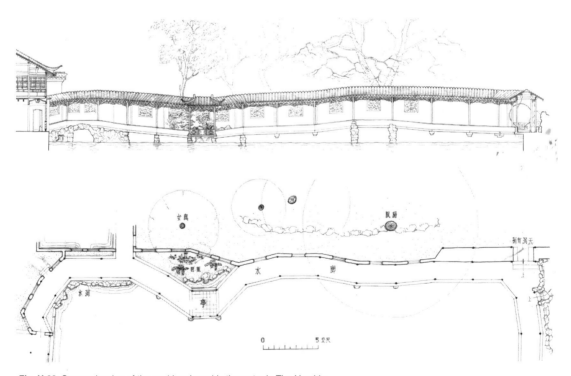

Fig. V-83 Survey drawing of the corridor alongside the water in The Humble Administrator's Garden.

258

Fig. V-84 Winding corridor in Lingering-Here Garden.

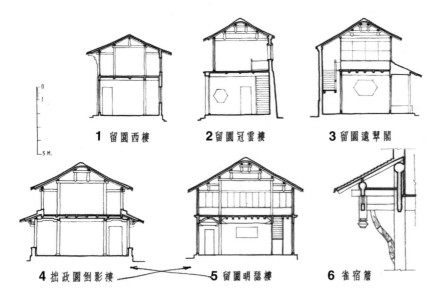

1 留園西樓　　2 留園冠雲樓　　3 留園遠翠閣

4 拙政園倒影樓　　5 留園明瑟樓　　6 雀宿簷

Fig. V-85 The structure of two-story buildings: **(1)** West Two-Storied Building, Lingering-Here Garden; **(2)** Cloud-Topping Two-Storied Building, Lingering-Here Garden; **(3)** Distant-Green Two-Storied Pavilion; **(4)** Bright-Zither Two-Storied Building; **(5)** Inverted-Image Two-Storied Building; **(6)** Birds-Nest-Like Eaves.

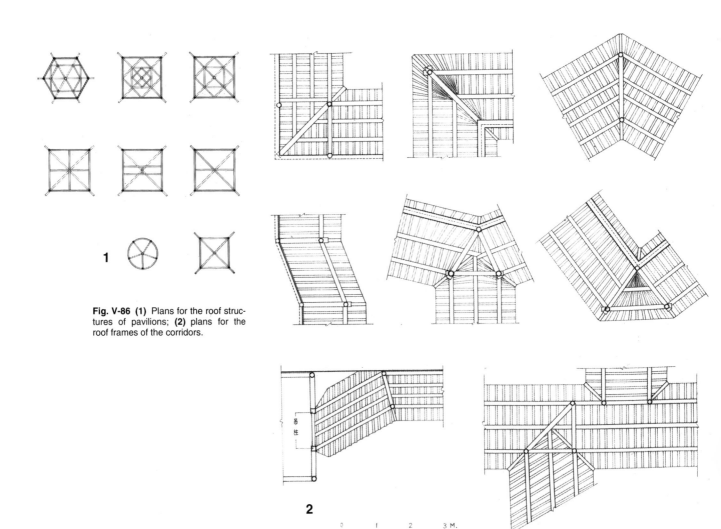

Fig. V-86 (1) Plans for the roof structures of pavilions; **(2)** plans for the roof frames of the corridors.

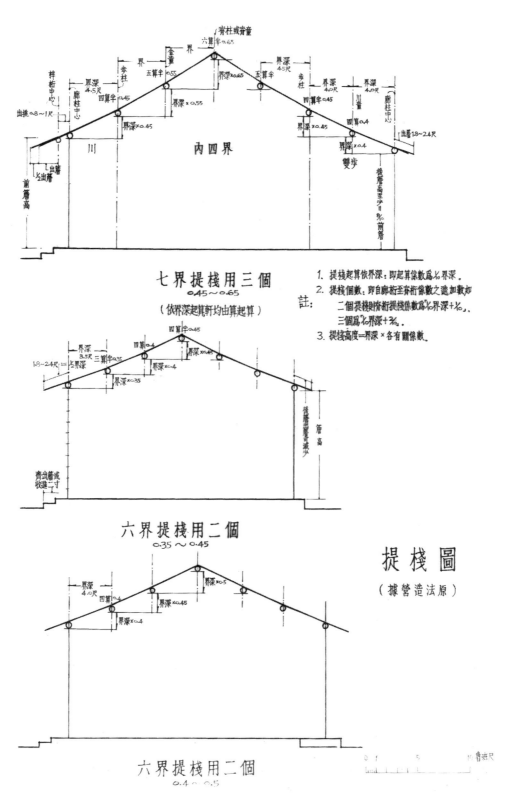

Fig. V-87 Drawings of rising-frameworks of roofs (otherwise known as raising-the-frames), according to *Rules of Architecture*.

Fig. V-88 Framework of the roof of House for the Aged Giants of Groves and Springs in Lingering-Here Garden.

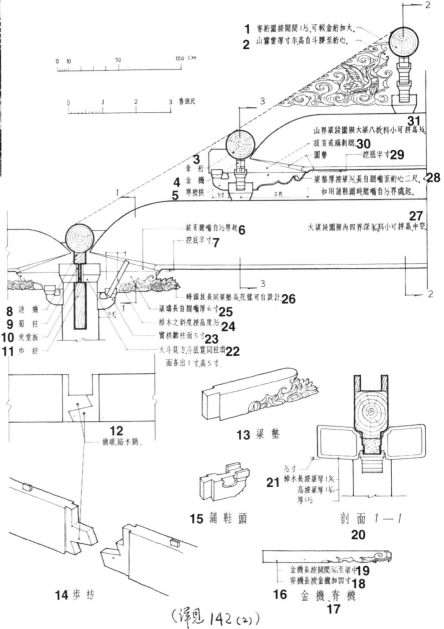

Fig. V-89. (1) The circumference of the ridge purlin can be broader than Jin-Heng (i.e., the purlin on the pillar between the ridge pillar and the pillar one span to the rear of the corridor pillar); (2) The decorative board's height is equal to the distance between the upper middle part of the wooden block and the center of the purlin; (3) The purlin on the pillar between the ridge pillar and the pillar one span to the rear of the corridor pillar; (4) a square wooden block under the purlin; (5) an arch to serve as a pad to hold one end of the beam; (6) the opening of the sawed-off end of flat timber may begin from one-half span; (7) bottom excavated 1.5 centimeters; (8) a small wooden block under the purlin; (9) a short wooden column area as partition; (10) partition board; (11) a small oblong wooden block on top of a small pillar; (12) peg; (13) pad under the beam; (14) timber on top of a pillar; (15) a short bow-shaped wooden board to serve as an arch to support the beam; (16) Jin-Ji: square wooden block under the purlin; (17) Ji-Ji: square wooden block under the ridge; (18) The length of the square wooden block under the ridge is that of the Jin-Ji plus 13 centimeters; (19) The length of the square wooden block under the purlin is the distance between two-tenths the bay and the center of the beam; (20) section; (21) The carved wooden board on the arched pads under the main beams is one and three-fifths as long as the thickness of the beam and as high as one and one-tenth to one and one-half the thickness of the beam; (22) The big wooden board is in the shape of a square; the bottom of it is as wide as the top of the pillar; (23) a solid arch, 15 centimeters from the surface of the pillar; (24) The degree of the obliqueness of the carved wooden board on the arched pads under the main beams is one-half its height; (25) The beam is extended from the sawed-off end of flat timber 20 centimeters thick; (26) The front part of the pad for the beam may be the same height as the pad itself; the flowery pattern on it may be freely designed; (27) The circumference of the main beam is three-fourths the depth of four span; if the timber is not large enough, another piece may be attached to make up for the height and it may be hollow in the center; (28) The pad for the beam is three-fifths the thickness of the beam and its length is 66 centimeters (between the sawed-off end of flat timber); if the short bow-shaped wooden block is used to serve as an arch, the opening of the sawed-off end of the flat timber begins from one-half span; (29) bottom excavated 1.5 centimeters; (30) the two ends of flat timber (one-fifth of which is sawed off); (31) The circumference of the top beam is eight-tenths the beam immediately underneath it; if the one piece of timber is not big enough, another piece one-fourth as big may be pieced together with it. (For further details, see **Fig. V-98(2)**.)

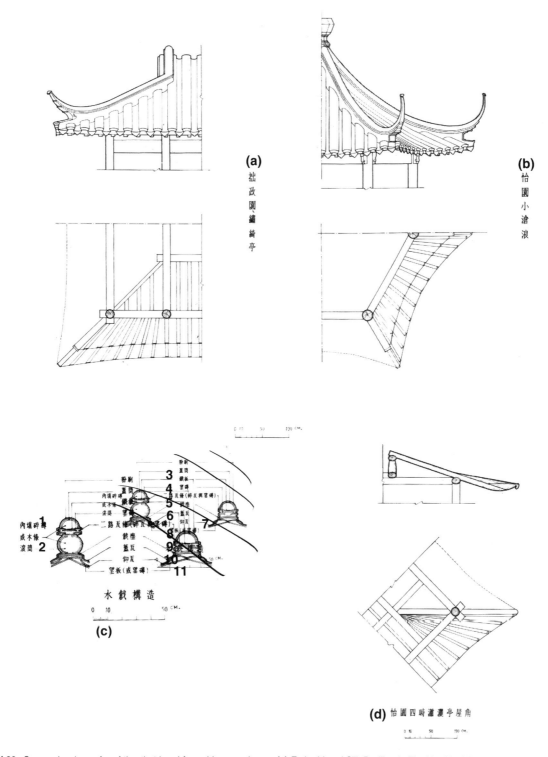

Fig. V-90. Survey drawings of roof-tips that bend from ridge prop-beam. **(a)** Embroidered-Silk Pavilion in The Humble Administrator's Garden. **(b)** Little-Surging-Wave Pavilion in Happy Garden. **(c)** Structure of roof-tips that bend from the ridge prop-beam. **(1)** Broken bricks and wooden strips filled therein, **(2)** rolling tube, **(3)** paint, **(4)** cover, **(5)** iron board, **(6)** brick placed above the rafter, **(7)** two-route brick slat, **(8)** beam seat, **(9)** brick to serve as cover, **(10)** brick facing upward, **(11)** wooden board facing upward (or brick placed above the rafters). **(d)** Roof-corner of Spirit-Unrestrained-through-the-Four-Seasons Pavilion, in the Happy Garden.

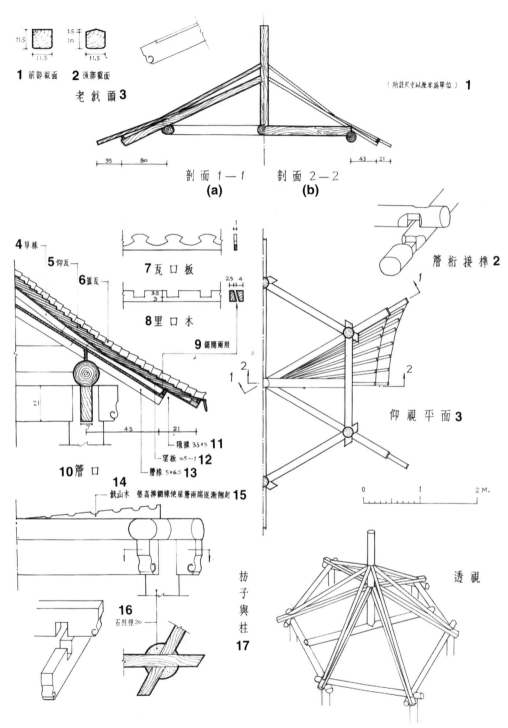

Fig. V-91. Structure of the roof frame of the Little-Surging-Wave Pavilion in Happy Garden. **(a) Section 1-1. (1)** Front section, **(2)** rear section, **(3)** ridge beam, **(4)** rafter, **(5)** tile facing upward, **(6)** tile serving as cover, **(7)** wooden board sawed into tile shape, to be placed on the eaves, **(8)** wooden strip between flying rafter and eaves rafter, **(9)** after sawing (to serve two purposes), **(10)** eaves, **(11)** flying rafter, **(12)** wooden board facing upward, **(13)** rafter to support the eaves, **(14)** toothlike, oblique wooden board to be placed under the eaves, **(15)** to be placed under the rafter at the corner eaves in order to make two ends of eaves jut upward, **(16)** diameter of stone pillar, **(17)** small oblong beam and pillar. **(b) Section 2-2. (1)** Measurement: centimeters, **(2)** tenons and mortises for the purlin on the eaves, **(3)** plan looking upward.

Fig. V-92 Outside view of roof-tips that bend from the small ridge prop-beam.

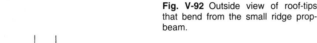

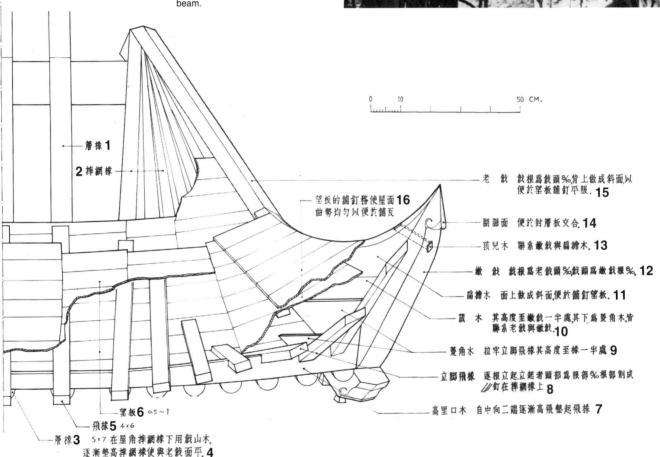

簷椽 **1**

2 捧網椽

望板的鋪釘務使屋面 **16**
曲勢均勻以便於鋪瓦

老 戧　戧根爲戧頭%背上做成斜面以
便於望板鋪釘平服. **15**

猢猻面　便於封簷板交合 **14**

孩兒木　聯系戧戧與扁擔木. **13**

嫩 戧　戧根爲老戧頭%戧頭爲嫩戧根%. **12**

扁擔木　面上做成斜面便於鋪釘望板. **11**

箴 木　其高度至嫩戧一半處其下爲菱角木皆
聯系老戧與嫩戧. **10**

菱角木　拉牢立腳飛椽其高度至椽一半處 **9**

立腳飛椽　逐根立起立起者頭都爲根部%根部削成
/// 釘在捧網椽上 **8**

高里口木　自中向二端逐漸高飛墊起飛椽 **7**

望板 **6** 0.5~1

飛椽 **5** 4×6

簷椽 **3**　5×7 在屋角捧網椽下用戧山木,
逐漸墊高捧網椽使與老戧面平. **4**

Fig. V-93. Drawing of the structure of roof-tip that bends from the small ridge prop-beam. (1) Eaves rafter, (2) flung-net rafter, (3) eaves rafter, (4) tooth-like oblique wooden board used under the flung-net rafter at the roof tip, making the rafter gradually higher until it reaches the same height as the oblique ridge beam, (5) flying rafter, (6) wooden board facing upward, (7) wooden board rising higher from its center, (8) standing flying rafter: each rafter is in standing posture, the top part being 8/10 of the root part; the root part is nailed onto the flung-net rafter, (9) water-chestnut-shaped wooden board holding fast the standing flying rafter; the board is one-half the height of the rafter, (10) sealing wooden board, the height of which is that of the branch prop beam; under it lies the water-chestnut-shaped wooden board, linking up the ridge beam with the branch prop beam, (11) flat eaves timber, the surface of which is oblique so that the wooden board, facing upward, may be nailed onto it, (12) branch beam, the root of which is 8/10 the end of the ridge beam; the end of the beam is 8/10 the root of the branch beam, (13) the shoulder pole wood and the wooden tenon nailed on the branch beam join the branch beam with flat eaves, (14) end of branch prop beam (which looks like a monkey's face) ready to be fitted to the wooden board at the end of the eaves, (15) ridge beam, the root of which is 8/10 the end; the back of the beam is oblique, so that flat boards, may be nailed onto the board facing upward, (16) nailing the wood boards facing upward makes the curvature of the roof top more even so that tiles may be paved thereon.

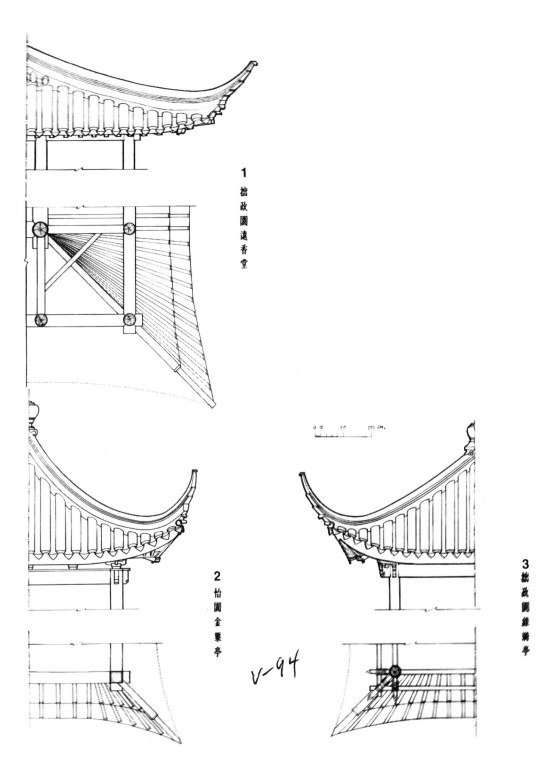

拙政園遠香堂

怡園金粟亭

拙政園綠漪亭

1

2

3

V-94

Fig. V-94 Survey drawing of the roof-tips that bend from the small ridge prop-beam: **(1)** Distant-Fragrance Hall, Humble Administrator's Garden; **(2)** Golden-Millet Pavilion, Happy Garden; **(3)** Green-Ripple Pavilion, Humble Administrator's Garden.

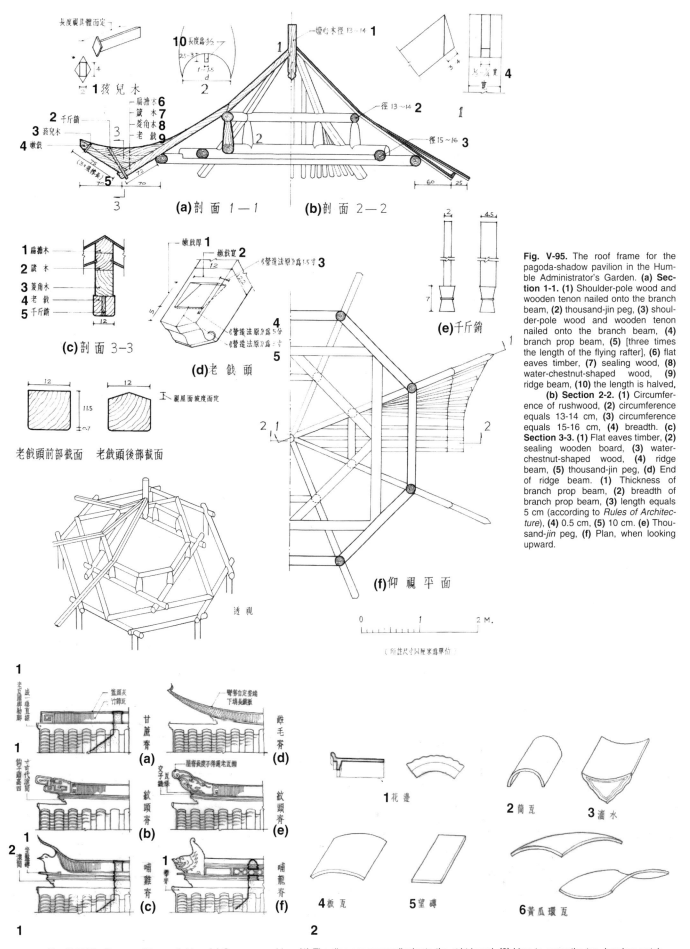

Fig. V-95. The roof frame for the pagoda-shadow pavilion in the Humble Administrator's Garden. **(a) Section 1-1. (1)** Shoulder-pole wood and wooden tenon nailed onto the branch beam, **(2)** thousand-jin peg, **(3)** shoulder-pole wood and wooden tenon nailed onto the branch beam, **(4)** branch prop beam, **(5)** [three times the length of the flying rafter], **(6)** flat eaves timber, **(7)** sealing wood, **(8)** water-chestnut-shaped wood, **(9)** ridge beam, **(10)** the length is halved,

(b) Section 2-2. (1) Circumference of rushwood, **(2)** circumference equals 13-14 cm, **(3)** circumference equals 15-16 cm, **(4)** breadth. **(c) Section 3-3. (1)** Flat eaves timber, **(2)** sealing wooden board, **(3)** water-chestnut-shaped wood, **(4)** ridge beam, **(5)** thousand-jin peg, **(d)** End of ridge beam. **(1)** Thickness of branch prop beam, **(2)** breadth of branch prop beam, **(3)** length equals 5 cm (according to *Rules of Architecture*), **(4)** 0.5 cm, **(5)** 10 cm. **(e)** Thousand-*jin* peg, **(f)** Plan, when looking upward.

Fig. V-96(1). Shapes of the roof ridge. **(a)** Sugar cane ridge: **(1)** The tiles are perpendicular to the skirt board, **(2)** Lime to cover the top, bamboo-notch tile. **(b)** Fret ridge: **(1)** End of hook, 13-cm high, may be used instead of roller tube. **(c)** Hen ridge: **(1)** Seated-plate brick, **(2)** roller tube. **(d)** Female bird-feather ridge: **(1)** The degree of the curve may be freely determined, the end of the ridge to be supported by a long iron board. **(e)** Fret ridge: **(1)** The inch or so of convex section between each two rows of tiles, **(2)** brick tips. **(f)** Dragon ridge: **(1)** The ridge where the front and the rear parts of the rooftop meet.
Fig. V-96(2). Details of tiles. **(1)** Decorative tiles used for the eaves, **(2)** top tile, **(3)** lower tile, **(4)** wooden-board tile, **(5)** brick facing upward, **(6)** cucumber-ring tile.

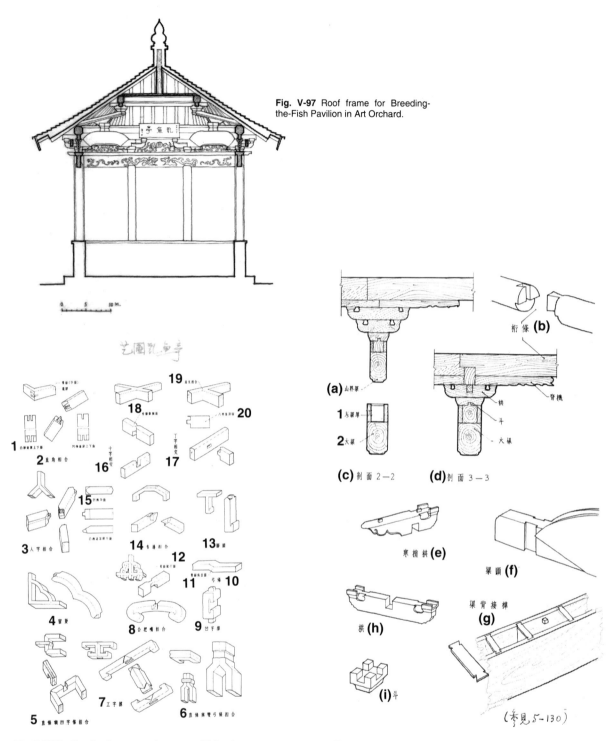

Fig. V-97 Roof frame for Breeding-the-Fish Pavilion in Art Orchard.

Fig. V-98(1). Details of tenons and mortises. **(1)** Depth of concave mortise, upward and downward, **(2)** meeting at right angles, **(3)** meeting in shape, **(4)** water-chestnut-shaped window, **(5)** meeting of straight strips with convex strips, **(6)** meeting of straight strips and double-bow-shaped strips, **(7)** I-shaped prop, **(8)** meeting of mouth-shaped wood, **(9)** convex prop, **(10)** bow-shaped strips, **(11)** concave and round surface, **(12)** plane as surface, **(13)** bottom end, **(14)** meeting of multiborders, **(15)** plane surface of convex mortise, **(16)** meeting at crossroad, **(17)** meeting in T shape, **(18)** convex and half round surface, **(19)** meeting in T shape, **(20)** surface of depth of concave mortise.

Fig. V-98(2). Details of tenons and mortises. **(a)** Girder beam; **(b)** purlin strips; **(c) Section 2-2: (1)** Thickness of 1/5 beam, **(2)** main beam; **(d) Section 3-3: (1)** Square wooden block under ridge, **(2)** bow-shaped wooden block on top of bearing block (*gong*), **(3)** bearing block (*dou*), **(4)** main beam; **(e)** An arch to serve as pad to hold one end of beam; **(f)** end of beam; **(g)** tenons and mortises on rear of beam; **(h)** bow-shaped wooden block, on top of bearing block (*gong*); **(i)** bearing block (*dou*).

268

Fig. V-99 The crane-shin-shaped ceiling of 36-Mandarin-Duck Hall in The Humble Administrator's Garden.

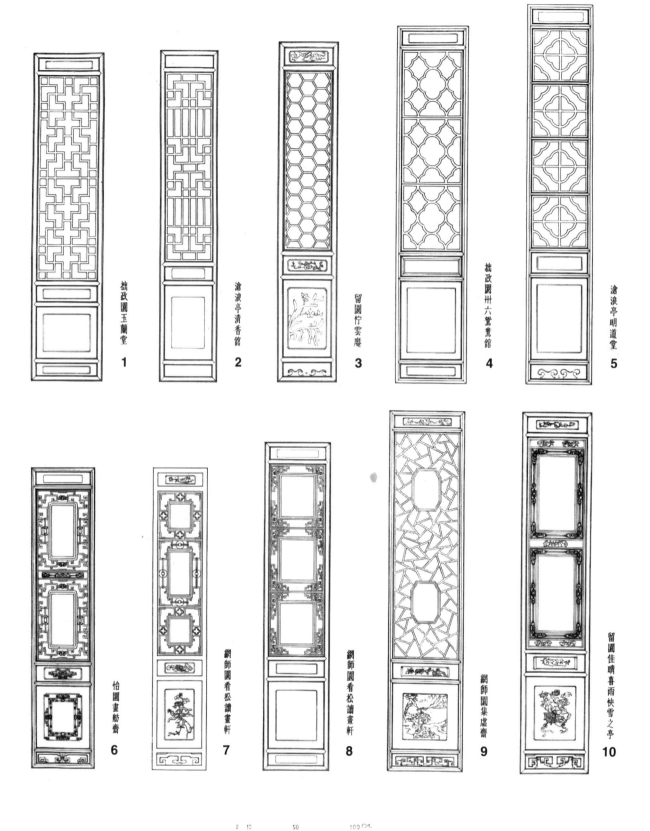

拙政園玉蘭堂 **1**

滄浪亭清香館 **2**

留園佇雲庵 **3**

拙政園卅六鴛鴦館 **4**

滄浪亭明道堂 **5**

怡園畫舫齋 **6**

網師園看松讀畫軒 **7**

網師園看松讀畫軒 **8**

網師園集虛齋 **9**

留園佳晴喜雨快雪之亭 **10**

Fig. V-100 (1) Drawings of lattice doors and screen partitions: **(1)** Magnolia Hall, Humble Administrator's Garden; **(2)** Fresh-Fragrance House, Surging-Wave-Pavilion Garden; **(3)** Lingering-Cloud House, Lingering-Here Garden; **(4)** 36-Mandarin-Duck Hall, Humble Administrator's Garden; **(5)** Comprehending-the-Doctrine Hall, Surging-Wave-Pavilion Garden; **(6)** Painting Landboat Study, Happy Garden; **(7)** Looking-at-Pine-and-Painting Hall, Retired Fisherman's Garden; **(8)** Looking-at-Pine-and-Painting Hall, Retired Fisherman's Garden; **(9)** Gathering-the-Void Study, Retired Fisherman's Garden; **(10)** Delight-in-Sunshine-and-Rain-and-Snow Pavilion, Lingering-Here Garden.

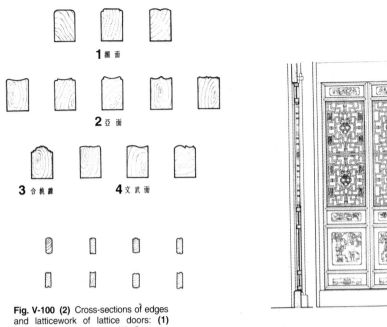

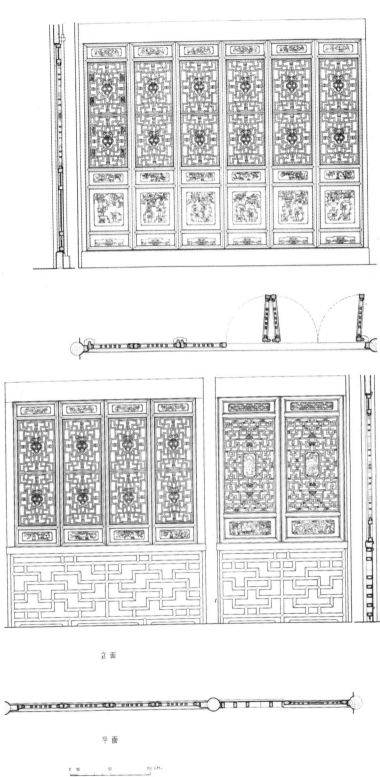

Fig. V-100 (2) Cross-sections of edges and latticework of lattice doors: **(1)** Convex and half-round; **(2)** Concave and round; **(3)** Small round thread; **(4)** Concave-and-round and convex-and-half-round, joined together.

1 捆 面

2 亞 面

3 合 桃 線   4 文 武 面

立 面

平 面

Fig. V-101 Drawings of the decorative devices in Salute-to-the-Peak Hall in Lingering-Here Garden.

Fig. V-102 Lattice doors in Delight-in-Sunshine-and-Rain-and-Snow Pavilion
in Lingering-Here Garden.

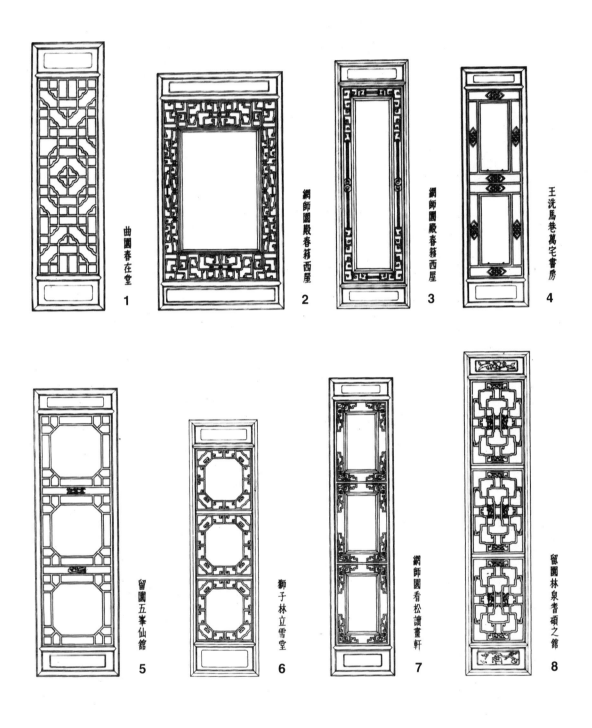

曲園春在堂 1

網師園殿春簃西屋 2

網師園殿春簃西屋 3

王洗馬巷萬宅書房 4

留園五峯仙館 5

獅子林立雪堂 6

網師園看松讀畫軒 7

留園林泉耆碩之館 8

0 10   50   100 CM

Fig. V-103 Drawings of windows and windows-above-balustrades: **(1)** Spring-Is-Here Hall, Winding Garden; **(2)** West room of Late-Spring Chamber, Retired Fisherman's Garden; **(3)** West room of Late-Spring Chamber, Retired Fisherman's Garden; **(4)** Study in the Residence of Wan, Wangxima Lane; **(5)** Five-Peak Celestial House, Lingering-Here Garden; **(6)** Standing-in-the-Snow Hall, Forest of Lions Garden; **(7)** Looking-at-Pine-and-Painting Hall, Retired Fisherman's Garden; **(8)** House for the Aged Giants of Groves and Springs, Lingering-Here Garden.

Fig. V-104 Window latticework for Restored-to-Me Study in Lingering-Here Garden.

Fig. V-105 Brick-framed tracery windows for Restored-to-Me Study in Lingering-Here Garden.

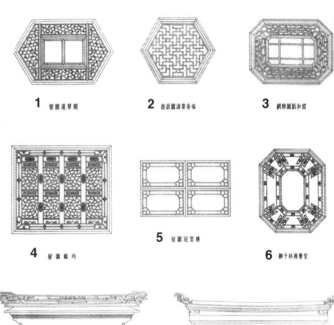

1 留園遠翠閣

2 拙政園海棠春塢

3 網師園撷秀樓

4 留園鶴所

5 留園冠雲樓

6 獅子林燕譽堂

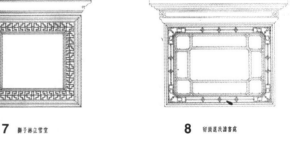

7 獅子林立雪堂

8 留園遠民讀書處

Fig. V-106 Drawings of brick-framed tracery windows: **(1)** Distant-Green Two-Storied Pavilion, Lingering-Here Garden; **(2)** Spring-Begonia-Cove House, Humble Administrator's Garden; **(3)** Pursuance-of-Harmony House, Retired Fisherman's Garden; **(4)** Crane Hall, Lingering-Here Garden; **(5)** Cloud-Topping Two-Storied Building, Lingering-Here Garden; **(6)** Famed-for-Swallow Hall, Forest of Lions Garden; **(7)** Standing-in-the-Snow Hall, Forest of Lions Garden; **(8)** Restored-to-Me Study, Lingering-Here Garden.

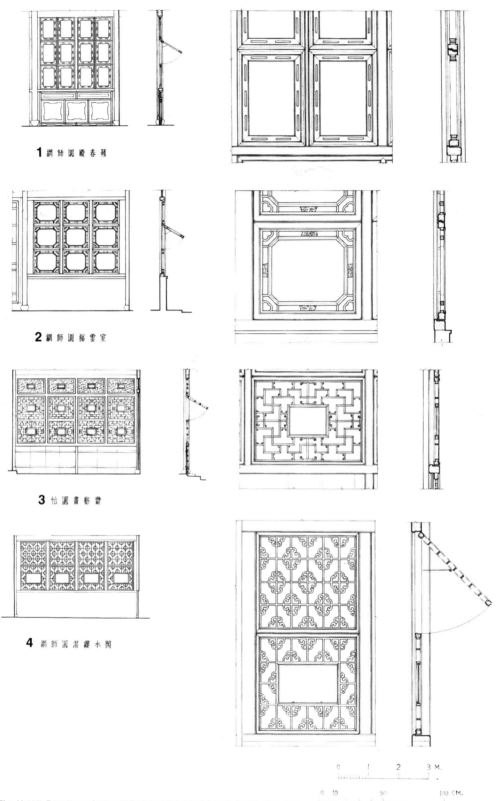

Fig. V-107 Drawings of upward-folding windows: **(1)** Late-Spring Chamber, Retired Fisherman's Garden; **(2)** Ladder-Cloud Chamber, Retired Fisherman's Garden; **(3)** Painting Landboat Study, Happy Garden; **(4)** Washing-Tassel Waterside Pavilion, Retired Fisherman's Garden.

1 網師園殿春簃

2 網師園梯雲室

3 怡園畫舫齋

4 網師園濯纓水閣

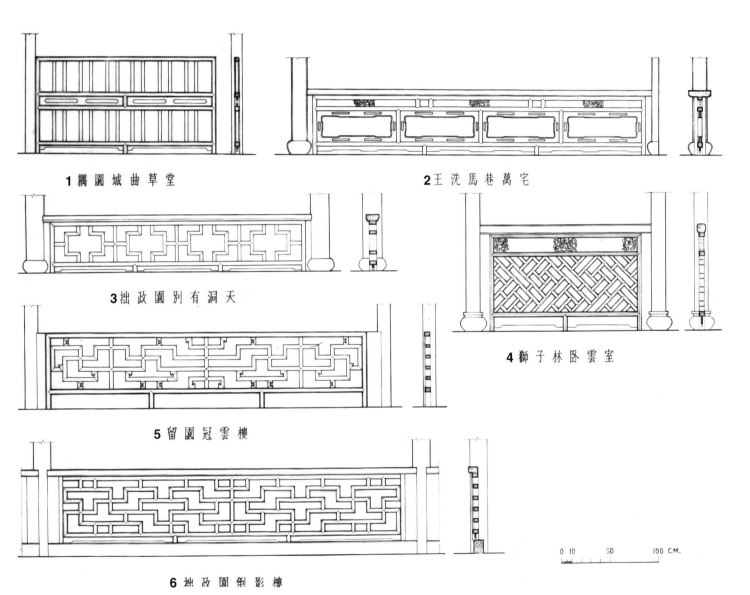

1 耦園城曲草堂

2 王洗馬巷萬宅

3 拙政園別有洞天

4 獅子林卧雲室

5 留園冠雲樓

6 拙政園倒影樓

0 10   50   100 CM.

Fig. V-108 Drawings of wooden balustrades: **(1)** City-Corner Cottage, Twin Garden; **(2)** Residence of Wan, Wangxima Lane; **(3)** Unique-Beauty Half-Pavilion, Humble Administrator's Garden; **(4)** Lying-in-the-Cloud Chamber, Forest of Lions Garden; **(5)** Cloud-Topping Two-Storied Building, Lingering-Here Garden; **(6)** Inverted-Image Two-Storied Building, Humble Administrator's Garden.

Fig. V-109 Balustrade for Gathering-the-Void Study in the Retired Fisherman's Garden.

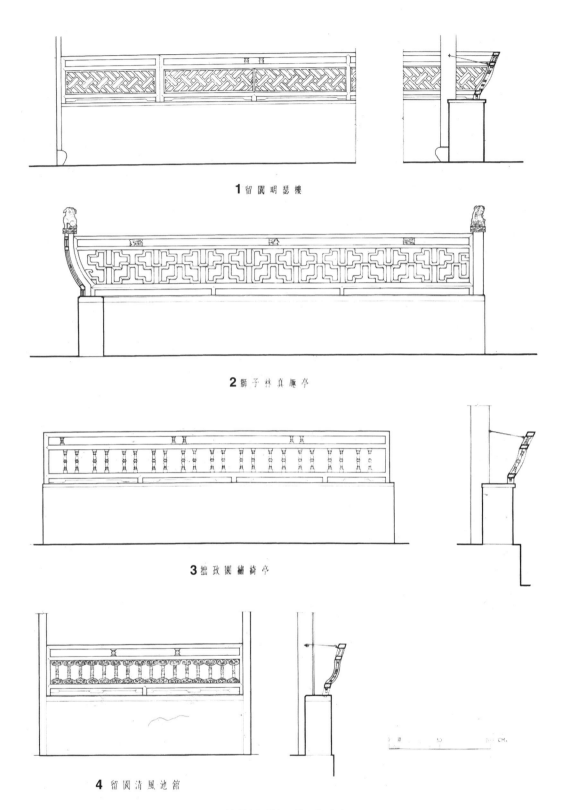

1 留園明瑟樓

2 獅子林真趣亭

3 拙政園繡綺亭

4 留園清風池館

Fig. V-110 Drawings of goose-neck chairs: **(1)** Bright-Zither Two-Storied Building, Lingering-Here Garden; **(2)** True-Interest Pavilion, Forest of Lions Garden; **(3)** Embroidered-Silk Pavilion, Humble Administrator's Garden; **(4)** Fresh-Breeze-Pool House, Lingering-Here Garden.

Fig. V-111 Goose-neck chairs in True-Interest Pavilion in Forest of Lions Garden.

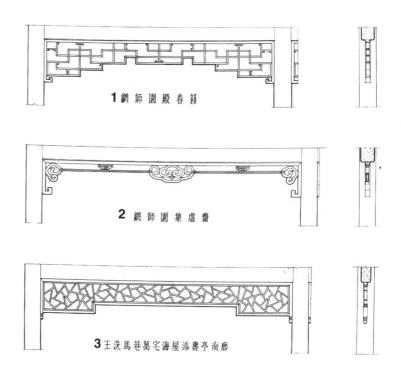

1 網師園殿春簃

2 網師園集虛齋

3 王洗馬巷萬宅海屋添壽亭南廊

Fig. V-112 Drawings of overhanging panels with flower patterns: **(1)** Late-Spring Chamber, Retired Fisherman's Garden; **(2)** Gathering-the-Void Study; **(3)** Corridor south of Haiwutianshou Pavilion, Residence of Wan, Wangxima Lane; **(4)** Famed-for-Swallow Hall, Forest of Lions Garden.

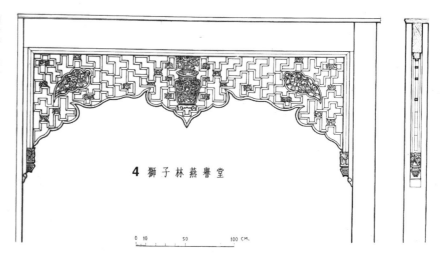

4 獅子林燕譽堂

0 10   50   100 CM.

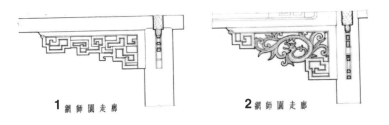

1 網師園走廊　　　　　2 網師園走廊

0　10　20　30 CM.

Fig. V-113 Drawings of overhanging panels with toothlike flower patterns: (1) Corridor, Retired Fisherman's Garden; (2) Corridor, Retired Fisherman's Garden; (3) Little-Surging-Wave Pavilion, Happy Garden; (4) Golden-Millet Pavilion, Happy Garden.

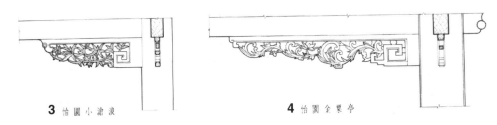

3 怡園小滄浪　　　　　4 怡園金粟亭

Fig. V-114 Decorations in House for the Aged Giants of Groves and Springs in Lingering-Here Garden.

Fig. V-115 Flower-pattern overhanging panels that reach to the floor in Ladder-Cloud Chamber in The Retired Fisherman's Garden.

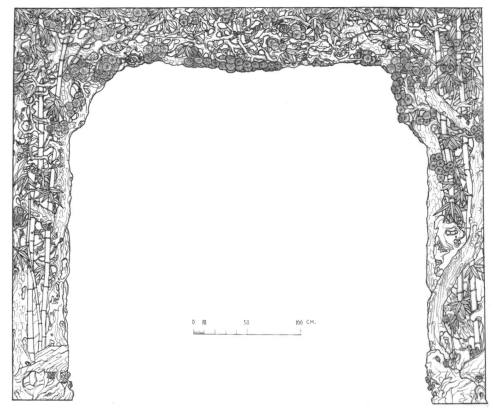

Fig. V-116 Drawing of flower-pattern hanging panels in Waterside-Pavilion-amid-the-Hillock-and-Pool, in Twin Garden.

0 10   50   100 CM.

282

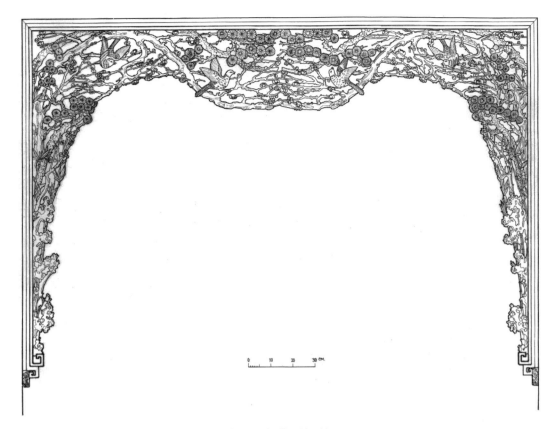

Fig. V-117 Flying panels in Lingering-to-Listen Pavilion in The Humble Administrator's Garden.

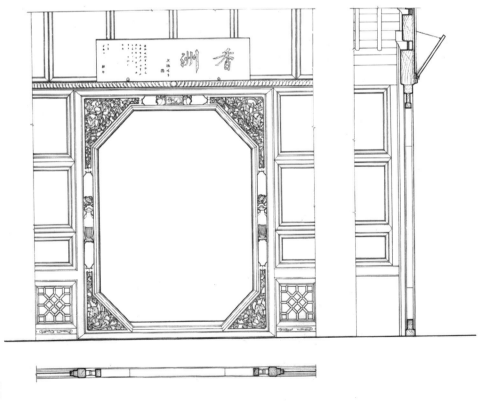

Fig. V-118 Overhanging panels that reach to the floor in Fragrant-Isle Landboat in The Humble Administrator's Garden.

Fig. V-119 Overhanging panels that reach to the floor in Five-Old-Pine Park in Forest of Lions Garden.

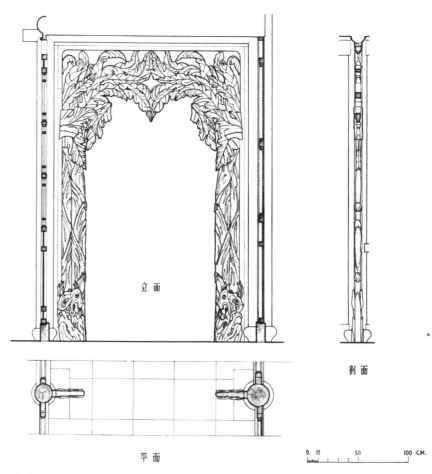

立面

剖面

平面

0 10   50   100 C.M.

Fig. V-120 Drawing of overhanging panels that reach to the floor in Five-Old-Pine Park in Forest of Lions Garden.

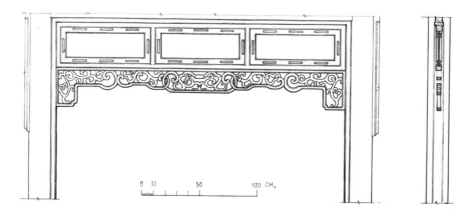

0 10   50   100 C.M.

Fig. V-121 Flying-panel in Late-Spring Chamber in The Retired Fisherman's Garden.

Fig. V-122 Flying-panel reaching to the floor in Five-Peak Celestial Hall in Lingering-Here Garden.

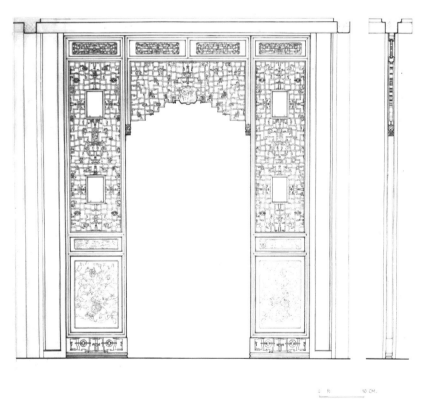

Fig. V-123 Drawing of flying-panel reaching to the floor in Five-Peak Celestial Hall.

Fig. V-124 Inside view of Famed-for-Swallow Hall in Forest of Lions Garden.

Fig. V-125 Tracery windows in the West Garden.

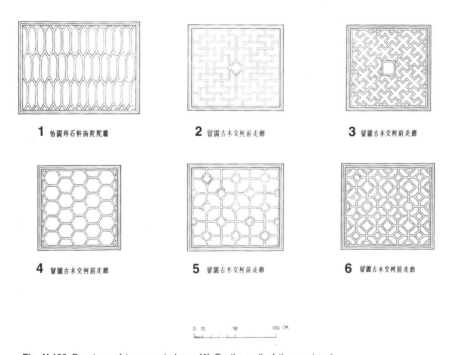

1 怡園拜石軒南院院牆   **2** 留園古木交柯前走廊   **3** 留園古木交柯前走廊

4 留園古木交柯前走廊   **5** 留園古木交柯前走廊   **6** 留園古木交柯前走廊

0 10   50   100 CM.

Fig. V-126 Drawings of tracery windows: **(1)** On the wall of the courtyard south of Bowing-to-the-Stone Hall, Happy Garden; **(2)**, **(3)**, **(4)**, **(5)**, and **(6)** Along the corridor in front of Old-Trees-Intertwining-One-Another, Lingering-Here Garden.

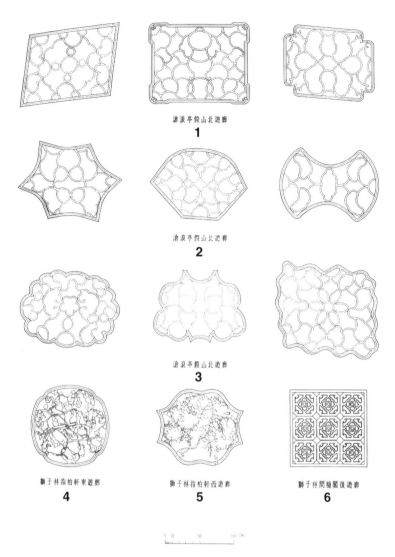

滄浪亭假山北遊廊
1

滄浪亭假山北遊廊
2

滄浪亭假山北遊廊
3

獅子林指柏軒東遊廊
4

獅子林指柏軒西遊廊
5

獅子林問梅閣後遊廊
6

Fig. V-127 Drawings of tracery windows: **(1)**, **(2)**, and **(3)** Along the corridor north of the rockery, Surging-Wave-Pavilion Garden; **(4)** Along the corridor east of Pointing-at-Cypress Hall, Forest of Lions Garden; **(5)** Along the corridor west of Pointing-at-Cypress Hall, Forest of Lions Garden; **(6)** Along the rear corridor of Asking-for-Plum-Tree Two-Storied Pavilion.

Fig. V-128 Tracery windows in Forest of Lions Garden.

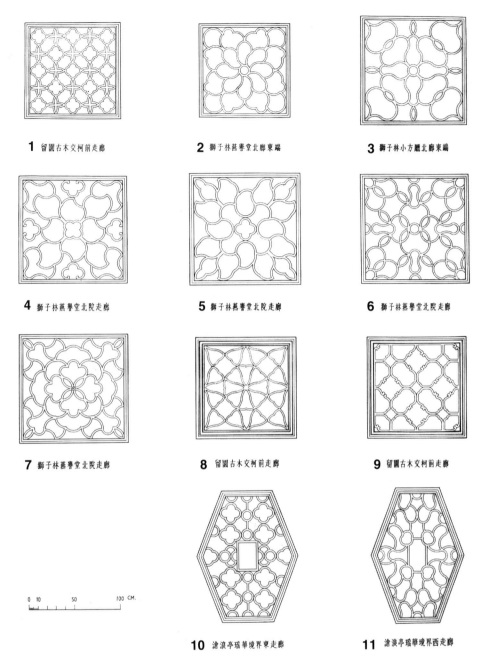

1 留園古木交柯前走廊   **2** 獅子林燕譽堂北廊東端   **3** 獅子林小方廳北廊東端

4 獅子林燕譽堂北院走廊   **5** 獅子林燕譽堂北院走廊   **6** 獅子林燕譽堂北院走廊

7 獅子林燕譽堂北院走廊   **8** 留園古木交柯前走廊   **9** 留園古木交柯前走廊

0 10   50   100 CM.

10 滄浪亭瑤華境界東走廊   **11** 滄浪亭瑤華境界西走廊

Fig. V-129 Drawings of tracery windows.

1. Along the front corridor of Old-Trees-Intertwining-One-Another, Lingering-Here Garden
2. East end of the corridor north of Famed-for-Swallow Hall, Forest of Lions Garden
3. East end of the corridor north of Little Square Hall, Forest of Lions Garden
4., 5., 6., and 7. Along the corridor in the courtyard north of Famed-for-Swallow Hall, Forest of Lions Garden
8., 9. Along the corridor in front of Old-Trees-Intertwining-One-Another, Lingering-Here Garden
10. Along the corridor east of the Land of Glistening-Jade, Surging-Wave-Pavilion Garden
11. Along the corridor west of Land of Glistening-Jade, Surging-Wave-Pavilion Garden

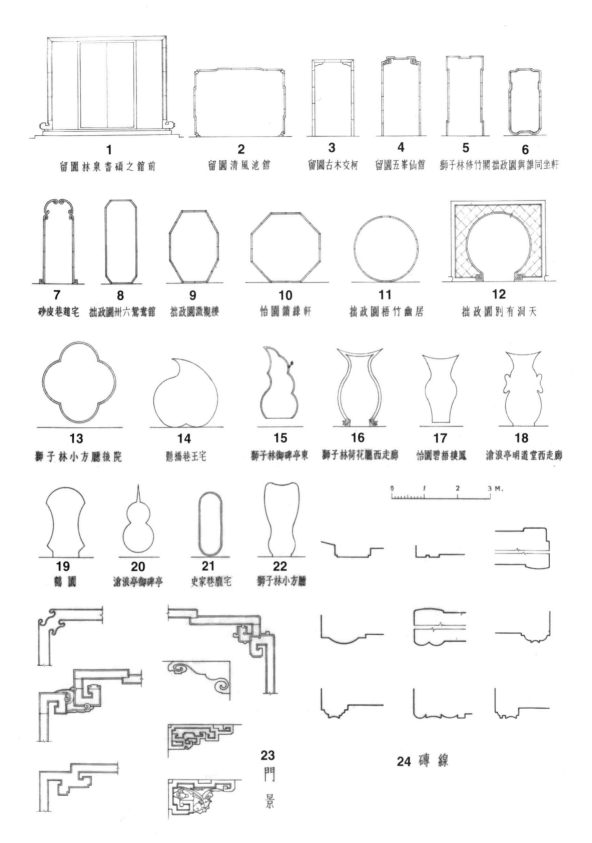

1 留園林泉耆碩之舘前
2 留園清風池舘
3 留園古木交柯
4 留園五峯仙舘
5 獅子林修竹閣拙政園與誰同坐軒

7 砂皮巷趙宅
8 拙政園卅六鴛鴦舘
9 拙政園澂觀樓
10 怡園鎖綠軒
11 拙政園梧竹幽居
12 拙政園別有洞天

13 獅子林小方廳後院
14 懸橋巷王宅
15 獅子林御碑亭東
16 獅子林荷花廳西走廊
17 怡園碧梧棲鳳
18 滄浪亭明道堂西走廊

19 鶴園
20 滄浪亭御碑亭
21 史家巷龐宅
22 獅子林小方廳

23 門景

24 磚線

Fig. V-130 Drawings of moon gates and their details.

1. In front of the House for the Aged Giants of Groves and Springs, Lingering-Here Garden
2. Fresh-Breeze-Pool House, Lingering-Here Garden
3. Old-Trees-Intertwining-One-Another, Lingering-Here Garden
4. Five-Peak Celestial House, Lingering-Here Garden
5. Tall-Bamboo Pavilion, Forest of Lions Garden
6. With-Whom-to-Sit Lounge, Humble Administrator's Garden
7. Residence of Zhao, Shapi Lane
8. 36-Mandarin-Duck Hall, Humble Administrator's Garden

9. Clearly-Viewing Two-Storied Building, Humble Administrator's Garden
10. Looking-up-at-Greenery Hall, Happy Garden
11. Pavilion amid-Secluded-Wutong-and-Bamboo, Humble Administrator's Garden
12. Unique-Beauty Half-Pavilion, Humble Administrator's Garden
13. Rear yard of Little Square Hall, Forest of Lions Garden
14. Residence of Wang, Xuanqiao Lane
15. East of Imperial Tablet Pavilion, Forest of Lions Garden
16. At the corridor west of Lotus Hall, Forest of Lions Garden

17. Green-Wutong-Sheltering-Phoenix House, Happy Garden
18. At the corridor west of Comprehending-the-Doctrine Hall, Surging-Wave-Pavilion Garden
19. Crane Garden
20. Imperial Tablet Pavilion, Surging-Wave-Pavilion Garden
21. Residence of Pang, Shijia Lane
22. Little Square Hall, Forest of Lions Garden
23. Flowery pattern over the gates
24. Brick moldings

Fig. V-131 Moon-shaped gate in a courtyard of Surging-Wave-Pavilion Garden.

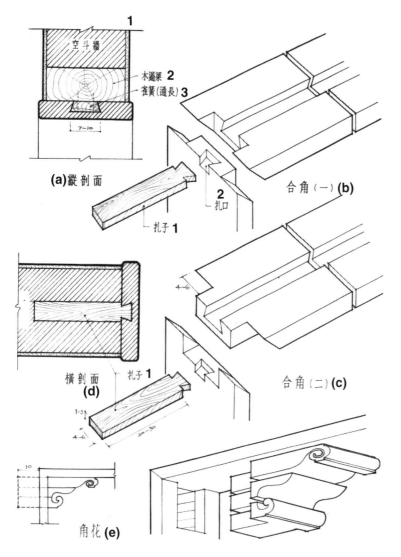

(a) 縱剖面

(d) 橫剖面 扎子**1**

角花 **(e)**

Fig. V-132. The structure for the frame of a gate piled with polished bricks: **(a)** longitudinal section: **(1)** hollow wall, **(2)** wood stretching beam, **(3)** tension spring; **(b)** corner of the door—1: **(1)** prick, **(2)** opening of the prick; **(c)** corner of the door **(d)** horizontal section: **(1)** prick; **(e)** flowery pattern at the corner.

Fig. V-133 Frame of a gate piled with polished bricks at the front of a residence in a lane near a bridge at the Fan Gate.

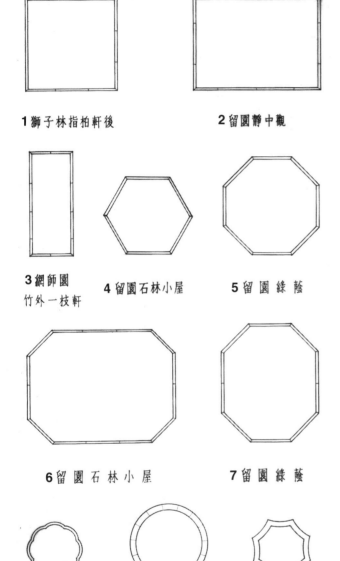

1 獅子林指柏軒後

2 留園靜中觀

3 網師園
竹外一枝軒

4 留園石林小屋

5 留園綠蔭

6 留園石林小屋

7 留園綠蔭

8 陸宅半園

9 獅子林複廊

10 陸宅半園

0 10   50   100 CM.

Fig. V-134 Drawings of casementless windows.

1. At the rear of Pointing-at-Cypress Hall, Forest of Lions Garden
2. Viewing-in-Quietness Lounge, Lingering-Here Garden
3. A-Branch-from-Bamboo Lounge, Retired Fisherman's Garden
4., 6. Small House in the Stone Forest, Lingering-Here Garden
5., 7. Green-Shade Lounge, Lingering-Here Garden
8., 10. Half-Garden in the Residence of Lu
9. Double-corridor, Forest of Lions Garden

Fig. V-135 Casementless windows at Fan-Shaped Pavilion in The Humble Administrator's Garden.

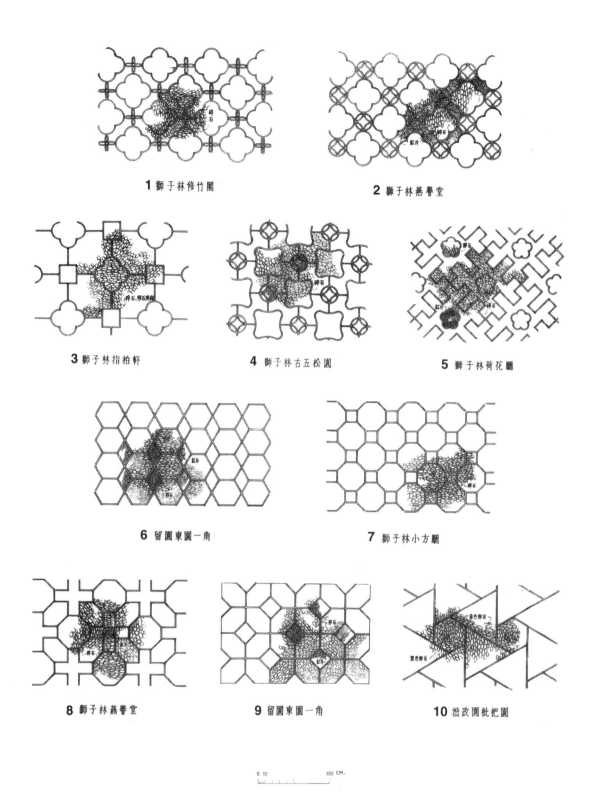

1 獅子林修竹閣   **2** 獅子林燕譽堂

3 獅子林指柏軒   **4** 獅子林古五松園   **5** 獅子林荷花廳

6 留園東園一角   **7** 獅子林小方廳

8 獅子林燕譽堂   **9** 留園東園一角   **10** 拙政園枇杷園

0 10   100 CM.

Fig. V-136 Drawings of pattern designs for ground pavements.

1. Tall-Bamboo Pavilion, Forest of Lions Garden
2. Famed-for-Swallow Hall, Forest of Lions Garden
3. Pointing-at-Cypress Hall, Forest of Lions Garden
4. Five-Old-Pine Park, Forest of Lions Garden
5. Lotus Hall, Forest of Lions Garden
6., 9. A corner of the East Garden, Lingering-Here Garden
7. Little Square Hall, Forest of Lions Garden
8. Famed-for-Swallow Hall, Forest of Lions Garden
10. Loquat Orchard, Humble Administrator's Garden

Fig. V-137 Flower-pattern pavement in Lingering-Here Garden.

Fig. V-138 Brick carvings atop the gate in The Retired Fisherman's Garden.

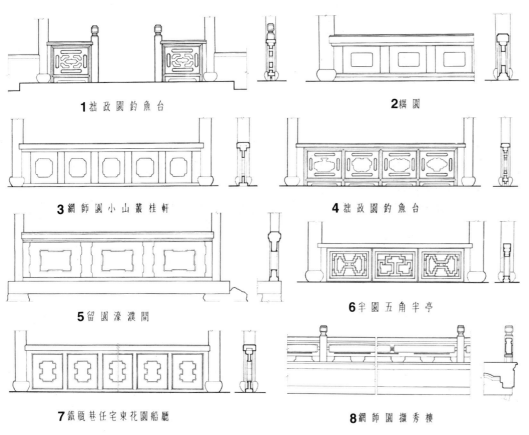

1 拙政園釣魚台

2 耦園

3 網師園小山叢桂軒

4 拙政園釣魚台

5 留園濠濮間

6 半園五角半亭

7 鐵瓶巷任宅東花園船廳

8 網師園攬秀樓

Fig. V-139 Drawings of brick balustrades: **(1)**, **(4)** Fishing-Terrace, Humble Administrator's Garden; **(2)** Twin Garden; **(3)** Little-Hillock-and-Laurel-Grove Hall; **(5)** River-Moat Pavilion, Lingering-Here Garden; **(6)** Pentagon Half-Pavilion, Half-Garden; **(7)** Landboat Hall of the east garden of the Residence of Ren, Iron-Bottle Lane; **(8)** Picking-Elegant-View Two-Storied Building.

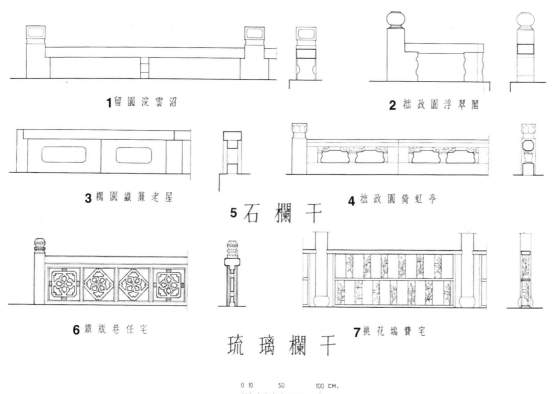

1 留園浣雲沼

2 拙政園浮翠閣

3 耦園織簾老屋

4 拙政園倚虹亭

5 石欄干

6 鐵瓶巷任宅

7 桃花塢費宅

琉璃欄干

0 10   50   100 CM.

Fig. V-140 Drawings of stone balustrades and glazed-tile balustrades: **(1)** Washing-Cloud Pool, Lingering-Here Garden; **(2)** Floating-Jade Two-Storied Pavilion; **(3)** Curtain-Weaving Old-Lodge, Twin Garden; **(4)** Leaning-on-the-Rainbow Pavilion, Humble Administrator's Garden: **(5)** Stone balustrades; **(6)** Residence of Ren, Iron-Bottle Lane; **(7)** Residence of Fei at Taohuawu.

Fig. V-141 Stone balustrades dating back to the Ming Dynasty in The Humble Administrator's Garden.

Fig. V-142 Stone table and stone seats in The Humble Administrator's Garden.

Fig. VI-1 Peonies in front of Distant-Fragrance Hall In The Humble Administrator's Garden.

Fig. VI-2 Garden scenery in the central part of The Humble Administrator's Garden.

Fig. VI-3 Trees planted on the shore of the pool in Happy Garden.

Fig. VI-4 Pavilion of Fragrant-Snow-and-Colorful-Clouds where the plum blossom is the major scenic object.

Fig. VI-5 Wutong and bamboo grove beside Pavilion Amid-Secluded-Wutong-and-Bamboo.

Fig. VI-6 Springtime scenery—peonies in Forest of Lions Garden.

Fig. VI-7 Summer scenery—wisteria in Happy Garden.

Fig. VI-8 Autumn scenery—chrysanthemums in The Humble Administrator's Garden.

Fig. VI-9 Winter scenery—wintersweet blossoms in The Retired Fisherman's Garden.

Fig. VI-10 Planted trees for all four seasons in the front courtyard of Little-Hillock-and-Laurel-Grove Hall in The Retired Fisherman's Garden.

Fig. VI-11 Magnolia in front of Magnolia Hall in The Humble Administrator's Garden.

Fig. VI-12 Big-leaf hydrangea beside Floating-Jade Two-Storied Pavilion in The Humble Administrator's Garden.

Fig. VI-13 Clover in Forest of Lions Garden.

Fig. VI-14 Winter jasmine along the shore of the pool in Happy Garden.

Fig. VI-15 Chinese trumpet creepers in Forest of Lions Garden.

Fig. VI-16 Wisteria in The Humble Administrator's Garden.

Fig. VI-17 Broad-leaf bamboo on the rockery in Surging-Wave-Pavilion Garden.

Fig. VI-18 Banana trees in front of Listening-to-the-Rain Hall in The Humble Administrator's Garden.

Fig. VI-19 Lacebark pines at the bridge in The Retired Fisherman's Garden.

Fig. VI-20 Straw-cape maples beside Little-Hillock-and-Laurel-Grove Hall in The Retired Fisherman's Garden.

Fig. VI-21 Wisteria on the rockery in Mountain Villa of Encircled Elegance.

Fig. VI-22 Camellias in front of Golden-Millet Pavilion in Happy Garden.

Fig. VI-23 Black pines in front of A-Branch-from-Bamboo Lounge in The Retired Fisherman's Garden.

Fig. VI-24 Grove of laurels beside Smelling-the-Fragrance-of-Osmanthus Lounge in Lingering-Here Garden.

Fig. VI-25 Chinese yew beside a pavilion in The Retired Fisherman's Garden.

Fig. VI-26 Courtyard scenery of Small Courtyard of Stone Forest in Lingering-Here Garden.

Fig. VI-27 Flowers, trees, and lake stones in front of Hoeing-on-the-Moon Hall in Happy Garden.

Fig. VI-28 Chinese Tianzhu and wintersweet in a small courtyard in Happy Garden.

Fig. VI-29 Flowers and trees in the rear courtyard of Five-Peak Celestial Hall in Lingering-Here Garden.

Fig. VI-30 Window scene at Late-Spring Chamber in The Retired Fisherman's Garden.

313

Fig. VI-31 Minute details of flowers of a tracery window in The Humble Administrator's Garden.

Fig. VI-32 Flowers and trees in front of Leaning-on-Jade Hall in The Humble Administrator's Garden.

Fig. VI-33 Flowers and trees in the front courtyard of Five-Peak Celestial Hall in Lingering-Here Garden.

Fig. VI-34 Surging-Wave Pavilion and the trees in its environs.

Fig. VI-35 Maple grove atop an earthen hill around Comfortable-Whistle Pavilion in Lingering-Here Garden.

Fig. VI-36 Trees beside a corridor in the western part of The Humble Administrator's Garden.

Fig. **VI-37** Lacebark pines and Wutong trees beside Lotus-Root-Fragrance Waterside Pavilion in Happy Garden.

Fig. **VI-38** Hillock and groves of trees in the central part of The Humble Administrator's Garden.

Fig. VI-39 Lacebark pines and the lotus pond beside the rockery in Happy Garden.

Fig. VI-40 Chinese hackberry tree atop the rockery in Lingering-Here Garden.

Fig. VI-41 Trees north of Little-Flying-Rainbow in The Humble Administrator's Garden.

Fig. VI-42 Flowers and trees beside the path along the pool in The Retired Fisherman's Garden.

Fig. VI-43 Flowers and trees along the pool shore south of Distant-Fragrance Hall in The Humble Administrator's Garden.

320

Fig. VI-44 Creepers along the pool in Happy Garden.

Fig. VI-45 Flowers, trees, and sleeping lilies along the pool in Carefree Garden.

Fig. VI-46 Lake stone parterre behind Lotus-Root-Fragrance Waterside Pavilion in Happy Garden.

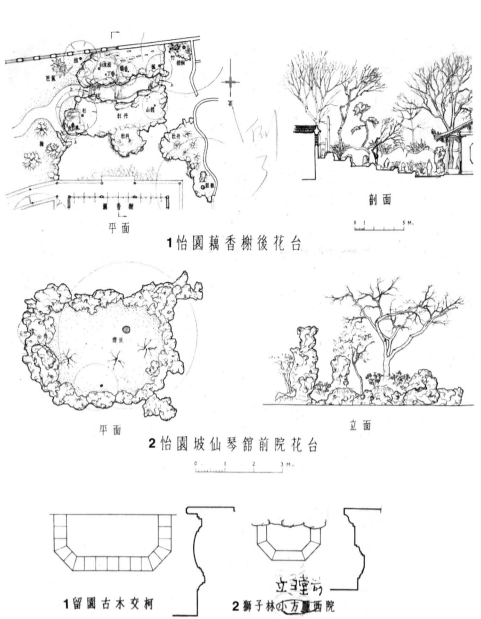

平面

剖面

1 怡園藕香榭後花台

0 1   5 M.

平面

立面

2 怡園坡仙琴館前院花台

0   1   2   3 M.

Fig. VI-47 Drawings of lake stone parterres: **(1)** Parterre at the rear of Lotus-Root-Fragrance Waterside Pavilion, Happy Garden; **(2)** Parterre in the front yard of Hill-Slope-Fairies Music House.

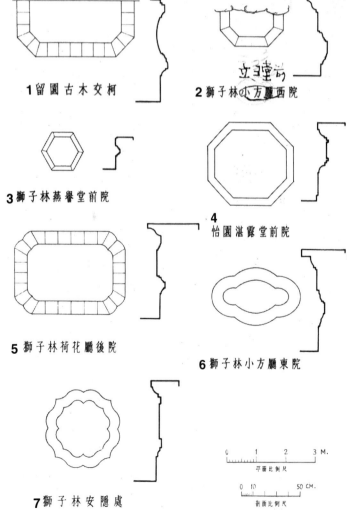

1 留園古木交柯

2 獅子林小方廳西院

3 獅子林燕譽堂前院

4 怡園湛露堂前院

5 獅子林荷花廳後院

6 獅子林小方廳東院

7 獅子林安隱處

0 1   2   3 M.
平面比例尺

0 10   50 CM.
剖面比例尺

Fig. VI-48 Drawings of regular-shaped parterres: **(1)** Old-Trees-Intertwining-One-Another, Lingering-Here Garden; **(2)** Front yard of Standing-in-the-Snow Hall, Forest of Lions Garden; **(3)** Front yard of Famed-for-Swallow Hall, Forest of Lions Garden; **(4)** Front yard of Crystal-Clear-Dew Hall, Happy Garden; **(5)** Back yard of Lotus Hall, Forest of Lions Garden; **(6)** East yard of Little Square Hall, Forest of Lions Garden; **(7)** Place of Hermitage, Forest of Lions Garden.

Fig. VI-49 Peonies in the parterre behind Lotus-Root-Fragrance Waterside Pavilion in Happy Garden.

Fig. VI-50 Large-size potted landscape in front of the Music Room in The Retired Fisherman's Garden.

Fig. VI-51 A pot of flowers in The Humble Administrator's Garden.

Fig. VII-1 Garden scenery in the central part of The Humble Administrator's Garden.

1

2

Fig. VII-2 Paintings of The Humble Administrator's Garden, drawn by Wen Zhenming of the Ming Dynasty. (1) the Little-Flying Rainbow; (2) the Little-Surging-Wave.

Fig. VII-3 Painting of The Humble Administrator's Garden, drawn by Fang Shishu of the Qing Dynasty.

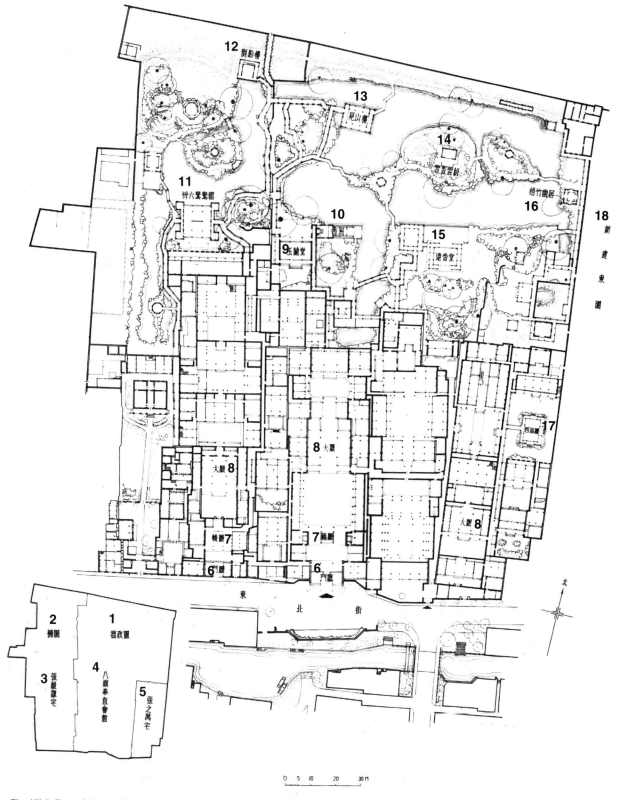

Fig. VII-5 Plan of the residential quarters and the garden in The Humble Administrator's Garden.

1. The Humble Administrator's Garden
2. Supplementary Garden
3. Residence of Zhang Lüqian
4. Guild Hall of Fengtian and Zhili Provinces of the "Eight Banners"
5. Residence of Zhang Zhiwan
6. Gate-Hall
7. Lounge
8. Hall
9. Magnolia Hall
10. Fragrant-Isle Landboat
11. 36-Mandarin-Duck Hall
12. Inverted-Image Two-Storied Building
13. Seeing-the-Hill Two-Storied Building
14. Pavilion of Fragrant-Snow-and-Colorful Clouds
15. Distant-Fragrance Hall
16. Pavilion amid-Secluded-Wutong-and-Bamboo
17. Facing-on-Four-Side Hall
18. Eastern part of the Garden

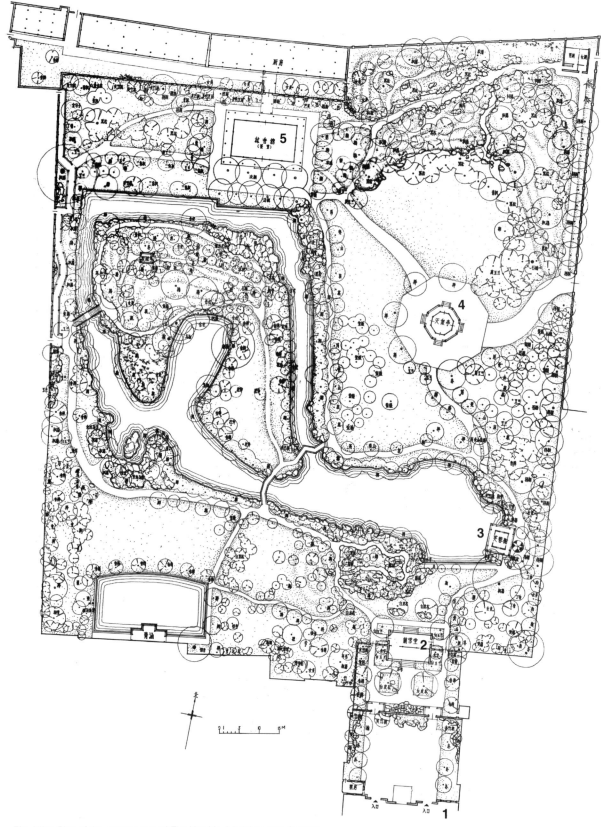

Fig. VII-6 Plan of the eastern part of The Humble Administrator's Garden:
(1) Entrance; (2) Orchid-Snow Hall; (3) Lotus Waterside Pavilion; (4) Heav-
enly-Springs Pavilion; (5) Sorghum-Fragrance House.

Fig. VII-7 Bird's eye view of the central part of The Humble Administrator's Garden **(1)**.

Fig. VII-8 Bird's eye view of the central part of The Humble Administrator's Garden **(2)**.

Fig. VII-9 Plan of the central and western part of The Humble Administrator's Garden.

1. Entrance
2. Inner-Gate
3. Distant-Fragrance Hall
4. Leaning-on-Jade Hall
5. Wind-from-the-Pine Pavilion
6. Little-Surging-Wave Watercourt
7. Little-Flying-Rainbow Corridor-Bridge
8. Pure-Will-and-Far-Reaching-Mind Study
9. Trust-Winning Pavilion
10. Fragrant-Isle Landboat
11. Clearly-Viewing Two-Storied Building

12. Magnolia Hall
13. Unique-Beauty Half-Pavilion
14. Winding-Path-under-Willow-Shade Corridor
15. Seeing-the-Hill Two-Storied Building
16. Pavilion of Fragrant-Snow-and-Colorful-Clouds
17. Northern-Hill Pavilion
18. Green-Ripple Pavilion
19. Pavilion amid-Secluded-Wutong-and-Bamboo
20. Leaning-on-the-Rainbow Pavilion
21. Embroidered-Silk Pavilion

22. Exquisite House
23. Spring-Begonia-Cove House
24. Fine-Fruit Pavilion
25. Listening-to-the-Rain Hall
26. 36-Mandarin-Duck Hall
27. 18-Datura Hall
28. With-Whom-to-Sit Lounge
29. Lingering-to-Listen Pavilion
30. Floating-Jade Two-Storied Pavilion
31. Inverted-Image Two-Storied Building
32. Pagoda-Shadow Pavilion

巷

15 昆山樓

18

17

16

19

20

香洲

4

3 遠香堂

7

9

5

8 6

2

1

21

23

22

24 25

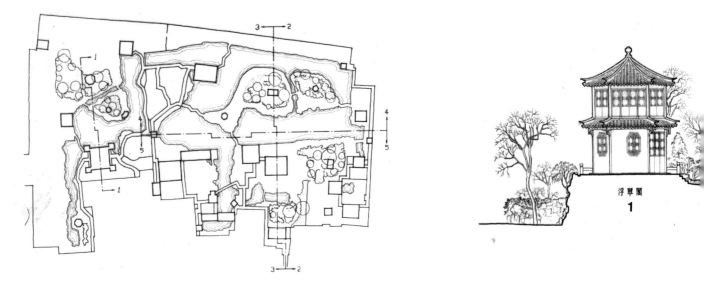

Fig. VII-10 Locations of the section drawings of the scenic spots in The Humble Administrator's Garden.

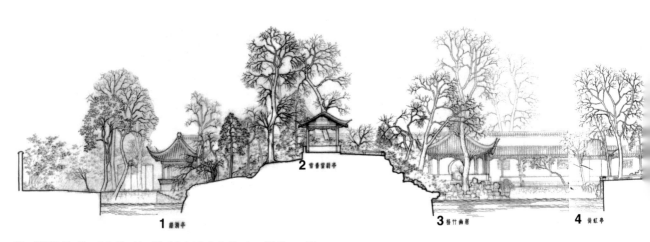

Fig. VII-12 Section 2-2, The Humble Administrator's Garden: **(1)** Green-Ripple Pavilion; **(2)** Pavilion of Fragrant-Snow-and-Colorful-Clouds; **(3)** Pavilion amid-Secluded-Wutong-and-Bamboo; **(4)** Leaning-on-the-Rainbow Pavilion; **(5)** Distant-Fragrance Hall; **(6)** Inner-Gate.

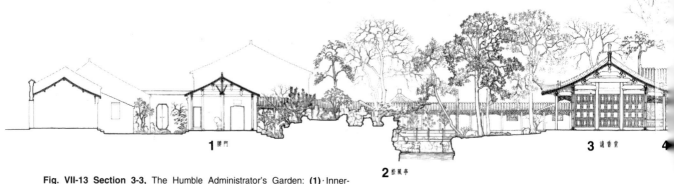

Fig. VII-13 Section 3-3, The Humble Administrator's Garden: **(1)** Inner-Gate; **(2)** Wind-from-the-Pine Pavilion; **(3)** Distant-Fragrance Hall; **(4)** Leaning-on-Jade Hall; **(5)** Unique-Beauty Half-Pavilion; **(6)** Breeze-from-the-Lotus-in-Four-Directions Pavilion; **(7)** Pavilion of Fragrant-Snow-and-Colorful Clouds; **(8)** Seeing-the-Hill Two-Storied Building.

笠亭

興誰同坐軒

2

3

洲六鸞寮館   十八曼陀羅花館

4   **5**

Fig. VII-11 Section 1-1, The Humble Administrator's Garden: **(1)** Floating-Jade Two-Storied Pavilion; **(2)** Bamboo-Hat Pavilion; **(3)** With-Whom-to-Sit Lounge; **(4)** 36-Mandarin-Duck Hall; **(5)** 18-Datura Hall.

遠香堂 **5**

6 腰門

7 雪香雲蔚亭

8 見山樓

5 到有洞天   **6** 待霜四面亭

1 且山楼   2 荷风四面亭

Fig. VII-14 Section 4-4, The Humble Administrator's Garden: **(1)** Seeing-the-Hill Two-Storied Building; **(2)** Breeze-from-the-Lotus-in-Four-Directions Pavilion; **(3)** Pavilion of Fragrant-Snow-and-Colorful-Clouds; **(4)** Northern-Hill Pavilion; **(5)** Green-Ripple Pavilion; **(6)** Pavilion amid-Secluded-Wutong-and-Bamboo.

1 倚虹亭   2 海棠春坞   3 绣绮亭   4 枇杷园   5 远香堂

Fig. VII-15 Section 5-5, The Humble Administrator's Garden: **(1)** Leaning-on-the-Rainbow Pavilion; **(2)** Spring-Begonia-Cove House; **(3)** Embroidered-Silk Pavilion; **(4)** Loquat Orchard; **(5)** Distant-Fragrance Hall; **(6)** Leaning-on-Jade Hall; **(7)** Little-Flying-Rainbow Corridor-Bridge; **(8)** Fragrant-Isle Landboat; **(9)** Clearly-Viewing Two-Storied Building; **(10)** Magnolia Hall; **(11)** Unique-Beauty Half-Pavilion.

334

3 雪香雲蔚亭　　　　**4** 北山亭　　　　**5** 綠漪亭　　　**6** 梧竹幽居

6 待玉軒　　　　**7** 小飛虹　　　　**8** 香洲　　　　**9** 澂爽樓　　　　**10** 玉蘭堂　　　**11** 別有洞天

Fig. VII-16 Entrance to the eastern part of The Humble Administrator's Garden.

Fig, VII-17 Rockery and pool in the eastern part of The Humble Administrator's Garden.

Fig. VII-18 Lotus Waterside Pavilion in the eastern part of The Humble Administrator's Garden.

Fig. VII-19 Outside scene south of Distant-Fragrance Hall in The Humble Administrator's Garden.

Fig. VII-20 Embroidered-Silk Pavilion in The Humble Administrator's Garden.

338

Fig. VII-21 Magnolia Hall in The Humble Administrator's Garden.

Fig. VII-22 View of the hillock and pool in the northeast, from Leaning-on-Jade Hall in The Humble Administrator's Garden.

Fig. VII-23 Distant-Fragrance Hall and Leaning-on-Jade Hall.

Fig. VII-24 Scenery northwest of the hillock and pool in the central part of The Humble Administrator's Garden.

Fig. VII-25 Scenery around Breeze-from-the-Lotus-in-Four-Directions Pavilion.

Fig. VII-26 Scenery north of Fragrant-Isle Landboat.

Fig. VII-27 Little-Flying-Rainbow at a distance.

Fig. VII-28 Bird's eye view of Little-Surging-Wave Watercourt.

343

Fig. VII-29 Unique-Beauty Half-Pavilion in the central part and Fit-to-Observe-Scenery-in-Two-Directions Pavilion in the western part of The Humble Administrator's Garden.

Fig. VII-30 Open corridor in Winding-Path-under-Willow-Shade in The Humble Administrator's Garden.

344

Fig. VII-31 Two-story corridor beside Seeing-the-Hill Two-Storied Building in The Humble Administrator's Garden.

Fig. VII-32 Looking eastward at Pavilion amid-Secluded-Wutong-and-Bamboo from the pool in the central part of The Humble Administrator's Garden.

345

Fig. VII-33 Looking northward from Pavilion amid-Secluded-Wutong-and-Bamboo.

Fig. VII-34 Scenery beside Embroidered-Silk Pavilion.

Fig. VII-35 Scenery north of Loquat Garden.

Fig. VII-36 Scenery in the environs of Waiting-for-the-Frost Pavilion (or North-Hill Pavilion), Green-Ripple Pavilion, and Pavilion amid-Secluded-Wutong-and-Bamboo.

347

Fig. VII-37 Full view of the hill and pool in the central part of The Humble Administrator's Garden.

Fig. VII-38 Full view of the hill and pool in the western part of The Humble
Administrator's Garden.

Fig. VII-39 The hill and pool north of 36-Mandarin-Duck Hall.

Fig. VII-40 Scenery in the environs of Fan-Shaped Pavilion and Inverted-Image Two-Storied Hall in the western part of The Humble Administrator's Garden.

Fig. VII-41 Looking southward at the scenery around Pagoda-Shadow Pavilion from Lingering-to-Listen Pavilion.

Fig. VIII-1 Paintings of Liu Shu Garden during the reign of Emperor Qianlong in the Qing Dynasty: **(1)** Painting by Wang Xuehao in the 54th year of the reign of Emperor Qianlong; **(2)** painting by Zhai Dakuan in the 59th year of the reign of Emperor Qianlong.

Fig. VIII-2 Picture of Cold-Emerald Mountain Villa, drawn by Liu Maogong in the middle of the Qing Dynasty (copy).

Fig. VIII-3 Site plan of Lingering-Here Garden.

1. Front-Gate
2. Ancestral Hall
3. Lobby
4. Hall
5. Green-Shade Lounge
6. Old-Trees-Intertwining-One-Another Courtyard
7. Winding-Creek Two-Storied Building
8. River-Moat Pavilion
9. West Two-Storied Building
10. Five-Peak Celestial House
11. Crane Hall
12. Place of Drawing-Water-from-Ancient-Well-to-Find-Rope
13. Salute-to-the-Peak Hall
14. House for the Aged Giants of Groves and Springs

15. Lingering-Cloud House
16. Washing-Cloud Pool
17. Cloud-Topping Terrace
18. Cloud-Topping Two-Storied Building
19. Cloud-Topping Peak
20. Restored-to-Me Study
21. Delight-in-Sunshine-and-Rain-and-Snow Pavilion
22. Distant-Green Two-Storied Pavilion
23. Small-Fabled-Immortals Abode
24. Bright-Zither Two-Storied Building
25. Encompassing-Jade Mountain House
26. Supreme-Happiness Pavilion
27. Comfortable-Whistle Pavilion
28. Unique-Beauty Half-Pavilion
29. Just-Right Pavilion
30. Lively-Place Waterside Pavilion

355

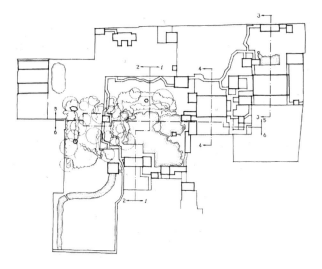

Fig. VIII-4 Locations of the section drawings of Lingering-Here Garden.

1 遠翠閣　　　　**2** 汲古得綆處　**3** 五峯仙

1 涵碧山房

4 清風池館　　5 西樓　　6 幸濂閣　　7 曲谿樓　　8 涵碧山房

Fig. VIII-5 Section 1-1, Lingering-Here Garden: **(1)** Distant-Green Two-Storied Pavilion; **(2)** Place of Drawing-Water-from-Ancient-Well-to-Find-Rope; **(3)** Five-Peak Celestial House; **(4)** Fresh-Breeze-Pool House; **(5)** West Two-Storied Building; **(6)** River-Moat Pavilion; **(7)** Winding-Creek Two-Storied Building; **(8)** Encompassing-Jade Mountain House.

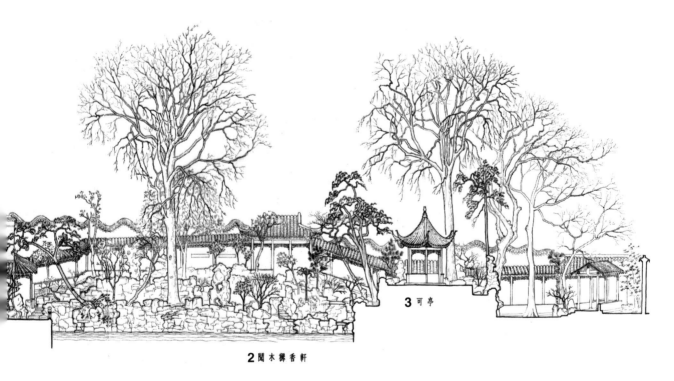

3 可亭　　2 聞木樨香軒

Fig. VIII-6 Section 2-2, Lingering-Here Garden: **(1)** Encompassing-Jade Mountain House; **(2)** Smelling-the-Fragrance-of-Osmanthus Lounge; **(3)** Just-Right Pavilion.

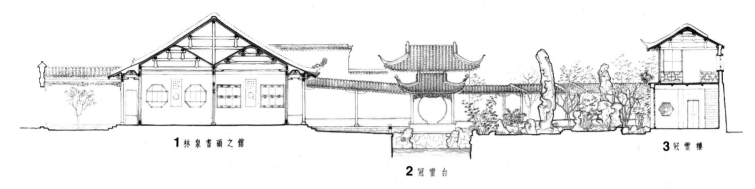

1 林泉耆硕之馆   **2** 冠云台   **3** 冠云楼

Fig. VIII-7 Section 3-3, Lingering-Here Garden: **(1)** House for the Aged Giants of Groves and Springs; **(2)** Cloud-Topping Terrace; **(3)** Cloud-Topping Two-Storied Building.

1 至乐亭   **2** 闻木樨香轩   **3** 可亭

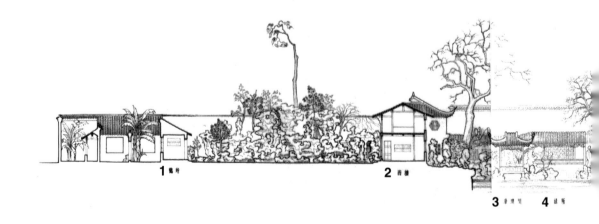

1 厕所   **2** 西楼   **3** 华步小筑   **4** 读经

Fig. VIII-8 Section 4-4, Lingering-Here Garden: **(1)** West Two-Storied Building; **(2)** Five-Peak Celestial House.

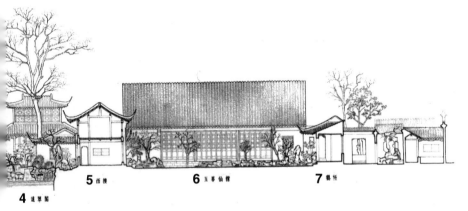

Fig. VIII-9 Section 5-5, Lingering-Here Garden: **(1)** Supreme-Happiness Pavilion; **(2)** Smelling-the-Fragrance-of-Osmanthus Lounge; **(3)** Just-Right Pavilion; **(4)** Distant-Green Two-Storied Pavilion; **(5)** West Two-Storied Building; **(6)** Five-Peak Celestial House; **(7)** Crane Hall.

Fig. VIII-10 Section 6-6, Lingering-Here Garden: **(1)** Crane Hall; **(2)** West Two-Storied Building; **(3)** River-Moat Pavilion; **(4)** Green-Shade Lounge; **(5)** Bright-Zither Two-Storied Building; **(6)** Encompassing-Jade Mountain House; **(7)** Smelling-the-Fragrance-of-Osmanthus Lounge; **(8)** Comfortable-Whistle Pavilion.

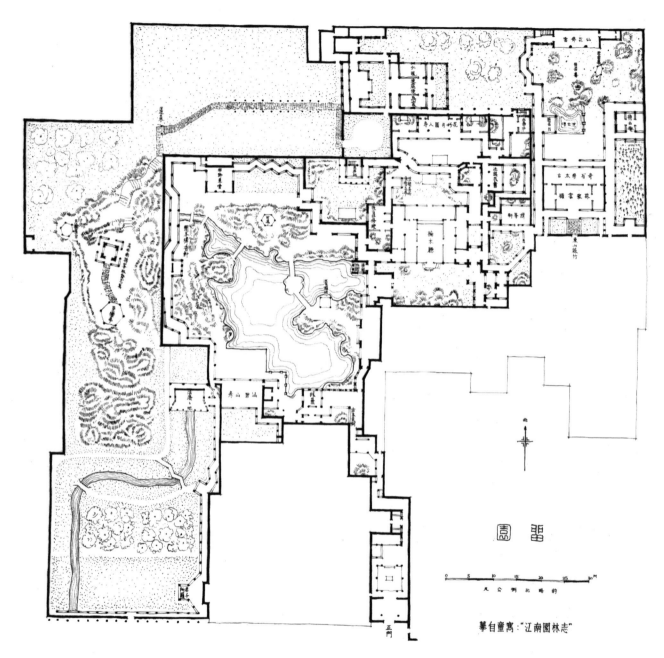

Fig. VIII-11 The original plan of Lingering-Here Garden. (*Copied from Records of Gardens South of the Changjiang River by Tong Jung.*)

Fig. VIII-12 Small courtyard, "Huabu Shaozhu"

Fig. VIII-13 Scenery in the environs of Bright-Zither Two-Storied Building in Lingering-Here Garden.

Fig. VIII-14 Scenery in the environs of Winding-Creek Two-Storied Building in Lingering-Here Garden.

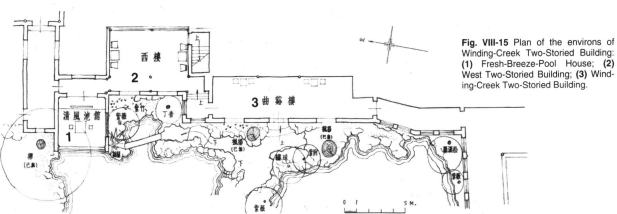

Fig. VIII-15 Plan of the environs of Winding-Creek Two-Storied Building: **(1)** Fresh-Breeze-Pool House; **(2)** West Two-Storied Building; **(3)** Winding-Creek Two-Storied Building.

清風池館

西樓

曲谿樓

Fig. VIII-16 Courtyard south of Five-Peak Celestial Hall.

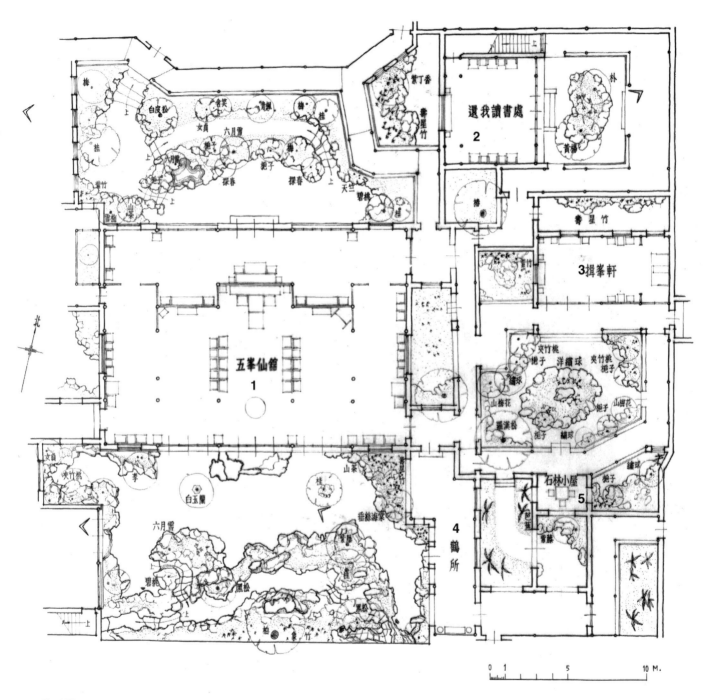

図中の文字:

椿　挂
上
白皮松　含笑　青楓　椿
女貞　六月雪　挂
上　把子　上
紫竹　山茶　探春　搾春　天竹　挂
雪柳　碧桃

紫丁香　書星竹

還我讀書處
2

林　黄楊

椿

書星竹

3揖峯軒

紫竹

夾竹桃
桅子　洋繡球　夾竹桃桅子
繡球
山樝花　桅子
羅漢松　桅子　繡球

繡球
桅子

石林小屋　5
芭蕉
紫藤

五峯仙館
1

女貞
夾竹桃
李
白玉蘭
桂
山茶
垂絲海棠

六月雪
碧桃　黑松
上
柏
黑松

4
鶴所

北

Fig. VIII-17 Plan of the environs of Five-Peak Celestial Hall: **(1)** Five-Peak Celestial House; **(2)** Restored-to-Me Study; **(3)** Salute-to-the-Peak Hall; **(4)** Crane Hall; **(5)** Small House in the Stone Forest.

0 1 5 10 M.

Fig. VIII-18 A corner of Small Courtyard of Stone Forest.

Fig. VIII-19 Scenery northwest of Courtyard of Cloud-Topping Peak.

Fig. VIII-20 Plan of the courtyard of Cloud-Topping Peak: **(1)** Cloud-Topping Two-Storied Building; **(2)** Cloud-Topping Peak; **(3)** Washing-Cloud Pool; **(4)** Cloud-Topping Terrace; **(5)** Delight-in-Sunshine-and-Rain-and-Snow Pavilion; **(6)** Salute-to-the-Peak Hall; **(7)** House for the Aged Giants of Groves and Springs; **(8)** Lingering-Cloud House.

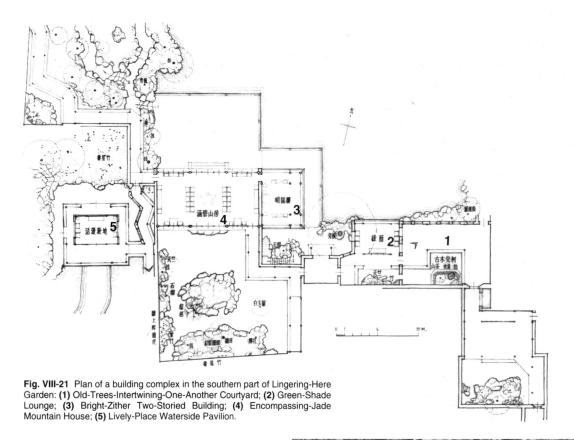

Fig. VIII-21 Plan of a building complex in the southern part of Lingering-Here Garden: **(1)** Old-Trees-Intertwining-One-Another Courtyard; **(2)** Green-Shade Lounge; **(3)** Bright-Zither Two-Storied Building; **(4)** Encompassing-Jade Mountain House; **(5)** Lively-Place Waterside Pavilion.

Fig. VIII-22 Comfortable-Whistle Pavilion in the western part of Lingering-Here Garden.

Fig. IX-1 Scenery west of the pool in Forest of Lions Garden.

Fig. IX-2 Painting of Forest of Lions Garden, drawn by Ni Yunlin.

374

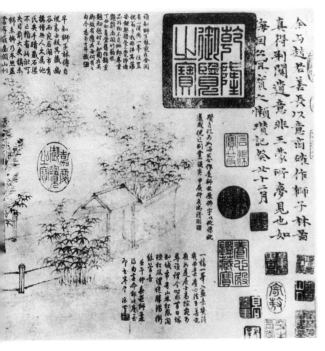

Fig. IX-3 A courtyard in front of Famed-for-Swallow Hall in Forest of Lions Garden.

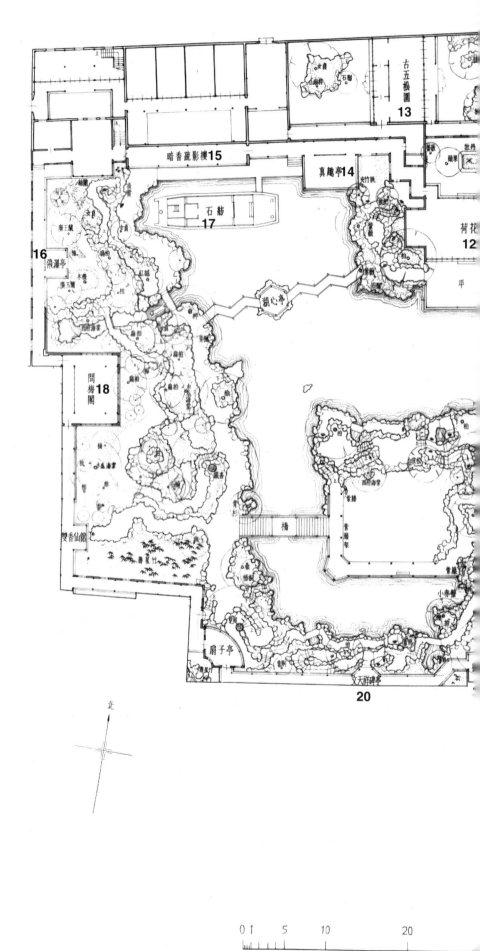

古五松園 13

暗香疎影樓 15

石舫 17

真趣亭 14

荷花 12

湖心亭

16 飛瀑亭

間梅閣 18

橋

扇子亭

文天祥碑亭

20

Fig. IX-4 Site plan of Forest of Lions Garden.

1. Entrance
2. Lobby
3. Ancestral Hall
4. Famed-for-Swallow Hall
5. Standing-in-the-Snow Hall
6. Little Square Hall
7. Pointing-at-Cypress Hall
8. Seeing-the-Hill Two-Storied Building
9. Lying-in-Cloud Chamber
10. Double-corridor
11. Tall-Bamboo Pavilion
12. Lotus Hall
13. Five-Old-Pine Park
14. True-Interest Pavilion
15. Hidden-Fragrance-and-Sparse-Shadow Two-
    Storied Building
16. Flying-Waterfall Pavilion
17. Stone Landboat
18. Asking-for-Plum-Tree Two-Storied Building
19. Fan Pavilion
20. Wen Tianxiang Memorial Tablet Pavilion
21. Imperial Tablet Pavilion

北

0 1   5   10   20

376

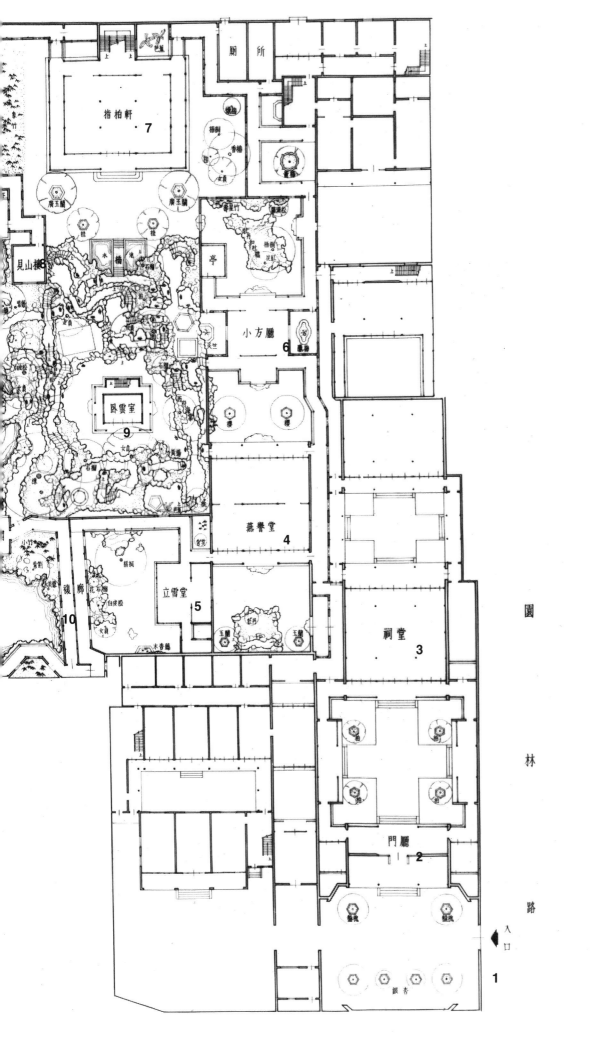

指柏軒 7

見山樓 8

小方廳 6

臥雲室 9

燕譽堂 4

立雪堂 5

復廊 10

祠堂 3

門廳 2

1

廁所

園

林

路

入口

文天祥碑亭 扇子亭
1 **2**

3 雙香仙館 橋**4**

問梅閣

Fig. IX-5 Section 1-1, Forest of Lions Garden: **(1)** Wen Tianxiang Memorial Tablet Pavilion; **(2)** Fan Pavilion; **(3)** Double-Fragrance Celestial House; **(4)** Bridge; **(5)** Asking -for-Plum-Tree Two-Storied Building; **(6)** Heart-of-the-Lake Pavilion; **(7)** Flying-Waterfall Pavilion; **(8)** Lotus Hall; **(9)** Five-Old-Pine Park.

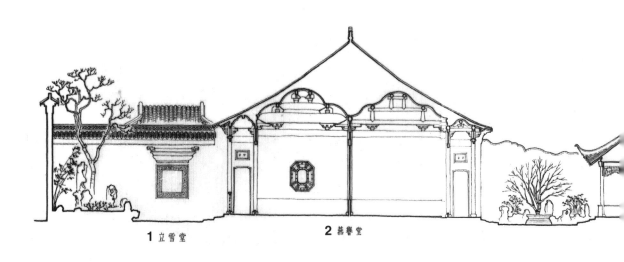

1 立雪堂   **2** 燕譽堂

Fig. IX-6 Section 2-2, Forest of Lions Garden: **(1)** Standing-in-the-Snow Hall; **(2)** Famed-for-Swallow Hall; **(3)** Little Square Hall.

378

湖心亭 **6** 飛瀑亭 **7** 荷花廳 **8** 古五松園 **9**

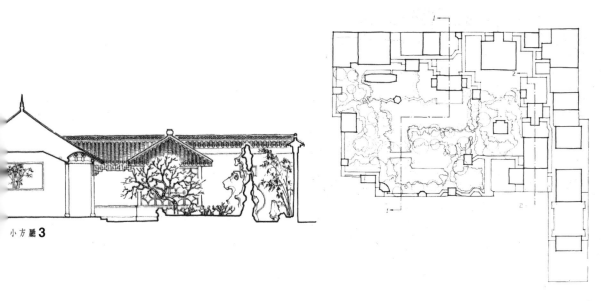

小方廳 **3**

Fig. IX-7 Locations of the section drawings of the scenic spots in Forest of Lions Garden.

Fig. IX-8 Full view of the hillock and pool in Forest of Lions Garden.

Fig. IX-9 Scenery northwest of the pool in Forest of Lions Garden.

Fig. IX-10 Lying-in-Cloud Chamber in Forest of Lions Garden.

Fig. IX-11 A corner of Pointing-at-Cypress Hall in Forest of Lions Garden.

Fig. X-1 Site plan of Surging-Wave-Pavilion Garden: **(1)** Front-Gate; **(2)** Facing-the-Water Lounge; **(3)** Surging-Wave Pavilion; **(4)** Watching-the-Fish Pavilion; **(5)** Comprehending-the-Doctrine Hall; **(6)** Land of Glistening-Jade; **(7)** Looking-at-the-Hill Two-Storied Building; **(8)** Delicate-Emerald Hall; **(9)** Memorial Hall for 500-Famous-Persons-of-Virtue; **(10)** Fresh-Fragrance House.

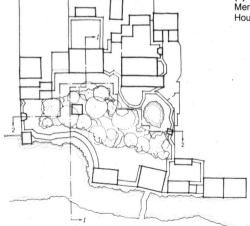

Fig. X-2 Locations of the section drawings of the scenic spots in Surging-Wave-Pavilion Garden.

1 明道堂   2 清香館   3 浦滇亭

1 大門

Fig. X-4 Section 2-2, Surging-Wave-Pavilion Garden: **(1)** Entrance; **(2)** Surging-Wave Pavilion; **(3)** Imperial Tablet Pavilion.

4 面水軒

5 滄浪勝蹟坊

0 1　　　5　　　　10 M.

2 滄浪亭

3

Fig. X-5 Painting of Surging-Wave-Pavilion Garden, drawn by Wang Hui during the reign of Emperor Kangxi of the Qing Dynasty.

Fig. X-6 Full view of the hillock and groves of Surging-Wave-Pavilion Garden.

Fig. X-7 Watching-the-Fish Pavilion in Surging-Wave-Pavilion Garden.

Fig. X-8 Along the shore of the pool, west of the main gate of Surging-Wave-Pavilion Garden.

390

Fig. X-9 A corner of Facing-the-Water Lounge.

Fig. X-10 The double corridor and the hillock in Surging-Wave-Pavilion Garden.

Fig. X-11 Fresh-Fragrance House of Surging-Wave-Pavilion Garden.

Fig. XI-1 Scenery in the central part of The Retired Fisherman's Garden.

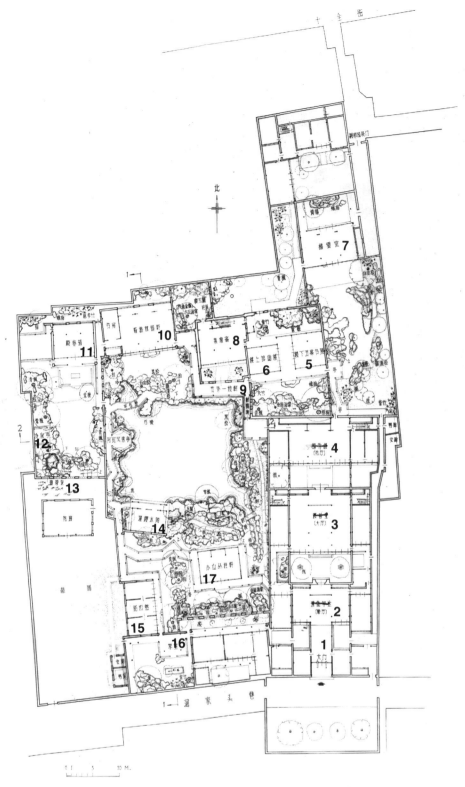

Fig. XI-2 Site plan of The Retired Fisherman's Garden.

1. Front-Gate
2. Lounge
3. Hall
4. Picking-Elegant-View Two-Storied Building
5. Five-Peak Study (ground floor)
6. Paintings Gallery (upper floor)
7. Ladder-Cloud Chamber
8. Gathering-the-Void Study
9. A-Branch-from-Bamboo Lounge
10. Looking-at-Pine-and-Painting Hall
11. Late-Spring Chamber
12. Cold-Springs Pavilion
13. Enclosing-Emerald Springs
14. Washing-Tassel Waterside Pavilion
15. Pursuance-of-Harmony House
16. Music Room
17. Little-Hillock-and-Laurel-Grove Hall

1 琴室　　　　2 小山叢桂軒　　　　3 濯纓水閣

Fig. XI-3 Section 1-1, The Retired Fisherman's Garden: (1) Music Room;
(2) Little-Hillock-and-Laurel-Grove Hall; (3) Washing-Tassel Waterside Pavilion; (4) Moon-Appearing-and-Breeze-Coming Pavilion; (5) Looking-at-Pine-
and-Painting Hall.

1 冷泉亭　　　2 殿春簃　　　3 月到風來亭　　　看松讀畫軒 4　　　集虚齋 5　　6 竹外一枝軒

Fig. XI-4 Section 2-2, The Retired Fisherman's Garden: (1) Cold-Spring
Pavilion; (2) Late-Spring Chamber; (3) Moon-Appearing-and-Breeze-Coming
Pavilion; (4) Looking-at-Pine-and-Painting Hall; (5) Gathering-the-Void Study;
(6) A-Branch-from-Bamboo Lounge.

5 香松讀畫軒

4 月到風來亭

Fig. XI-5 Bird's eye view of the central part of The Retired Fisherman's Garden.

Fig. XI-6 Scenery northeast of the pool in The Retired Fisherman's Garden.

Fig. XI-7 Washing-Tassel Waterside Pavilion in The Retired Fisherman's Garden.

Fig. XI-8 A corner of Little-Hillock-and-Laurel-Grove Hall in The Retired Fisherman's Garden.

Fig. XI-9 Cold-Springs Pavilion in The Retired Fisherman's Garden.

Fig. XI-10 Late-Spring Chamber in The Retired Fisherman's Garden.

Fig. XII-1 Full view of the hillock and pool of Happy Garden.

1

Fig. XII-2 Paintings of Happy Garden in the Qing Dynasty: **(1)** Lotus-Root-Fragrance Waterside Pavilion; **(2)** Golden-Millet Pavilion; **(3)** Facing-the-Cliff Pavilion.

2

3

405

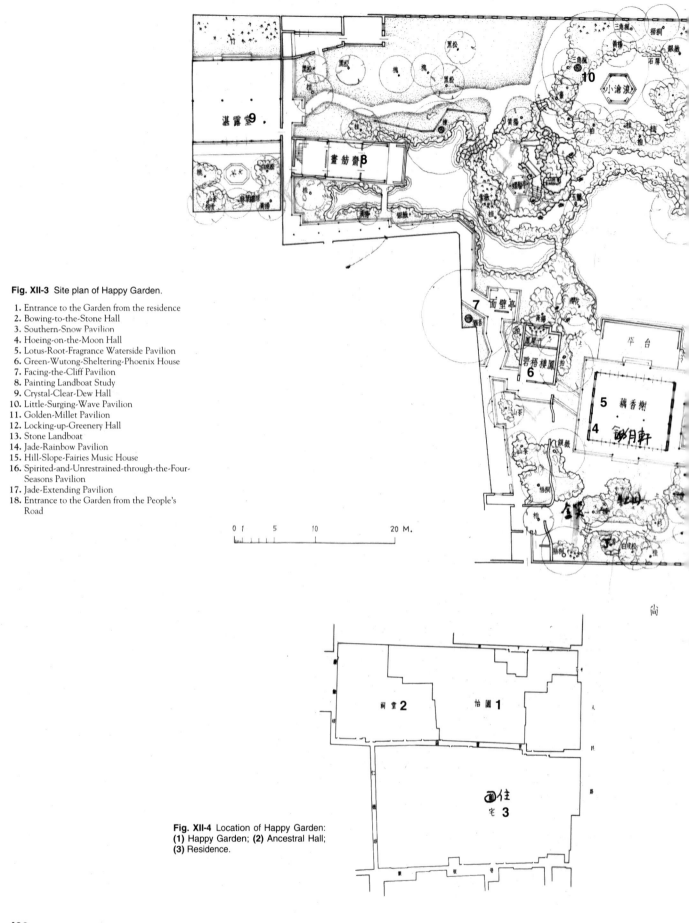

Fig. XII-3 Site plan of Happy Garden.

1. Entrance to the Garden from the residence
2. Bowing-to-the-Stone Hall
3. Southern-Snow Pavilion
4. Hoeing-on-the-Moon Hall
5. Lotus-Root-Fragrance Waterside Pavilion
6. Green-Wutong-Sheltering-Phoenix House
7. Facing-the-Cliff Pavilion
8. Painting Landboat Study
9. Crystal-Clear-Dew Hall
10. Little-Surging-Wave Pavilion
11. Golden-Millet Pavilion
12. Locking-up-Greenery Hall
13. Stone Landboat
14. Jade-Rainbow Pavilion
15. Hill-Slope-Fairies Music House
16. Spirited-and-Unrestrained-through-the-Four-
    Seasons Pavilion
17. Jade-Extending Pavilion
18. Entrance to the Garden from the People's
    Road

0 1   5   10   20 M.

Fig. XII-4 Location of Happy Garden:
(1) Happy Garden; (2) Ancestral Hall;
(3) Residence.

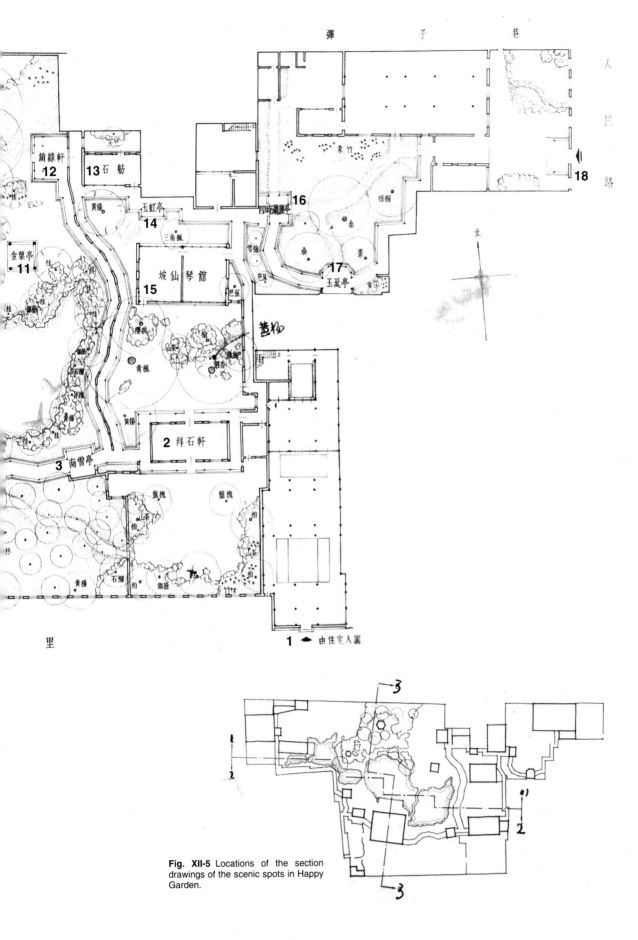

彈　　子　巷

鎖綠軒
12

13 石軸

天牡

玉虹亭
14

黃楊

三角楓

16

四時瀟灑亭

桑

梧桐

金粟亭
11

桂
桂
桂
桂

雪梅
芭蕉

坡仙琴館
15

芭蕉

17
玉延亭

北

櫻桃

青楓

黃楊

銀杏

黃楊

2 拜石軒

蟠槐

盤槐

柏

山茶

3 南雪亭

柏

黃楊

石榴

柏

銀杏

1 由住宅入園

里

人民路

18

3

2

2

3

Fig. XII-5 Locations of the section drawings of the scenic spots in Happy Garden.

Fig. XII-6 Section 1-1, Happy Garden: **(1)** Crystal-Clear-Dew Hall; **(2)** Painting Landboat Study; **(3)** Snail-Shaped Coiled-Hair Pavilion; **(4)** Little-Surging-Wave Pavilion; **(5)** Golden-Millet Pavilion; **(6)** Hill-Slope-Fairies Music House.

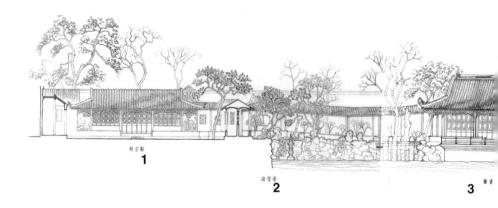

Fig. XII-7 Section 2-2, Happy Garden: **(1)** Bowing-to-the-Stone Hall; **(2)** Southern-Snow Pavilion; **(3)** Lotus-Root-Fragrance Waterside Pavilion; **(4)** Green-Wutong-Sheltering-Phoenix House; **(5)** Bridge.

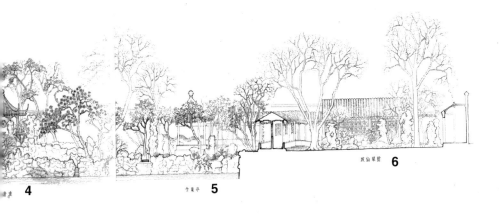

4　　　　　5　　　　　宓仙翠罷 6

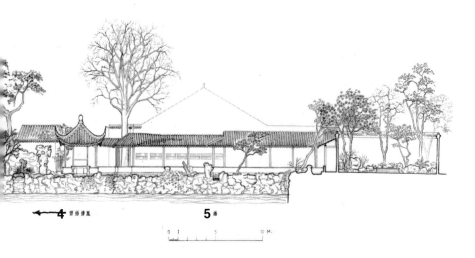

←4 穿海樓凡　　　　　5 樓

0 1　　　5　　　　10 M.

2 藕香榭

Fig. XII-8 Section 3-3, Happy Garden: **(1)** Little-Surging-Wave Pavilion; **(2)**
Lotus-Root-Fragrance Waterside Pavilion.

Fig. XII-9 Scenery at the entrance courtyard of Happy Garden.

Fig. XII-10 Bird's eye view of Happy Garden.

Fig. XII-11 A corner of the hillock and pool of Happy Garden.

Fig. XII-12 Lotus-Root-Fragrance Waterside Pavilion in Happy Garden.

Fig. XII-13 Water bay beside Painting Landboat Study and Snail-Shaped Coiled-Hair Pavilion in Happy Garden.

Fig. XII-14 Scenery east of the pool in Happy Garden.

Fig. XIII-1 Scenery in the eastern part of Twin Garden.

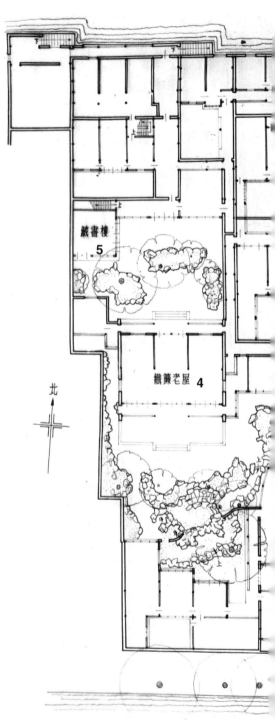

藏書樓
5

織簾老屋
4

北

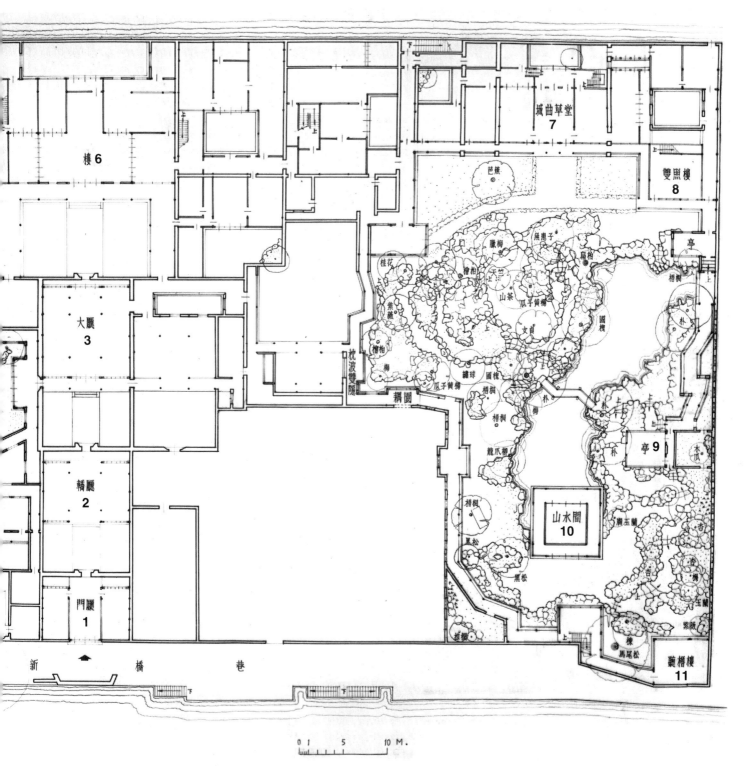

Fig. XIII-2 Site plan of Twin Garden: **(1)** Entrance, lobby; **(2)** Lounge; **(3)** Hall; **(4)** Curtain-Weaving Old-Lodge; **(5)** Two-Storied Library; **(6)** Two-Storied Building; **(7)** City-Corner Cottage; **(8)** Double-Shining Two-Storied Building; **(9)** Pavilion; **(10)** Waterside Pavilion-amid-the-Hillock-and-Pool; **(11)** Listening-to-the-Scull Two-Storied Building.

Fig. XIII-3 Entrance to the East Garden of Twin Garden.

418

Fig. XIII-4 City-Corner Cottage and rockery in Twin Garden.

Fig. XIII-5 Double-Shining Two-Storied Building.

Fig. XIII-6 Waterside Pavilion-amid-the-Hillock-and-Pool.

Fig. XIII-7 Listening-to-the-Scull Two-Storied Building in Twin Garden.

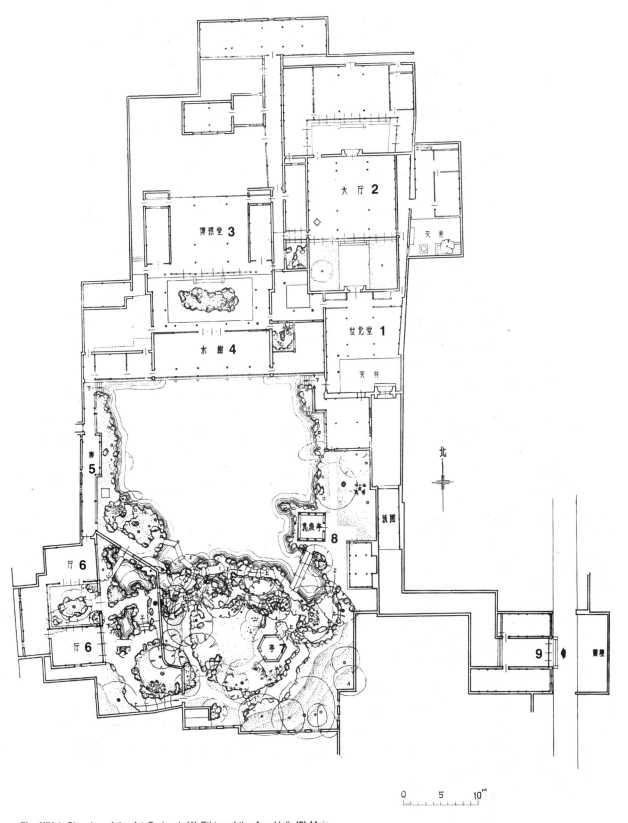

大厅 **2**

博雅堂 **3**

天井

世伦堂 **1**

水榭 **4**

天井

北

廊 **5**

乳鱼亭

筑圃

8

厅 **6**

亭 **7**

厅 **6**

9

黄壁

0   5   10ᴹ

Fig. XIV-1 Site plan of the Art Orchard: **(1)** Ethics-of-the-Age Hall; **(2)** Main Hall; **(3)** Rich-in-Learning Hall; **(4)** Waterside Pavilion; **(5)** Corridor; **(6)** Hall; **(7)** Pavilion; **(8)** Breeding-the-Fish Pavilion; **(9)** Entrance.

Fig. XIV-2 A corner of a courtyard in the Art Orchard.

Fig. XIV-3 Piled rockery south of the pool in the Art Orchard.

Fig. XIV-4 Full view southwest of the hill and pool of the Art Orchard.

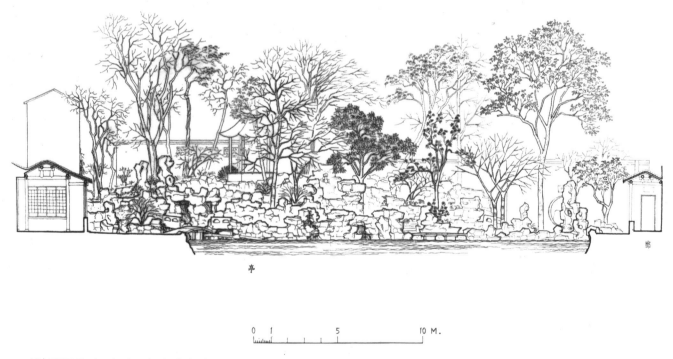

0 1   5   10 M.

Fig. XIV-5 Section drawing, the Art Orchard.

424

Fig XV-1 Full view of the lake stone rockery in Mountain Villa of Encircled Elegance.

425

0　1　　　　5 M.

Fig. XV-2 Section drawing, Mountain Villa of Encircled Elegance: Replenishing-Autumn Mountain Lodge.

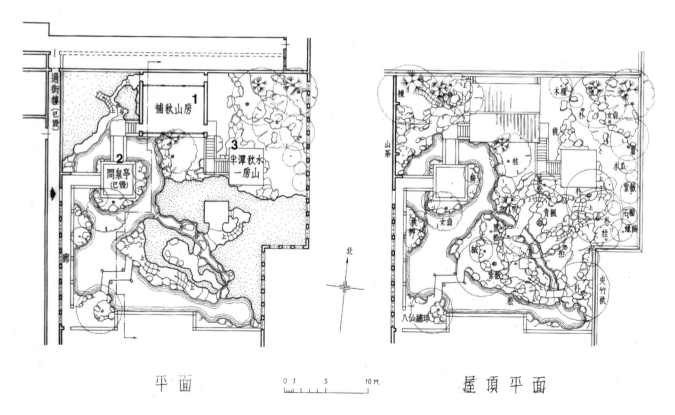

平 面　　　0　1　　5　　　10 M.　　屋 頂 平 面

Fig. XV-3 Site plan of Mountain Villa of Encircled Elegance: **(1)** Replenishing-Autumn Mountain Lodge; **(2)** Asking-for-the-Springs Pavilion; **(3)** Half-Pond-of-Autumn-Water Hill-House.

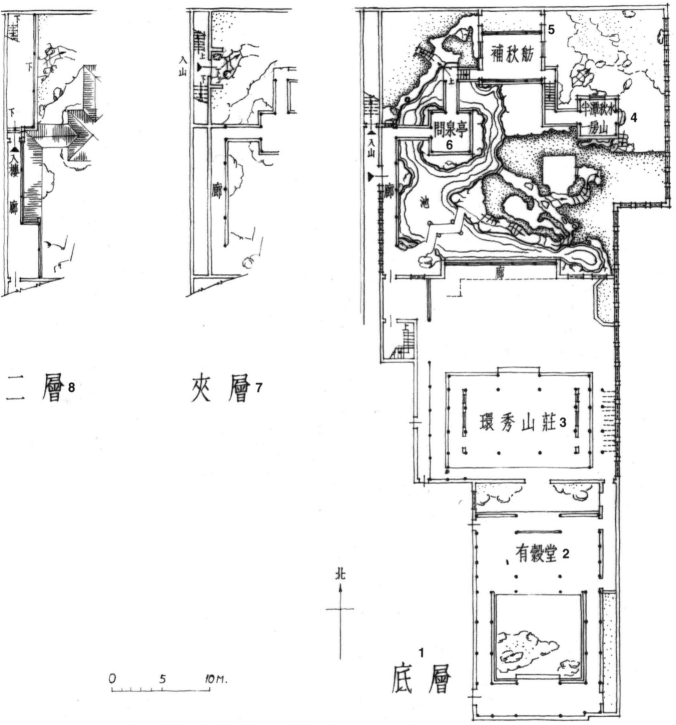

二 層 8　　　夾 層 7

北

0　　5　　10 M.

底 層 1

Fig. XV-4 Original plan of Mountain Villa of Encircled Elegance: **(1)** Ground floor; **(2)** Plenty-of-Grain Hall; **(3)** Mountain-Villa-of-Encircled-Elegance Hall; **(4)** Half-Pond-of-Autumn-Water Hill House; **(5)** Replenishing-Autumn Landboat; **(6)** Asking-for-the-Springs Pavilion; **(7)** Mezzanine floor; **(8)** Upper floor.

Fig. XV-5 Entrance to the gully southeast of the lake stone rockery in Mountain Villa of Encircled Elegance.

Fig. XV-6 Viewing the northwestern corner from inside the gully in Mountain Villa of Encircled Elegance.

Fig. XV-7 Rocky cliff in Mountain Villa of Encircled Elegance.

Fig. XV-8 Outside view of Replenishing-Autumn Landboat in Mountain Villa of Encircled Elegance.

Fig. XVI-1 Site plan of Mountain Villa of Embracing Emerald: **(1)** Inner front-gate; **(2)** Mountain-Villa-of-Embracing-Emerald Hall; **(3)** Hanhan Springs; **(4)** Embracing-Emerald Two-Storied Pavil-ion; **(5)** Asking-for-the-Springs Pavil-ion; **(6)** Harnessing-the-Moon Lounge; **(7)** Scholar's Retreat amid-the-Fairies'-Billows; **(8)** Seeing-off-Spring Cham-ber.

Fig. XVI-2 Bird's eye view of Mountain Villa of Embracing Emerald.

1月駕軒

Fig. XVI-3 Section 1-1, Mountain Villa of Embracing Emerald: (1) Harness-ing-the-Moon Lounge; (2) Scholar's Retreat amid-the-Fairies'-Billows.

2聽瀾精舍

剖面 1-1

0 1   5   10 M.

0   1   2   3 M

Fig. XVI-4 Section 2-2, Mountain Villa of Embracing Emerald.

Fig. XVI-5 Scholar's Retreat amid-the-Fairies'-Billows.

Fig. XVI-6 Harnessing-the-Moon Lounge.

Fig. XVI-7 Mountain Villa of Embracing Emerald and Tiger-Hill Pagoda.

Fig. XVII-1 Pavilion and winding corridor in Crane Garden.

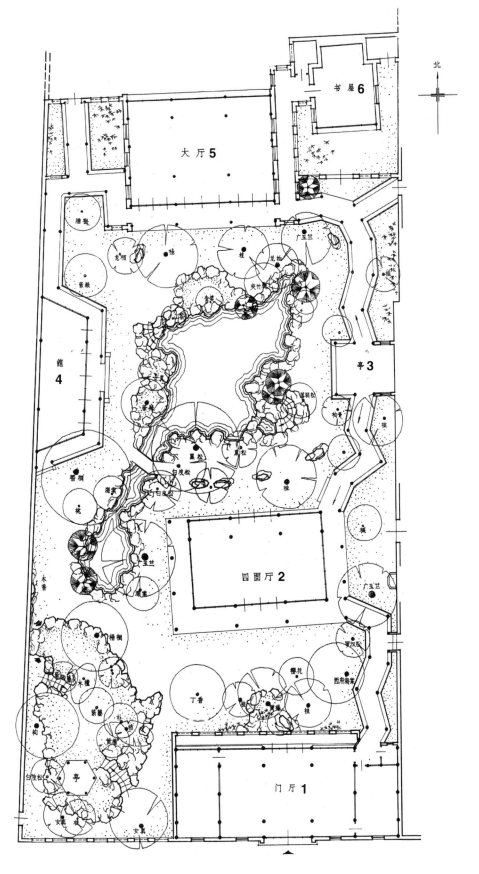

Fig. XVII-2 Site plan of Crane Garden: **(1)** Entrance, lobby; **(2)** Facing-Four-Sides Hall; **(3)** Pavilion; **(4)** House; **(5)** Main Hall; **(6)** Study.

Fig. XVII-3 Main hall of Crane Garden.

Fig. XVII-4 Scenery north of Facing-Four-Sides Hall of Crane Garden.

Fig. XVII-5 Scenery west of the pool of Crane Garden.

Fig. XVIII-1 Rest pavilion and winding corridor in Carefree Garden.

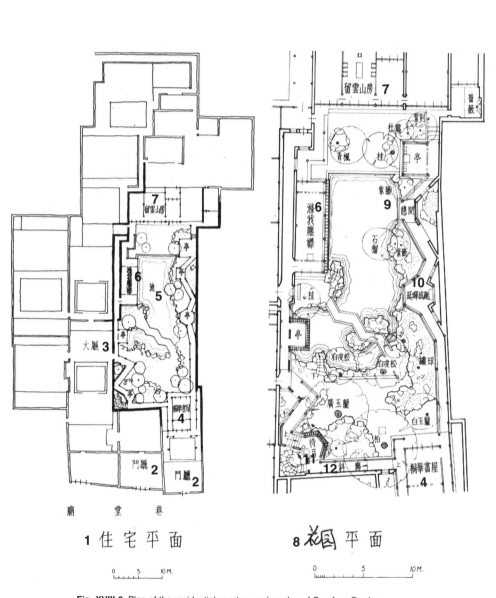

廟　堂　巷

1 住宅平面

8 花園平面

0   5   10 M.

0   5   10 M.

Fig. XVIII-2 Plan of the residential quarters and garden of Carefree Garden: **(1)** Plan of the residence; **(2)** Lobby; **(3)** Hall; **(4)** Parasol-Flower Studio; **(5)** Pool; **(6)** Washing-My-Dusty-Clothing Pavilion; **(7)** Lingering-Cloud Hill House; **(8)** Plan of the garden; **(9)** Rest Pavilion; **(10)** Extending-Splendor-to-Induce-Delight Pavilion; **(11)** Waiting-for-the-Moon Pavilion; **(12)** Oblique Corridor.

Fig. XVIII-3 Full view of the northeastern part of Carefree Garden.

Fig. XVIII-4 Section drawing, Carefree Garden: **(1)** Oblique Corridor; **(2)** Waiting-for-the-Moon Pavilion; **(3)** Washing-My-Dusty-Clothing Pavilion; **(4)** Lingering-Cloud Hill House.

1 斜廊　　待月 2

3 濯我尘缨

Fig. XVIII-5 Scenery south of Lingering-Cloud Hill House in Carefree Garden.

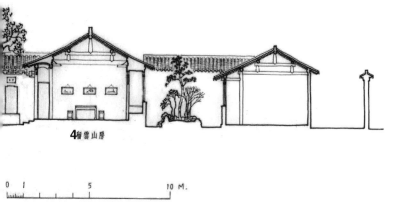

4 留雲山房

0 1   5   10 M.

Fig. XVIII-6 Extending-Splendor-to-Induce-Delight Pavilion in Carefree Garden.

Fig. XIX-1 Scenery south of the pool in Kettle Garden.

Fig. XIX-2 Bird's eye view of Kettle Garden.

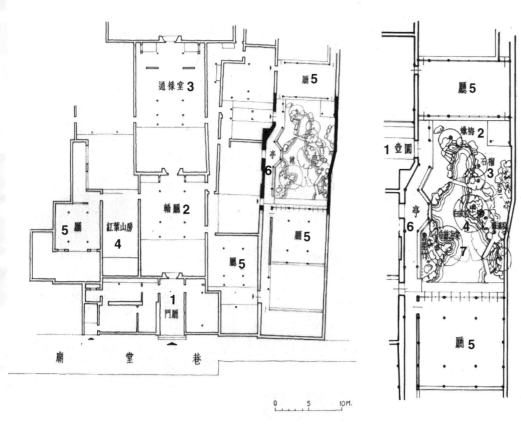

Fig. XIX-3 Plan of the residential quarters of Kettle Garden: **(1)** Entrance, lobby; **(2)** Lounge; **(3)** Approaching-to-Happiness Hall; **(4)** Red-Leaf Hill-Lodge; **(5)** Hall.

Fig. XIX-4 Plan of the garden part of Kettle Garden: **(1)** Entrance to the garden; **(2)** Wintersweet; **(3)** Pomegranate; **(4)** Lacebark Pine; **(5)** Hall; **(6)** Pavilion; **(7)** Begonia.

Fig. XIX-5 The hall north of the pool of Kettle Garden.

Fig. XX-1 Scenery in front of Green-Juniper Pavilion.

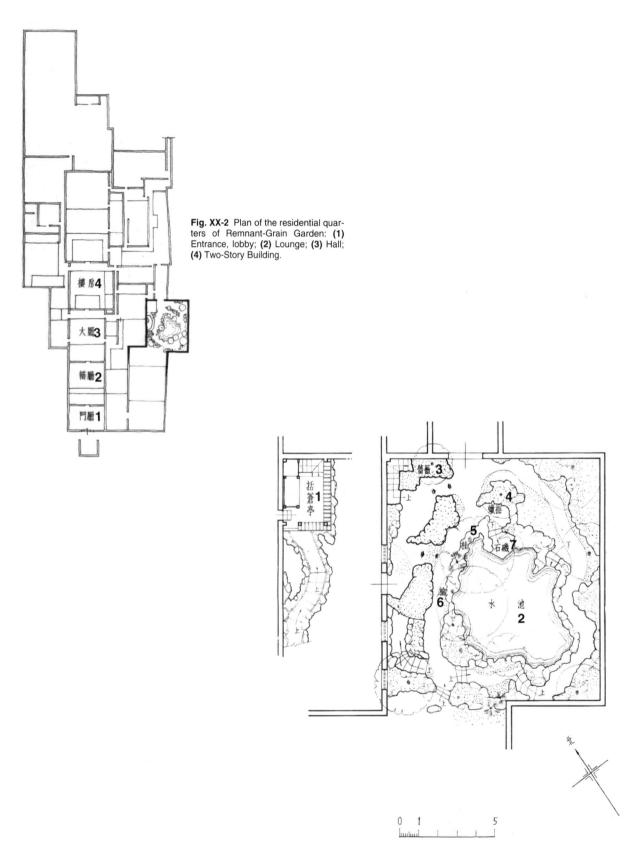

Fig. **XX-2** Plan of the residential quarters of Remnant-Grain Garden: **(1)** Entrance, lobby; **(2)** Lounge; **(3)** Hall; **(4)** Two-Story Building.

樓房4

大廳3

轎廳2

門廳1

括蒼亭1

薔薇3

蠟梅4

桂5

石磯7

水 池 2

榆6

北

0   1   5

Fig. **XX-3** Plan of the garden part of Remnant-Grain Garden: **(1)** Green-Juniper Pavilion; **(2)** Pool; **(3)** Rose; **(4)** Wintersweet; **(5)** Laurel; **(6)** Elm; **(7)** Projecting-over-the-Water rock.

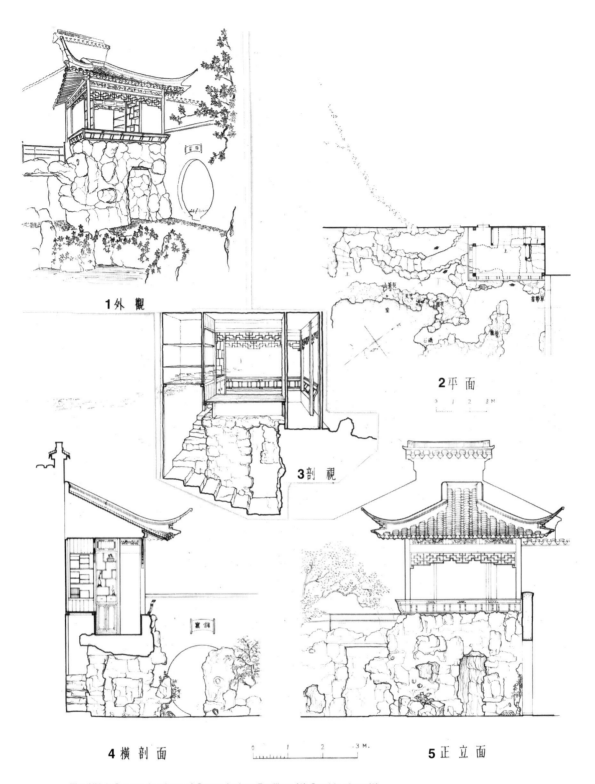

1 外 观

2 平 面

3 剖 视

4 横 剖 面

5 正 立 面

Fig. XX-4 Survey drawings of Green-Juniper Pavilion: **(1)** Outside view; **(2)** Plan; **(3)** Cross-section in perspective; **(4)** Cross-section; **(5)** Front elevation.

Fig. XX-5 Scenery at a wall corner in Remnant-Grain Garden.

Fig. XXI-1 Scenery south of the courtyard of a residence in Wangxima Lane.

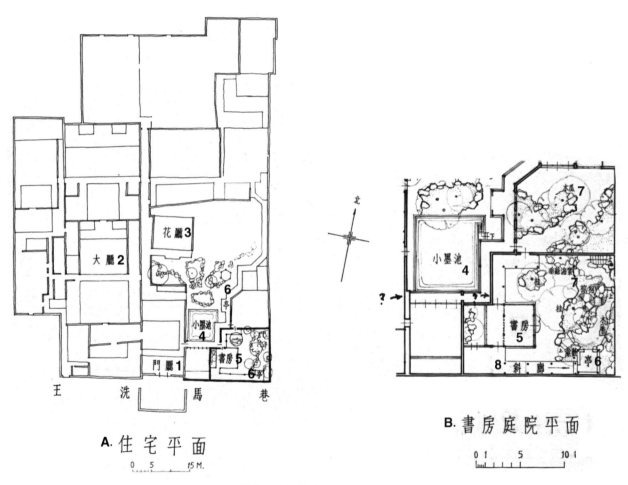

A. 住宅平面

0 5 15 M.

B. 書房庭院平面

0 1 5 10 1

北

門廳 1　大廳 2　花廳 3　小墨池 4　書房 5　亭 6

王　洗　馬　巷

小墨池 4　書房 5　斜廊 8　亭 6

Fig. XXI-2 Site plan of a residence in Wangxima Lane: (A) Plan of the Residence; (B) Plan of the courtyard and studio: **(1)** Entrance, lobby; **(2)**, **(3)** Hall; **(4)** Pool; **(5)** Studio; **(6)** Pavilion; **(7)** Trees and flowers; **(8)** Oblique corridor.

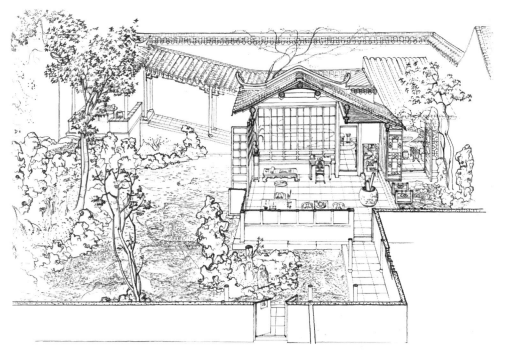

Fig. XXI-3 Perspective view of the studio and courtyard in Wangxima Lane.

Fig. XXI-4 Scenery east of the studio and courtyard of a residence in Wangxima Lane.

459